SPORT COMPACT
PERFORMANCE

By Jay Storer

ABCDE
FGHIJ
KLMNO
PQRST

Haynes Publishing Group
Sparkford Nr Yeovil
Somerset BA22 7JJ
England

Haynes North America, Inc
861 Lawrence Drive
Newbury Park
California 91320 USA

Acknowledgements

We are grateful for the help and cooperation of APC (American Products Company), 22324 Temescal Canyon Rd. Corona, CA 92883 (www.4apc.net), who supplied many of the custom car photographs used throughout this book, Steve Rothenbuehler at Dynamic Autosports, Inc., 23901 Remme Ridge, Lake Forest, CA 92630 (www.dynamicautosports.com), who provided valuable insight into the world of Sport Compact customizing, and to the many sport compact owners who offered their vehicles for photography at various shows and events during the winter and spring of 2003. Special thanks to Charles Gutmann and Team Speedtrix for making their cars available and assisting with research.

Cover photo: Photo used with permission by Lund International, Honda Civic project vehicle for Auto Vent shade, www.autoventshade.com.

Printed by **J H Haynes & Co Ltd,**
Sparkford, Yeovil, Somerset BA22 7JJ, England.

© Haynes North America, Inc. 2003
With permission from J.H. Haynes & Co. Ltd.

ISBN 1 56392 506 0
Library of Congress Control Number 2003108353

While every attempt is made to ensure that the information in this manual is correct, no liability can be accepted by the authors or publishers for loss, damage, or injury caused by any errors in, or omissions from, the information given

03-208

Be **careful** and know the **law**!

1 This manual contains information on modifying vehicles for high performance and racing. When these modifications are made, safety is often compromised. Racing should never be attempted on public highways, but only at purpose-built racetracks, adhering strictly to all safety regulations.

2 Advice on safety procedures and precautions is contained throughout this manual, and more specifically within the Safety section towards the back of this book. You are strongly recommended to note these comments, and to pay close attention to any instructions that may be given by the parts supplier.

3 Haynes recommends that vehicle modification should only be undertaken by individuals with experience of vehicle mechanics; if you are unsure as to how to go about the modification, advice should be sought from a competent and experienced individual. Any questions regarding modification should be addressed to the product manufacturer concerned, and not to Haynes, nor the vehicle manufacturer.

4 The instructions in this manual are followed at the risk of the reader who remains fully and solely responsible for the safety, roadworthiness and legality of his/her vehicle. Thus Haynes is giving only non-specific advice in this respect.

5 When modifying a car it is important to bear in mind the legal responsibilities placed on the owners, drivers and modifiers of cars. If you or others modify the car you drive, you and they can be held legally liable for damages or injuries that may occur as a result of the modifications.

6 The safety of any alteration and its compliance with construction and use regulations should be checked before a modified vehicle is sold as it may be an offense to sell a vehicle which is not roadworthy.

7 Any advice provided is correct to the best of our knowledge at the time of publication, but the reader should pay particular attention to any changes of specification to the vehicles, or parts, which can occur without notice.

8 Alterations to a vehicle should be disclosed to insurers and licensing authorities, and legal advice taken from the police, vehicle testing centers, or appropriate regulatory bodies.

9 Various makes of vehicle are shown being modified. Some of the procedures shown will vary from make to make; not all procedures are applicable to all makes. Readers should not assume that the vehicle manufacturers have given their approval to the modifications.

10 Neither Haynes nor the manufacturers give any warranty as to the safety of a vehicle after alterations, such as those contained in this book, have been made. Haynes will not accept liability for any economic loss, damage to property or death and personal injury other than in respect to injury or death resulting directly from Haynes' negligence.

Contents

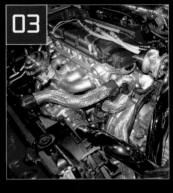

05

Ignition Systems 60

06

Induction Systems 72

07

Fuel System 82

08

Valvetrain 92

13

Engine Durability 164

14

Engine Swapping 172

15

Gauges and monitoring engine performance 178

16

Driveline Upgrades 192

Engine performance

It's been said "speed is just a question of how much you want to spend." There's a lot of truth in this statement. People with big incomes and racers with sponsors can afford to build 7-second cars. But remember also that speed comes with compromise, and an engine built to make 600 horsepower at the racetrack is not going to idle smoothly, get good gas mileage or go 200,000 miles between overhauls. Performance modifications are frequently called "upgrades," but we need to keep in mind that the *performance* is what's being upgraded, and often you'll have to give up some of the smooth, reliable and economical operation that sport-compact cars are famous for.

So it's best to have a plan for your project, even if you don't have all the money to do everything right away. Perhaps the best compromise is a car that is fast enough to race on the weekend, but is still practical to drive to work every day. Many upgrades, such as an exhaust header, cat-back system, and air-intake tube give "free" horsepower, meaning the only downside is more engine noise (actually a plus for most of us). These upgrades are also relatively inexpensive and are "no-brainers" for any sport-compact build-up. When you get into nitrous, turbos and superchargers, you'll be spending more money and also getting into more risk of engine damage. Camshafts and cylinder head work will reduce your car's low-speed driveability and frequently decrease your gas mileage. Often, when these modifications are designed to increase high-rpm horsepower, you'll actually lose some low-rpm power.

Many upgrades work best only when combined with other upgrades. For example, if you install a high-performance ignition coil and wires to your otherwise stock engine, they'll look nice, but probably won't add any power. These devices are designed to provide ultra-high voltage to overcome high cylinder pressures created by high-compression, turbocharging or supercharging. At the normal pressures created by your stock engine, your old ignition components were plenty adequate.

So it's more than just whether or not the parts fit. It's also important to make sure that the upgrades are appropriate to the "application." If you install an exhaust system and cat-back exhaust system, you'll almost surely get a performance increase, maybe even one that you can feel in the seat of your pants. But how much increase? Magazine ads are very specific with horsepower numbers, but it's

important to understand that these numbers may not apply to your application. Why? Because a new free-flowing exhaust system will do wonders for a car with engine mods and a restrictive stock exhaust. On the other hand, those same components will do little for a bone-stock engine with a decent system from the factory.

This interrelation of components is why it's important to talk with a tuner or knowledgeable engine builder before you get out the tools. Figure out how much power and performance you want, how much street driving you plan to do, and how much you have to spend. A tuner who has experience on sport-compact cars will guide you to the best values for your situation. So, what are you waiting for? There's plenty of horsepower out there just waiting for a home under your hood.

Choosing a Tuner

Who needs a tuner? Well, at some point, anyone interested in building a quality, reliable performance car will. There is always going to be someone out there who knows a little, or a lot, more than you do about transforming a stock street machine into a high-performance vehicle. A qualified tuner fully grasps "The Big Picture," how everything under the hood works as a system, how each system is interdependent with every other system and how a malfunction in one system affects the performance of other systems. All of this complexity makes tuning a modern vehicle challenging. This is especially true when aftermarket high performance parts are thrown into the mix.

If you've read this far, you have probably already started calling and emailing tuning firms with questions about the modifications you want to make to your project vehicle. Maybe you're still looking for a tuner. If so, this section will help you choose a good one. But even if you already have a tuner, this section will help you determine whether he's the right tuner for you. Is he a good technical consultant whose advice you can count on, a teacher from whom you can learn how to set up your car and a businessman whom you can trust? Yeah? Cool.

But first impressions can be misleading. Tuners have to make a living just like the rest of us, so at some point in their relationship with a customer they have to make some money. Many tuners don't just tune cars. They also sell high-performance products. So being a tuner is a balancing act: a good tuner dispenses advice about how to go faster, and he also sells the goods and services to make it happen. You are hiring this guy to help you improve your vehicle's performance. He's going to tell you how to get there, and much of his advice will be free. But he's a businessman, and he's in business to make money. Sure, he wants to have fun, and hang out with other enthusiasts, but he does have a bottom line. So keep this in mind when you're searching for the perfect tuner.

What should you look for in a tuner? Someone who is honest, knowledgeable and affordable, someone who will help you prioritize your modification plans, who will step up and do the job for you when it's over your head but who will also willingly step aside when he thinks you can handle the job yourself. Maybe you can't judge a book by its cover, but you can rate a prospective tuner by answering the following questions.

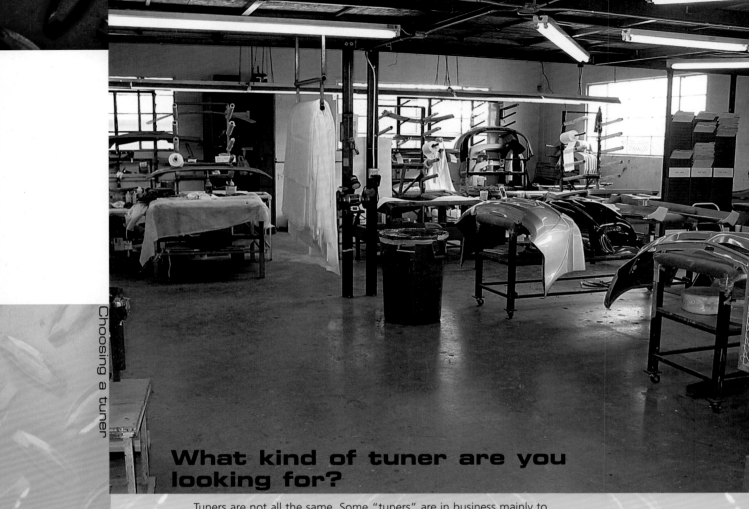

What kind of tuner are you looking for?

Tuners are not all the same. Some "tuners" are in business mainly to sell high-performance hardware. These guys often know something about the speed equipment that they sell (some of the tuners in this category actually know quite a lot), and some of them will even install the products you buy from them on your car. But they often don't provide tuning services such as flow bench and dyno work, custom machining, welding or fabricating. In the initial stages of a project (when you're upgrading the wheels, tires, brakes, suspension and installing bolt-on high-performance mods) a tuner of this type might be perfectly satisfactory.

Other tuners are more "hands-on." They don't just sell speed products. They act as technical consultants to their customers, sell them the products and/or services they need to improve their car's performance and then install the product or make the necessary modifications. If you're not already blessed with mechanical ability and plenty of tools, get yourself a full-service tuner. What you need is someone who can serve you not only as your technical guru but who can help you reach your performance goals by doing some or all of the work for you. Novices often waste thousands of dollars on inappropriate modifications because they don't take into consideration how one modification affects another modification. The hands-on, full-service tuner can save you a lot of aggravation and money in the early stages of designing and building your project vehicle because he'll help you make good decisions on expensive upgrades that require some planning.

Does the tuner know what he's talking about?

There are no shortcuts to becoming a good tuner. The best ones are standing on top of the tallest piles of broken parts. Basically, all tuning knowledge springs from the same well. Breakthroughs are rare. Nobody gets to the top in The Tuner's Game unless he's willing to take chances, try out new ideas, add what works to his performance repertoire and eliminate what doesn't. Before establishing a business relationship with a tuner, try to get a sense of whether your vehicle is just another rung on the ladder for him to gain more knowledge. Make sure that his broken-parts-phase is behind him. Don't become an unwitting guinea pig for someone who's still learning. You are looking for an Enlightened One, a member of the elite inner circle of guys who pretty much know everything about how to design and build your dream car. Settling for less could actually prove to be more expensive in the long run.

To the real tuner, there are two kinds of experiences: good experiences and . . . learning experiences. When a modification works the way it's supposed to, that's a good experience. When it doesn't, that's a learning experience. A good tuner isn't afraid to make mistakes, but he doesn't repeat those mistakes. He learns from them and moves on. And good tuners use their own vehicles, not customers' cars, to research and develop new products and services. If you decide to work with a tuner who intends to use your vehicle as a test-bed for new ideas and/or products, make sure that you get paid for this

service, perhaps in the form of free or discounted parts and labor.

When asked about his background, a novice tuner looking for new customers might fudge the truth a bit. An experienced tuner who has been in business for awhile won't need to. If his shop is neat, clean and filled with hand, power and machine tools and clean and craftsmanlike vehicles, and if his office is filled with trophies from the track and photos of smiling customers standing proudly next to their project vehicles, then stick around and ask him some questions. A good tuner has nothing to hide (except his most closely held speed secrets!) and he'll be happy to tell you how he got to where he is.

Ask a prospective tuner about his educational background and his experience and training. Some tuners might bristle when asked this question, but if you're going to spend thousands of dollars at this establishment, you need to judge for yourself whether the "tuner" standing before you is really qualified to modify your car, or tell you how to do it. Did he start out taking auto shop classes in high school? Did he study auto mechanics at a community college? Is he a certified ASE (Automotive Service Excellence) technician? Is he an ASE-certified Master Automotive Technician (CMAT)? Does he have dealership experience? Did he work for or own an independent garage? Did he ever work for a professional big-time drag racing or roadracing team? His answers to these questions will tell you whether this tuner has devoted a chunk of his life to cars, or whether he's simply out to make a buck.

Some of the best tuners have gained their special knowledge and skills while working for an automotive manufacturer

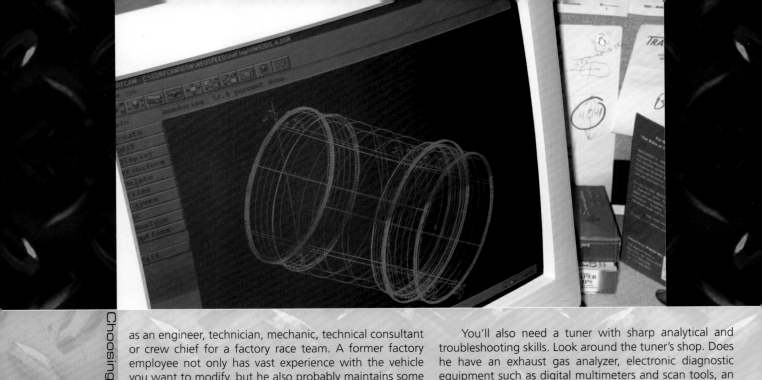

as an engineer, technician, mechanic, technical consultant or crew chief for a factory race team. A former factory employee not only has vast experience with the vehicle you want to modify, but he also probably maintains some connection to the factory, even if it's a backdoor, i.e. unofficial, relationship. This connection often enables these tuners to gain insights into the inner workings of, say, the engine management system, unavailable to their competitors. While tuners with factory connections aren't really necessary in the initial stages of a project, their special knowledge can be invaluable once you start pumping up the horsepower of your engine, especially if you're planning to keep it street legal.

Some people will tell you that tuning is art; some will tell you that it's science; some will tell you it's both. But it's neither. Tuning is engineering. That's not to say that one must have a degree in mechanical engineering to become a successful tuner. Most tuners are probably not engineers. But the good ones have "engineering minds," i.e. they understand physics, mechanics, hydraulics, pneumatics, electricity, etc. well enough to define a problem in engineering terms, and then solve it the way an engineer would.

Look for a tuner with experience not only in turning wrenches but also in machining, welding and fabricating. Or look for a tuner with people in his firm who have these skills. A tuner or shop with machining, welding and fabricating skills will be able to do a three-angle valve job or make you that special bracket without relying on subcontractors or sending you to a cross-town shop that you're not familiar with.

You'll also need a tuner with sharp analytical and troubleshooting skills. Look around the tuner's shop. Does he have an exhaust gas analyzer, electronic diagnostic equipment such as digital multimeters and scan tools, an oscilloscope, a dynamometer and a flow bench? If he doesn't, he's not going to be able to tune a modern high-performance vehicle. When you see this type of equipment in a tuner's shop, you know that this guy has some analytical and troubleshooting skills. These tools are too expensive to buy just to impress customers. When things go wrong, a skilled troubleshooter will save you money. Because he has fully grasped The Big Picture, i.e. he knows how everything works together and how one thing affects another, he can approach problems systemically and then solve them logically.

Look for a tuner with satisfied customers. If your friends drive vehicles similar or identical to yours, and if they're having success at the strip or the track with modifications made by a particular tuner, then that tuner is probably a good guy to start with. If you're interested in seeking help from someone farther from home, ask around at the strip or at car club or social gatherings. A tuner's reputation for knowing, or not knowing, what he's doing gets around pretty quickly. Word-of-mouth advertising should be part of your search, but don't make it the only part. People pleased with the work done by their own tuner might be tempted to exaggerate somewhat. But people displeased with work recently done might also exaggerate, so you've got to take this anecdotal advice for what it is - hearsay. However, there's no question that people vote with their dollars. Tuners with happy customers probably can provide more good tuning advice than tuners with unhappy customers.

Can the tuner deliver what he's promising?

Most tuners start out as self-employed small businessmen who "do it all" with a small or nonexistent staff. But as they become established and successful, smart tuners usually hire skilled and knowledgeable technicians to remedy any gaps in their capabilities, thereby enabling them to become full-service tuning shops. (Some tuners, however, surround themselves with "yes-men" who just try to keep the boss happy; stay away from these shops.) If possible, try to get to know some of the key people who work for a prospective tuner. Are they happy and excited about their work and about working for this particular tuner? If they're not, then you might be less than happy here as a long-term customer. And ask employees the same kinds of general questions you've asked their boss about their education and training. This isn't as hard as it might sound. Employees are usually hired for their expertise in one area, such as welding, fabrication or machining, so it's not that difficult to assess their qualifications. A tuner who's really proud of his staff will probably brag a little about their accomplishments.

Good tuners get results; bad ones don't. So look at a prospective tuner's track record. If you're hoping to improve the handling and braking of your car, look for a tuner with roadracing experience. Braking and handling upgrades that work well on the track also work well on the street. If more straight-line performance is what you want, then look for a tuner with drag racing experience. Most tuning shops that market themselves as horsepower specialists have a drag racing vehicle (or they sponsor one) which they use to try out new ideas and develop new products in competition. If a tuning firm's dragster has already earned a championship or two using his speed products, then that tuner probably knows some things that you don't. In other words, if a tuner has achieved success in competition, or if his customers have achieved similar success, then what works for them will probably work for you.

Is the tuner local?

Most tuners are set up for mail order, and when you're buying wheels, tires, suspension components, tune-up parts or bolt-on performance goodies, mail order prices can be hard to beat. But, if you're planning to do modifications that require precision machining, welding, fabrication or actual tuning, don't get into a long-distance relationship with a tuner unless absolutely necessary. Even if his reputation is sterling, you don't want to get involved in lengthy emails, phone calls and rewrapping and returning custom parts that don't fit or don't work.

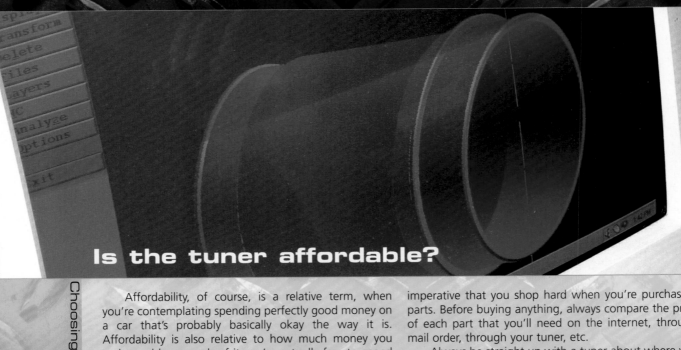

Is the tuner affordable?

Affordability, of course, is a relative term, when you're contemplating spending perfectly good money on a car that's probably basically okay the way it is. Affordability is also relative to how much money you make and how much of it you're actually free to spend on your car. And it's relative to what you intend to do to your vehicle. Some modifications are more cost effective than others. There are people in this sport with $20,000 in their engines. Are those engines twice as powerful as a $10,000 engine? Probably not, but you'd be amazed how many people spend megabucks on one part of their car, only to ignore the rest of it because they're broke! A good tuner will sit you down before you spend a penny and have you do a "build sheet," which is an overview of what you want to do your car, and how much each modification is going to cost. The total cost of some projects can get into five figures pretty quickly, so it's imperative that you shop hard when you're purchasing parts. Before buying anything, always compare the price of each part that you'll need on the internet, through mail order, through your tuner, etc.

Always be straight up with a tuner about where you want to go with your project and let him know what you can really, really afford. This is your hobby (okay, maybe it's your obsession!), so don't let it snowball to the point that it interferes with essential living expenses such as rent or mortgage payments, car payments, credit card debt, etc. Figure out how much money a month you can realistically afford to spend on your project and then divide that into the total estimated cost of the project and you'll know roughly how long it's going to take to get there. And you'll know the true meaning of affordability!

Is the tuner easy to get along with?

Most tuners are helpful and supportive. But some are eccentrics or egomaniacs.
This is probably unavoidable in a field that's filled with self-made, self-promoting small businessmen whose success is tied to their accomplishments. If you find that your tuner is patronizing or talking down to you, lecturing you or grumbling about the stupidity of other customers and/or his competitors, get rid of him. You want results, not therapy. A truly hard-working professional doesn't have the time to talk trash about his customers or fellow tuners. He's too busy taking care of business.

Does the tuner do the work on time?

Project vehicles are like new buildings. In the building trade, the progress of a new home or office building proceeds in spurts, with long intervals of waiting for the building code inspector to sign off the most recently completed phase of the project, punctuated by brief bursts of activity. In the tuning trade, project vehicles progress in a similar fashion, with long intervals of waiting - for parts, rebuilds, custom fabrication, etc. - punctuated by feverish bursts of activity installing them when they arrive. So patience is a virtue that you must have, or learn to cultivate, if you're going to undertake the challenge of putting together a project vehicle with the help of a tuner.

But patience-as-a-virtue notwithstanding, nobody wants a tuner who is unable, or unwilling, to deliver goods or services in a timely manner, particularly if the project vehicle is also the daily driver. Be realistic. If you can't afford to be without your car for lengthy periods of time, either obtain a back-up car, or look for a tuner who's willing to work on your car when you don't need it, like evenings, or weekends, or holidays. Some more complex projects - like engine or transaxle rebuilds or swaps - are unavoidably time-consuming, so find a tuner who will take the time he needs to do the job right, but no longer. Timeliness is not something you can always determine up front, but if you've hooked up with a procrastinator, it will become apparent soon enough.

The Flowbench:
The tuner's wind tunnel

If you're looking for a tuner to re-work your cylinder head for optimum airflow, look for one who owns and knows how to use a flowbench.

Since the power output of an engine is directly proportional to the amount of air it can inhale, a good tuner will try to remove all resistance to airflow in the induction system so that the engine can pack as much mixture into the combustion chambers as possible. In order to do so he must be able to measure the volume of air flowing through the intake manifold and the cylinder head so that he can quantify the results of his modifications. The device that he uses to measure airflow through the intake manifold and the cylinder head(s) is known as a flowbench. For tuners, the flowbench is an essential tool. Without it, you're just guessing how much power the cylinder head modifications will make.

Dynamometers

Horsepower talk is cheap when you're sitting around, kicking tires and telling lies with your buddies. If a friend claims a certain amount of horsepower for his vehicle, there's no way to verify such a claim without subjecting it to the ultimate tuning tool: the dynamometer. A dynamometer is a device that can accurately measure horsepower. There are two kinds of automotive dynamometers: engine dynos and chassis dynos.

Engine dynamometers

Engine development work is easier with the engine removed from the vehicle and installed on an engine dynamometer. An engine dyno is capable of "loading" the engine as if it were being run while installed in the vehicle. Engine dynos can provide a very accurate picture of an engine's power output because they measure power at the flywheel, with no power losses through the transmission/transaxle or driveline. This means, of course, that the engine must be removed from the vehicle and installed on the dyno. Then all the auxiliary systems - fuel supply, electrical supply, exhaust extraction, intake air for combustion, air flow for cooling, coolant temperature control, throttle actuation, etc. - must be provided. Because of these requirements, engine dynos are usually installed in enclosed, soundproof "test cells" that can provide the engine with these auxiliary systems. Despite the complexity of setting up an engine dyno/test cell site, engine dynos are popular with automobile manufacturers and OEM engine developers because of the degree of control over the test parameters made possible by isolating the engine from the vehicle. Serious developers and researchers want repeatability (consistent results from test to test) unaffected by factors that can't be controlled by the tester. They also want the capability to install special testing sensors and to make easy adjustments and changes to the test engine. For these reasons, engine dynamometers are used extensively by automobile manufacturers to develop new engines, and to test them for reliability and endurance. Engine dynos are not used much by aftermarket tuners because testing an engine out of the vehicle isn't practical for most tuning shops, or affordable for most customers.

Chassis dynamometers

If a tuner proudly shows off his dynamometer when you "take the tour" of his shop, chances are it will be a chassis dyno. The chassis dynamometer is the dyno of choice for most tuners because it allows them to test an engine's performance without removing it from the vehicle. The typical chassis dyno uses a series of big rollers that are connected to some type of power absorber capable of controlling the load that's applied to the rollers. To measure horsepower, you simply drive the vehicle onto the dyno, position it so that the drive wheels are resting on top of the rollers, start the engine, put it in gear and record the data. The chassis dyno operator can dial a specific amount of load into the rollers to simulate acceleration, passing or going up a steep hill. The main advantage of a chassis dyno is that you don't have to remove the engine to dyno it. This, of course, simplifies both the testing procedure itself and the setup for the testing. Another advantage is that the chassis dyno delivers "real world" numbers, i.e. it reflects the actual horsepower at the drive wheels, not the horsepower at the crankshaft. The disadvantage of a chassis dyno is that the results aren't that consistent or repeatable because of the factors - driveline losses, and tire wear, pressure and temperature - that influence each dyno run.

Engine
compartment
dress-up

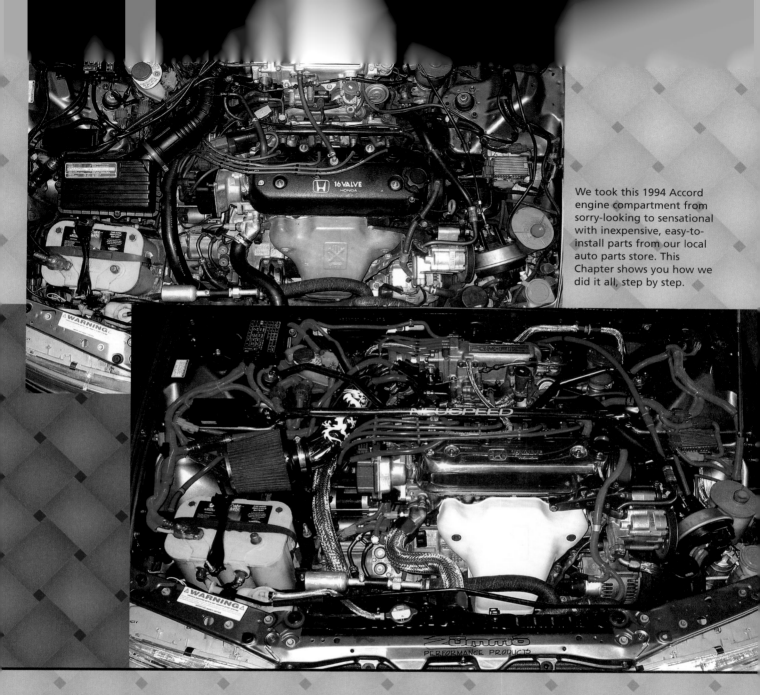

We took this 1994 Accord engine compartment from sorry-looking to sensational with inexpensive, easy-to-install parts from our local auto parts store. This Chapter shows you how we did it all, step by step.

Open the hood on a sport compact car and what do you see? Black plastic air filter housing, black air intake duct, black battery, black radiator and heater hoses, black vacuum hoses, black fuse box, black electrical harnesses, black accelerator and cruise control cables, black valve cover (with, of course, a black oil filler cap), black . . . well, black everything. Black, black, black everywhere! A sea of black! It's as if the engine compartment was dressed for a funeral or some other somber occasion.

Show-car engine compartments don't look like midnight in a coal mine, so why should yours? Look how we transformed the engine compartment shown above - this only took a few hundred bucks and a couple of weekends.

Detail your engine compartment

before dressing it up

Before we talk about things you can do to dress up your engine compartment, let's take a few minutes to discuss engine compartment detailing, which is a good thing to do even if you never spend a penny to trick out the engine bay.

After 20,000 or 30,000 miles, an engine usually begins to leak a little coolant or engine oil. Brake fluid, power-steering fluid and transmission fluid leaks might also appear. As the miles click through the odometer, these little leaks slowly spread out, dirt and road grime start sticking to the areas covered by oil, and the engine gets dirty. Some of the leaking fluids, if they're not regularly removed, can degrade paint, plastic and rubber. Batteries can also be messy. A bad voltage regulator can allow the alternator to overcharge the battery, which can spit highly corrosive sulfuric acid onto painted surfaces. Battery connections must also be cleaned regularly, or one day you'll hear that dreaded "click-click," which means that you're not playing with a full 12 volts.

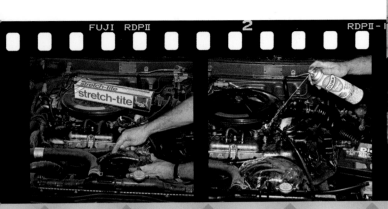

Engine washing

In a basic wash and detail, a clean engine might need nothing more than a simple soaping up and hosing down. If you can't remove the accumulated dirt and grime this easily, stronger measures are called for. Chemical cleaners for degreasing engines are available at your local auto parts store, and there are even some effective household cleaners. Most oven cleaners work well on heavy grease deposits on your engine. And many household liquid or spray cleaners like 409, or Simple Green, will also work in most cases. Be sure to observe all the cautions on the container, and wear rubber gloves and eye protection when hosing off this stuff. Some of these cleaners are caustic and most can damage your eyes and skin. If you accidentally splash some cleaner in your eyes or on your skin, rinse it out or off immediately!

Engine cleaners from the auto parts store are even more effective than household cleaning agents. Gunk is a widely-available brand that has been used for many years, and the newer Castrol SuperClean, is also excellent. Some of the automotive engine cleaners are available in both spray and foam, the latter of which is good at staying in place on vertical surfaces such as timing covers, firewalls and fenderwells.

Pressure washing

On engines with heavy grease deposits, it's helpful to have some kind of pressure to help loosen the deposits. Renting or buying a pressure-washer is the best solution if you're willing to spend the money.

The local coin-op carwash is an ideal place to detail your engine, if it's still legal. There's plenty of pressure, hot water and even soapy water to wash off the chemicals before rinsing with clear water. But because of the accumulated sludge in the drains at the-washing bays of some coin-op carwashes, the government has cracked down in recent years on carwash owners. If there's a "No Engine Washing" sign at your local coin-op carwash, go somewhere else. At carwashes that still allow engine cleaning, the owners have invested in expensive sludge traps and filters that prevent hosed-off grease from contaminating the water supply.

Steam cleaning

The third option is to take your car to a place that does engine steam cleaning. Before the general availability of good consumer engine cleaners in spray cans, this was the only option, and you had to "know where to go" to even find a carwash that did engine steam-cleaning. As its name implies, this process involves a pressure spray of really hot water and solvent. It does a superb job of removing baked-on grease and dirt from engines, transaxles and running gear. Many professional modifiers and tuners make the steam-cleaner their first stop when starting a new project.

Steam cleaning, if you can find a shop that still does it, cleans everything extensively. The only drawbacks are that it can remove paint from the engine or from painted accessories if the paint is already beginning to flake or peel off from age, chemical exposure or heat, and can also damage rubber components if you're not careful. But if you're going to go all the way with engine compartment detailing, this shouldn't matter that much because you will eventually refinish most components anyway.

Moisture

Another problem with pressure washing and steam cleaning is moisture, which isn't good for ignition and fuel system components. Keeping critical components dry during engine cleaning is a precaution that should be taken no matter what wash method you use - hose, pressure-wash or steam. Of course, the best plan is to avoid getting water on sensitive components in the first place, but with steam cleaning it's pretty much unavoidable! Steamy, pressurized water can get inside your distributor cap and other places that you think are completely sealed. Your engine might start but run poorly after a steam bath, or it might not start at all. So have some WD-40 and some clean rags handy. You might have to dry out the distributor cap or the boots at the ends of the coil wire and each spark plug wire.

To keep them from getting wet in the first place protect the coil, the distributor and the carburetor or throttle body. These can be effectively covered with household aluminum foil, plastic bags or "stretch-type" plastic food wrap.

Remove the big chunks first

After bagging or otherwise protecting vital components, use a paint stirring stick or an old plastic-coated kitchen spatula to scrape away the heavier concentrations of grease. Look in crevices and places where dirt collects easily. The more buildup you can remove this way, the fewer applications of cleaner you'll have to make. Don't use screwdrivers or other sharp metal tools or putty knives to remove the grease, or you take a chance on scraping off painted surfaces on the engine or components.

Not too hot!

In most cases it's not a good idea to detail a hot engine. Some enthusiasts like to clean an engine while it's still hot because the heat makes the chemicals work faster at loosening dirt. But some normally-hot components such as the exhaust manifold (and turbocharger, if you have one) can crack if they're exposed to a sudden bath of cold water when the part is really hot. If you're doing your cleanup at the coin-op carwash, let the engine cool off before starting the underhood detailing.

Use lots of cleaner

Begin your underhood cleanup by applying a liberal coat of cleaner everywhere, even on areas that you don't think are that dirty. Douse the firewall, inner fender panels, radiator and all around the engine. Work your way down to the parts of the chassis that are exposed in the engine compartment. Most engine

cleaning products work best if they are not allowed to dry out completely before rinsing. If you notice that warmer areas seem to be drying out, spray them again with cleaner and let the cleaner work for the interval specified by the cleaner manufacturer. If you don't allow the cleaner to do its work long enough to thoroughly soak the stuff you're trying to remove, you'll have to repeat the process. Use a parts-cleaning brush with a long wooden handle and stiff bristles to scrub the cleaner into areas of baked-on grease.

Since you are probably using strong cleaners for your underhood session, make sure that you either mask off your fenders and cowl, or wash down those areas with carwash soap and water right after the engine work. The cleaner and sludge you hose off can get on your paint and cause wax streaking, if not paint damage, when left on too long.

Inspect and clean rubber hoses, vacuum lines and cables

After a thorough cleaning, inspect all of your engine compartment hoses and vacuum lines. If some of your hoses are noticeably spongy or soft, it's time to replace them. If all your rubber hoses are in good shape, they can be made to look like new very easily. Clean them with a rag and any tire or rubber cleaner, then wipe them off with a silicone protectant. You'll be amazed at how fresh they look! Do NOT use cleaners or protectants on drivebelts; it can cause them to slip and squeal. Spark plug wires that have become greasy from handling during plug changes are also easily cleaned

Braided metal hose covers

Braided covers are available from automotive retailers in a variety of lengths and diameters. Typical cover kits include six feet of material for vacuum lines, fuel hoses or heater hoses. Radiator hose covers are available in three or six foot lengths, each of which is available in 1-1/2 inch or 1-3/4 inch diameters.

Most aftermarket manufacturers of stainless-look braided cover kits also include anodized aluminum "clamps" which look just like the more expensive fittings used on racecar plumbing. Except that they're just aluminum rings, machined to look like big nuts, which fit over a standard hose clamp (which you can easily hide by putting it on the side of the hose that nobody will ever see).

Before heading for your nearest automotive retailer to buy braided covering, it's a good idea to measure the hoses and/or lines you plan to cover. You need to determine how many feet you will need for each diameter hose or line you want to cover. If you don't know exactly how much braided covering you're going to need, some manufacturers offer starter kits with a little bit of everything. For example, each of the two kits that we used to dress up the engine compartment of a 1994 Honda Accord included lengths of braided cover for 3 feet of vacuum line, 4 feet of fuel line, 12 feet of heater hose and 4-1/2 feet of radiator hose. Each kit also included four fuel line clamps, four heater hose clamps, two upper radiator hose clamps and four shrink sleeves for vacuum lines. Other kits are similarly versatile. Okay, ready? Let's get started!

Installation on radiator hoses

01 First, unpack your kit and make sure that everything you'll need is included. Most of these kits don't include elaborate instructions, but after we walk you through some typical covering procedures, you'll wonder why you didn't tackle this job sooner!

02 Wait until the engine cools off completely. Drain the engine coolant (refer to your Haynes manual if necessary), then loosen the hose clamp at the radiator and slide it back . . .

03 . . . loosen the clamp at the thermostat housing and slide it back . . .

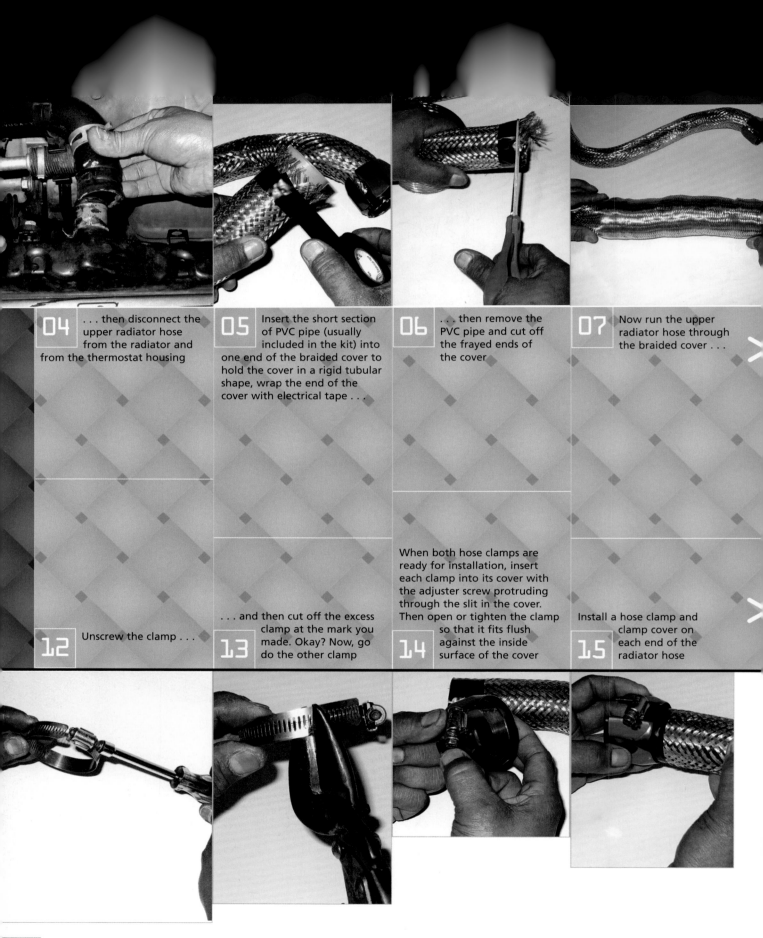

04 . . . then disconnect the upper radiator hose from the radiator and from the thermostat housing

05 Insert the short section of PVC pipe (usually included in the kit) into one end of the braided cover to hold the cover in a rigid tubular shape, wrap the end of the cover with electrical tape . . .

06 . . . then remove the PVC pipe and cut off the frayed ends of the cover

07 Now run the upper radiator hose through the braided cover . . .

12 Unscrew the clamp . . .

13 . . . and then cut off the excess clamp at the mark you made. Okay? Now, go do the other clamp

14 When both hose clamps are ready for installation, insert each clamp into its cover with the adjuster screw protruding through the slit in the cover. Then open or tighten the clamp so that it fits flush against the inside surface of the cover

15 Install a hose clamp and clamp cover on each end of the radiator hose

08 . . . tape the end . . .

09 . . . and cut off the excess

10 Install a hose clamp on one end of the newly covered radiator hose and snug it down so that it fits perfectly. Don't tighten it so much that it begins to compress the hose. You're determining how much of the clamp to cut off, because the part of the clamp that sticks out from the adjuster screw won't fit underneath the clamp cover, and you don't want anyone to see an unsightly clamp exposed. Very unprofessional!

11 Slide the clamp off the end of the hose and mark the point at which the clamp sticks out from the adjuster screw. Mark it right at the screw

16 Here's what your covered and clamped upper radiator hose should look like

17 Carefully install the radiator hose between the radiator and the thermostat housing . . .

18 . . . then tighten the hose clamps at both ends

19 One upper radiator hose done! Now repeat this entire procedure for the lower radiator hose!

Installation on PCV hoses

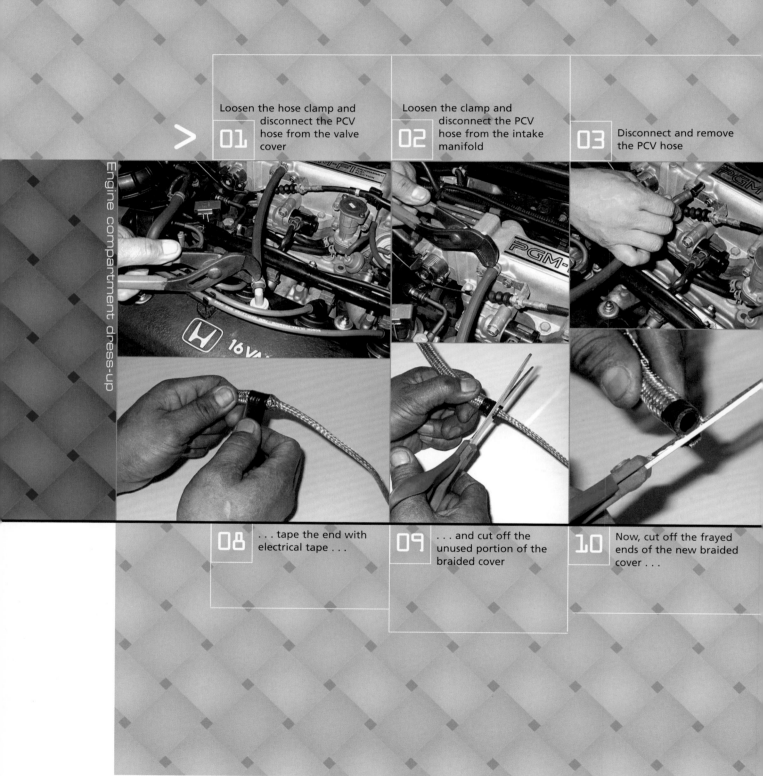

Engine compartment dress-up

01 Loosen the hose clamp and disconnect the PCV hose from the valve cover

02 Loosen the clamp and disconnect the PCV hose from the intake manifold

03 Disconnect and remove the PCV hose

08 . . . tape the end with electrical tape . . .

09 . . . and cut off the unused portion of the braided cover

10 Now, cut off the frayed ends of the new braided cover . . .

04 Insert one end of the PCV hose into the new braided metal cover . . .

05 Wrap a piece of electrical tape around the end of the braided metal cover . . .

06 . . . work the PCV hose through the braided cover until the hose is completely covered . . .

07 . . . pull on the braided cover to make sure that it's a tight fit over the PCV hose so that the braided cover won't bunch up later . . .

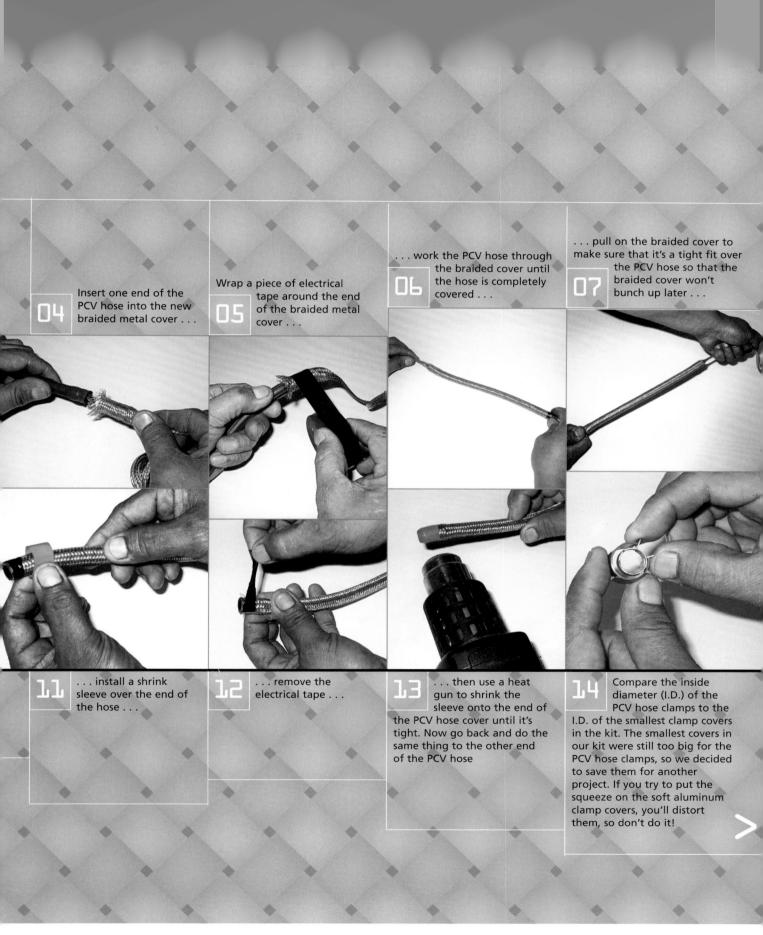

11 . . . install a shrink sleeve over the end of the hose . . .

12 . . . remove the electrical tape . . .

13 . . . then use a heat gun to shrink the sleeve onto the end of the PCV hose cover until it's tight. Now go back and do the same thing to the other end of the PCV hose

14 Compare the inside diameter (I.D.) of the PCV hose clamps to the I.D. of the smallest clamp covers in the kit. The smallest covers in our kit were still too big for the PCV hose clamps, so we decided to save them for another project. If you try to put the squeeze on the soft aluminum clamp covers, you'll distort them, so don't do it!

>

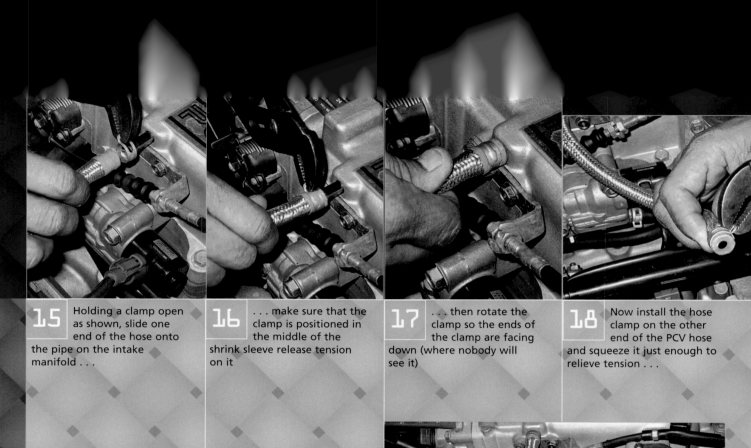

15 Holding a clamp open as shown, slide one end of the hose onto the pipe on the intake manifold . . .

16 . . . make sure that the clamp is positioned in the middle of the shrink sleeve release tension on it

17 . . . then rotate the clamp so the ends of the clamp are facing down (where nobody will see it)

18 Now install the hose clamp on the other end of the PCV hose and squeeze it just enough to relieve tension . . .

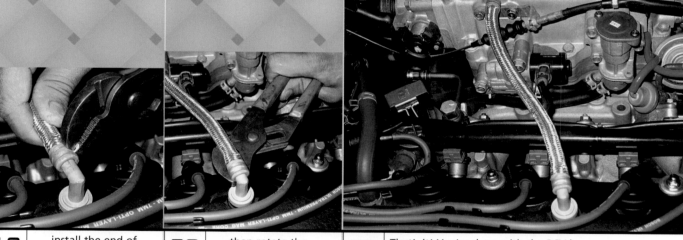

19 . . . install the end of the PCV hose onto the pipe on the valve cover . . .

20 . . . then rotate the ends of the clamp down where they're less noticeable

21 That's it! You're done with the PCV hose

Replace the dipstick and the oil filler cap with billet

01 Remove the old oil filler cap

02 Install the new cap. You won't find too many engine dress-up swaps any easier than this!

Most replacement dipsticks look better than the stock unit, but the ones with billet handles are among the prettiest, so we selected a blue-anodized billet-handled dipstick for our engine compartment dress-up project.

And while you're at it, why not add a matching oil filler cap? Get a billet cap! Anodized in the color of your choice, of course. We opted for - you guessed it - blue!

01 Yank out the old dipstick . . .

02 . . . make sure that the old unit and the new model are the same dimensions . . .

. . . then install the new dipstick. Check out this beautiful blue-anodized, billet handled model! A nice touch for any engine

03

Wiring and small hoses

Wiring covers can protect your wiring from damage, in addition to making it look good. And replacing your old, rotting vacuum hoses with long-life silicone hoses may even fix a vacuum leak that's causing your engine to run poorly. And you've got to get some high-performance silicone spark-plug wires in a matching color. You'll be enhancing your car's performance as well as giving it a cool look.

Installing silicone vacuum hoses

01 First, break out your new silicone hose kit(s). The owner of this project car wanted something blue, so we rounded up some popular kits in the various diameters we would need

02 Where to start? Well, if you're going to replace all the old vacuum hoses, just pick a hose! We started with some small vacuum hoses in the vicinity of the throttle body. Disconnect one hose at a time (so you don't get confused and reattach the new silicone hose incorrectly) from the throttle body . . .

03 . . . and from the metal pipe at the other end

04 Compare the inside diameter (I.D.) of the new silicone hose to the I.D. of the old vacuum hose and make sure that they're the same. You can get away with using a slightly smaller I.D. than the stock you're replacing because it produces an even tighter fit. But don't ever replace an old hose with a new vacuum hose that has a larger I.D. than the stock hose, or you'll end up with a major problem

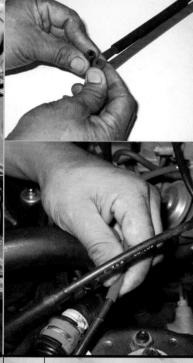

05 Using the old vacuum hose as a template, mark off a piece of the new silicone hose the same length . . .

06 . . . and cut it off

07 Okay, push one end of the new silicone vacuum hose onto the pipe on the throttle body . . .

08 . . . and the other end on the pipe at, well, the other end

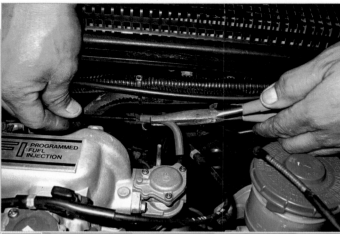

09 Okay, wanna do another one? How 'bout that little short elbow-shaped piece connecting the two metal pipes, right behind this diaphragm?

10 Pull the hose off one pipe . . .

11 . . . and then pull it off the other pipe

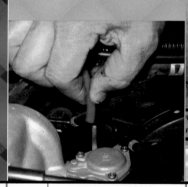

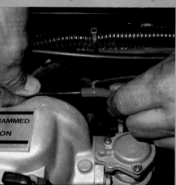

12 Using the old vacuum hose as a template, cut off an equal length of silicone hose, make sure that the I.D.s are the same then install the new piece on one pipe . . .

13 . . . and on the other pipe

14 Okay, got the idea? Go ahead, do that little short piece in the foreground, between the diaphragm and the throttle body. Now keep going! Pretty soon, a sea of blue will slowly begin to wash over this once clean but dull engine compartment

Installing silicone spark plug wires

Disconnect the first spark plug wire and boot from its corresponding spark plug. The boots on some vehicles are rather long, and sometimes difficult to disconnect. Do not pull on the wire itself; pull only on the boot. Auto parts stores sell special plier-like tools with plastic coated tips that wrap around and grip the spark plug boot, making it easier to remove

02

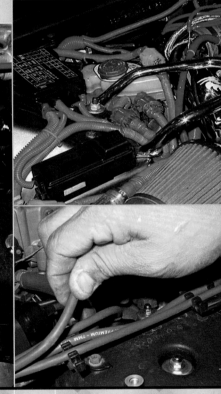

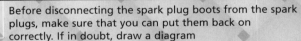

01 Before disconnecting the spark plug boots from the spark plugs, make sure that you can put them back on correctly. If in doubt, draw a diagram

03 Disengage the first spark plug wire from any cable guides on the valve cover or anywhere between the distributor and the spark plugs

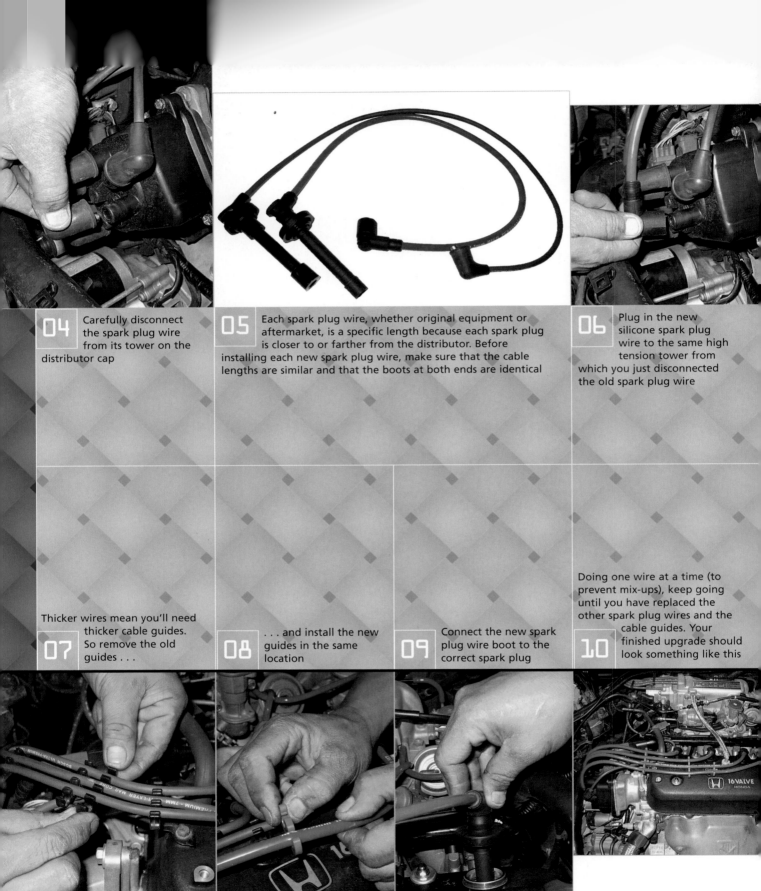

04 Carefully disconnect the spark plug wire from its tower on the distributor cap

05 Each spark plug wire, whether original equipment or aftermarket, is a specific length because each spark plug is closer to or farther from the distributor. Before installing each new spark plug wire, make sure that the cable lengths are similar and that the boots at both ends are identical

06 Plug in the new silicone spark plug wire to the same high tension tower from which you just disconnected the old spark plug wire

07 Thicker wires mean you'll need thicker cable guides. So remove the old guides . . .

08 . . . and install the new guides in the same location

09 Connect the new spark plug wire boot to the correct spark plug

10 Doing one wire at a time (to prevent mix-ups), keep going until you have replaced the other spark plug wires and the cable guides. Your finished upgrade should look something like this

Replacing the breather hose with a filter

Another colorful upgrade is to eliminate that unsightly rubber breather hose and replace it with a trick baby air filter. Breather filters are available in blue, red, yellow and chrome, and look like miniature versions of the big K & Ns used on tuned intake systems. But do yourself a favor. Before you run out and buy a breather filter, make sure that it's legal. You don't want to fail the visual part of a smog test over a breather filter.

 01 Loosen the hose clamp . . .

 02 . . . and disconnect the PCV fresh air inlet hose from the pipe on the valve cover

03 Install the new PCV air filter . . .

 04 . . . and tighten the hose clamp securely

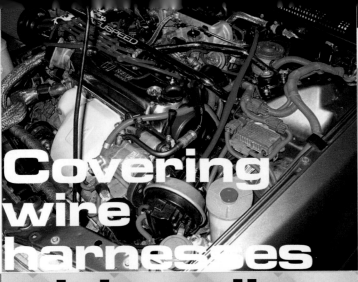

Covering wire harnesses with split loom

01 If the harness is already covered by the old black plastic stuff, remove it first

02 Install the new split loom over the harness . . .

Plastic split-loom is easy to install and looks great. It will help protect your wiring and is easy to remove for servicing. You'll never realize how many wires you have until you have to cover them - but don't worry, this one's easy!

03 . . . and tape the end (the end that you're not going to cut) with electrical tape

04 Keep pushing the new split loom onto the harness until you reach an electrical connector or anything that serves as a natural stopping point for a continuous section of split loom. We stopped here because of a junction in the harness, at which point the harness splits off into two smaller harnesses. At this point, pull off the end of the split loom and cut it (but don't tape it yet)

05 Okay, now cover the two smaller harness with split loom and then cut them to fit

06 Now go back and wrap the junction for the three sections of split loom with electrical tape. That's all there is to it! Keep going until you've covered every harness in the engine compartment with new split loom!

Replacing the accelerator cable

The accelerator cable isn't something you would normally think of replacing unless it breaks or is sticking. But take a minute to just look at this aftermarket cable, which is clad in genuine braided stainless steel. Are you going to sit around and wait until the stock cable breaks to install one just like it? Not! You're going to rush out, buy one and install it right now!

01 When you get home from your automotive retailer, break out your new braided stainless steel accelerator cable kit, make sure that everything is there and then read the instructions included with the kit

02 Here's the stock accelerator cable setup. If you've never replaced an accelerator cable before, take a few minutes to study the cable installation on your car. Note the routing of the cable from the firewall to the throttle cam on the throttle body. Your new aftermarket cable must be routed just like this, except that it'll look better. A lot better!

03 First, disengage the accelerator cable from any cable guides on the intake manifold or on the valve cover

04 Using a pair of wrenches, loosen the accelerator cable adjustment nut and the locknut at the cable bracket . . .

05 . . . then disengage the accelerator cable from the cable bracket

06 Disengage the plug on the forward end of the cable from its slot in the throttle cam

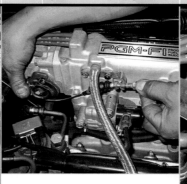

07 Now go inside the car, stick your head under the dash and, using a flashlight, locate the lower end of the accelerator cable, where it connects to the upper end of the accelerator pedal. Disengage the plug on the lower end of the cable from its slot in the accelerator pedal. Now, back in the engine compartment, pull the cable through the firewall

08 Okay, that takes care of the old accelerator cable. Now grab the new cable and, using an Allen wrench, loosen the set screw and remove the cable end plug from the end of the cable . . .

09 . . . then pull the cable out of its braided steel covering . . .

10 . . . and remove the nut from the threaded fitting

>

Hold up the forward end of the braided steel sheathing in its installed position and mark the point on the sheathing which parallels the end of the threaded assembly you just installed . . .

. . . but before cutting off the excess sheathing, make sure that the sheathing is correctly routed, just like it will be routed when the cable is installed and hooked up to the throttle body. Don't cut the sheathing too short, which will strain the cable if an engine mount starts to head south and allows the engine to move around. Instead, give yourself a little wiggle room by leaving a few inches of extra sheathing. If your guesstimate turns out to be a little too generous, you can always cut if off later

After you have verified that your mark is more or less where it should be, wrap a little piece of tape around the braided sheathing at the mark, then cut off the excess sheathing

Remove the tape from the sheathing, pull the little cable ferrule out of the threaded fitting at the cable bracket (the ferrule that you inserted into the big nut on the threaded fitting back in Step 14, remember?) and slide the little ferrule onto the sheathing

>

15
16
17
18

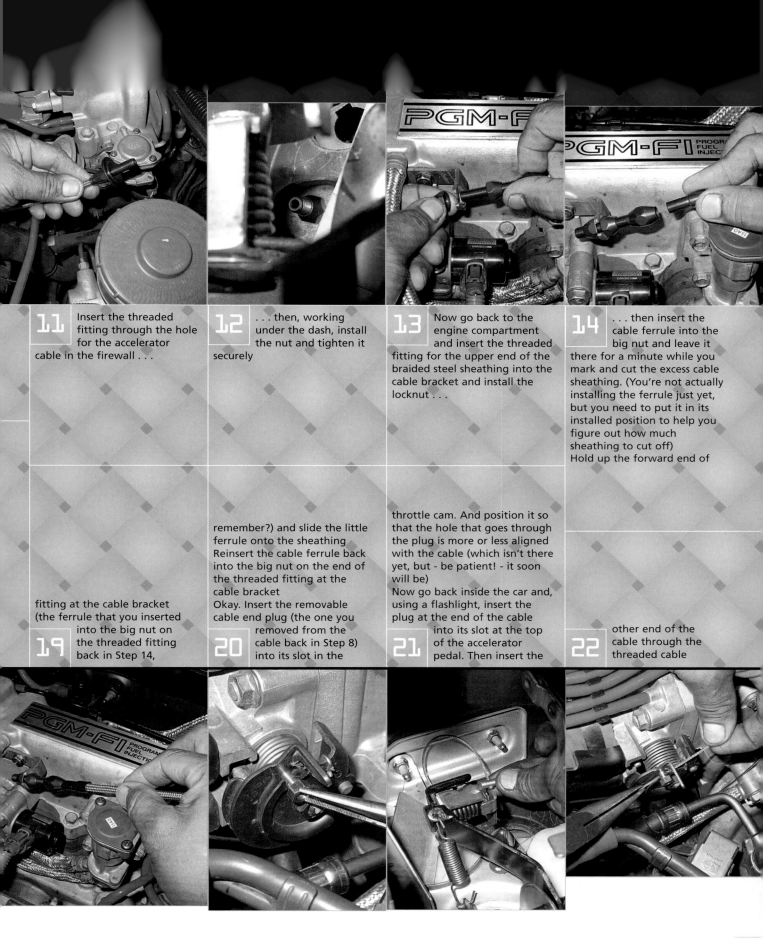

11 Insert the threaded fitting through the hole for the accelerator cable in the firewall . . .

12 . . . then, working under the dash, install the nut and tighten it securely

13 Now go back to the engine compartment and insert the threaded fitting for the upper end of the braided steel sheathing into the cable bracket and install the locknut . . .

14 . . . then insert the cable ferrule into the big nut and leave it there for a minute while you mark and cut the excess cable sheathing. (You're not actually installing the ferrule just yet, but you need to put it in its installed position to help you figure out how much sheathing to cut off)
Hold up the forward end of

fitting at the cable bracket (the ferrule that you inserted into the big nut on the threaded fitting

remember?) and slide the little ferrule onto the sheathing
Reinsert the cable ferrule back into the big nut on the end of the threaded fitting at the cable bracket
Okay. Insert the removable cable end plug (the one you removed from the cable back in Step 8)

throttle cam. And position it so that the hole that goes through the plug is more or less aligned with the cable (which isn't there yet, but - be patient! - it soon will be)
Now go back inside the car and, using a flashlight, insert the plug at the end of the cable into its slot at the top of the accelerator pedal. Then insert the

other end of the cable through the threaded cable

19 back in Step 14,

20 into its slot in the

21

22

> 23 . . . pull the excess cable out the other side of the end plug . . .

24 . . . then tighten the end plug set screw to hold the cable

25 Cut off the excess cable. You won't be able to cut off the excess flush with the end plug, but just cut off as much as you can

26 Remove the end plug from its slot in the throttle cam and finish the job

27 Once the cable has been cut off flush with the end plug, retighten the setscrew. Make sure that it's tight!

28 Insert the end plug back into its socket in the throttle cam and thread the cable onto the cable guide that goes around the perimeter of the throttle cam

29 Insert the threaded fitting back into the cable bracket . . .

30 . . . and install the locknut to secure the fitting to the cable bracket. Then refer to your Haynes manual and adjust the accelerator cable freeplay in accordance with the manufacturer's specifications. That's it!

Polished valve covers

The traditional route for upgrading the appearance of your valve cover has always been to replace it. But that's because there wasn't much you could do with the typical stamped steel valve cover, which was usually painted in an exciting . . . black (which inevitably wore off, leaving you with a rusty stamped steel valve cover). So you went out and bought a nice aluminum valve cover to replace the stock unit.

Nowadays, though, a lot of sport compact cars are already equipped with an aluminum valve cover. Trouble is, it's not polished, or anodized. It's often just painted in a crinkle-finish black paint. It won't rust like one of those cheap old steel valve covers, but it won't get any better looking with time, either. Which is why we decided that the black valve cover on this Honda had to go. But instead of replacing it, we simply removed the black paint and had it polished by a local shop. The results speak for themselves.

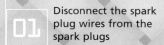

01 Disconnect the spark plug wires from the spark plugs

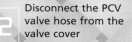

02 Disconnect the PCV valve hose from the valve cover

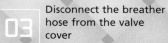

03 Disconnect the breather hose from the valve cover

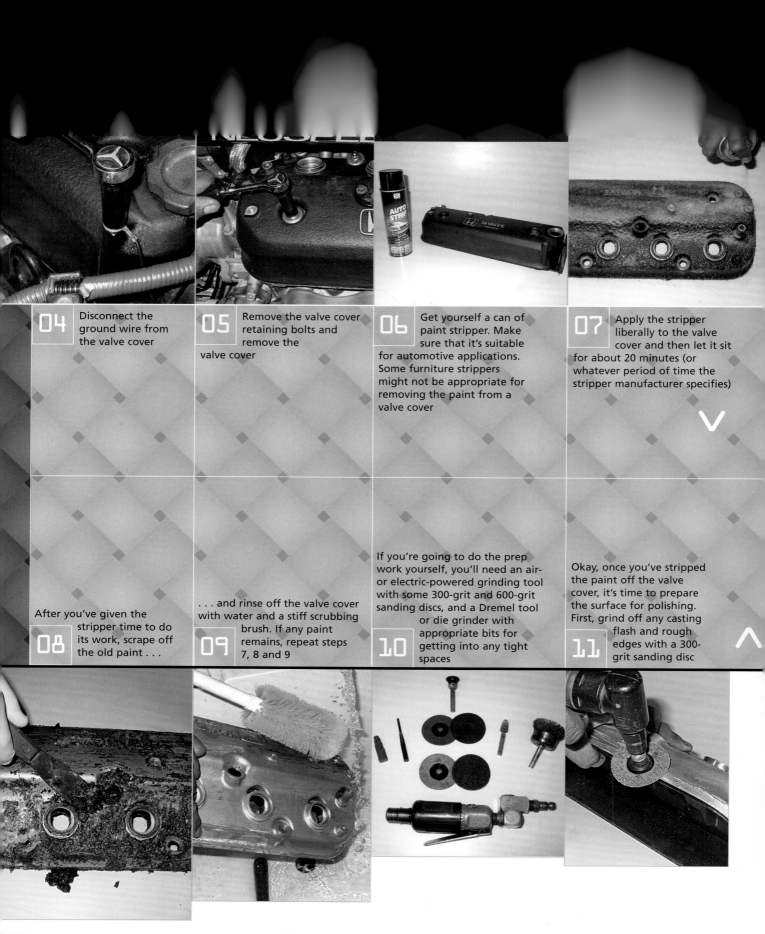

04 Disconnect the ground wire from the valve cover

05 Remove the valve cover retaining bolts and remove the valve cover

06 Get yourself a can of paint stripper. Make sure that it's suitable for automotive applications. Some furniture strippers might not be appropriate for removing the paint from a valve cover

07 Apply the stripper liberally to the valve cover and then let it sit for about 20 minutes (or whatever period of time the stripper manufacturer specifies)

∨

08 After you've given the stripper time to do its work, scrape off the old paint . . .

09 . . . and rinse off the valve cover with water and a stiff scrubbing brush. If any paint remains, repeat steps 7, 8 and 9

10 If you're going to do the prep work yourself, you'll need an air- or electric-powered grinding tool with some 300-grit and 600-grit sanding discs, and a Dremel tool or die grinder with appropriate bits for getting into any tight spaces

11 Okay, once you've stripped the paint off the valve cover, it's time to prepare the surface for polishing. First, grind off any casting flash and rough edges with a 300-grit sanding disc

∧

12 Then switch to a 600-grit sanding disc to produce a smoother finish

13 Use a Dremel tool to get into any tight spots

14 Here are some typical tools of the trade for polishing aluminum. You'll also need some metal polishing compound (available at most automotive retailers)

15 Switch to a 3M cutting pad and remove any scratches caused by the grinding discs

16 We borrowed some typical blocks of polishing "rouge" (compound) from our local polishing shop to show you what the pros use. Each compound is different, and is designed to bring out the color or shine of certain metals. The black compound is for stainless steel surfaces; white is for "final finish" polishing; green is for chrome; and brown is for aluminum. (Of course, as a do-it-yourselfer, you won't need this many compounds, unless you plan to start polishing for a living!)

17 All right, enough talk. Let's get started. Add some (brown) polishing compound to the buffing pad . . .

18 . . . and start polishing the valve cover!

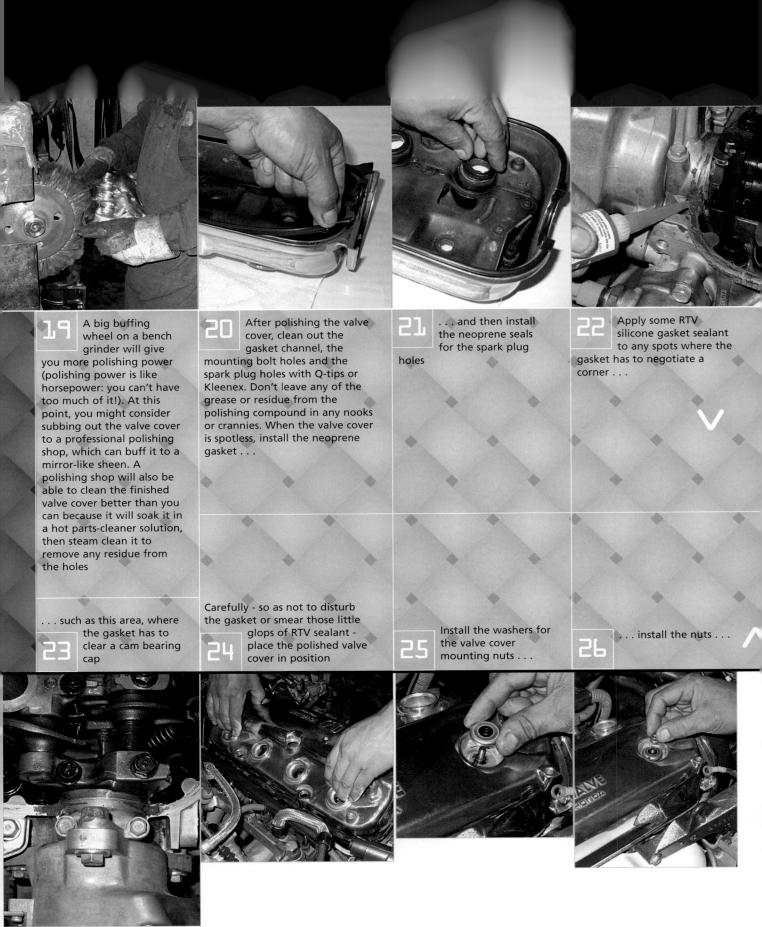

19 A big buffing wheel on a bench grinder will give you more polishing power (polishing power is like horsepower: you can't have too much of it!). At this point, you might consider subbing out the valve cover to a professional polishing shop, which can buff it to a mirror-like sheen. A polishing shop will also be able to clean the finished valve cover better than you can because it will soak it in a hot parts-cleaner solution, then steam clean it to remove any residue from the holes

20 After polishing the valve cover, clean out the gasket channel, the mounting bolt holes and the spark plug holes with Q-tips or Kleenex. Don't leave any of the grease or residue from the polishing compound in any nooks or crannies. When the valve cover is spotless, install the neoprene gasket . . .

21 . . . and then install the neoprene seals for the spark plug holes

22 Apply some RTV silicone gasket sealant to any spots where the gasket has to negotiate a corner . . .

23 . . . such as this area, where the gasket has to clear a cam bearing cap

24 Carefully - so as not to disturb the gasket or smear those little glops of RTV sealant - place the polished valve cover in position

25 Install the washers for the valve cover mounting nuts . . .

26 . . . install the nuts . . .

44

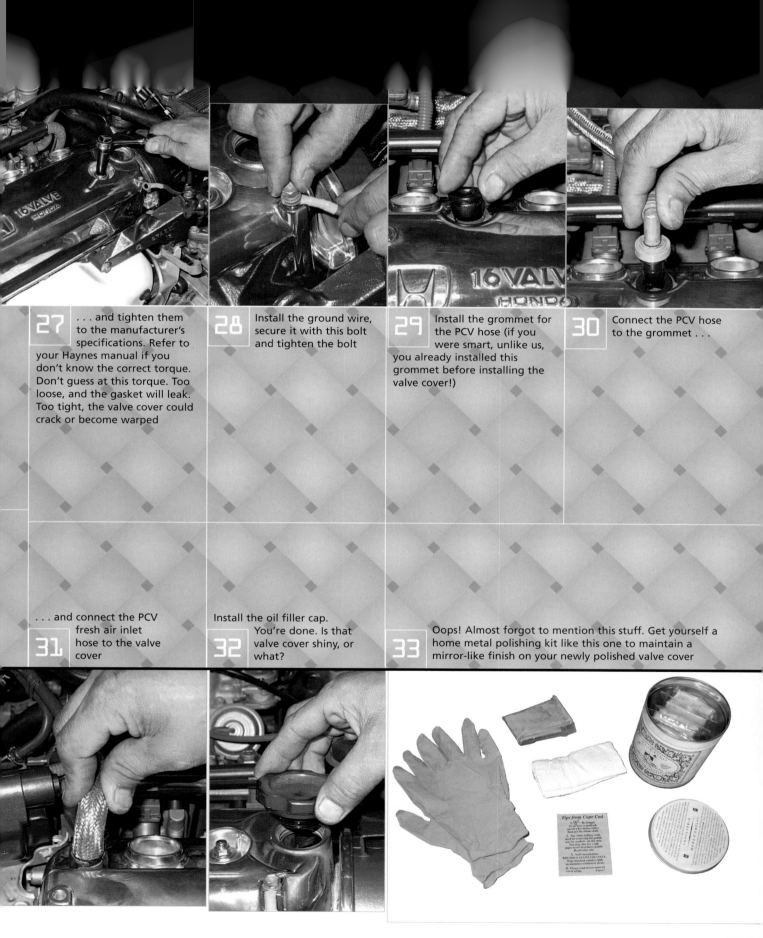

27 . . . and tighten them to the manufacturer's specifications. Refer to your Haynes manual if you don't know the correct torque. Don't guess at this torque. Too loose, and the gasket will leak. Too tight, the valve cover could crack or become warped

28 Install the ground wire, secure it with this bolt and tighten the bolt

29 Install the grommet for the PCV hose (if you were smart, unlike us, you already installed this grommet before installing the valve cover!)

30 Connect the PCV hose to the grommet . . .

31 . . . and connect the PCV fresh air inlet hose to the valve cover

32 Install the oil filler cap. You're done. Is that valve cover shiny, or what?

33 Oops! Almost forgot to mention this stuff. Get yourself a home metal polishing kit like this one to maintain a mirror-like finish on your newly polished valve cover

Painting an exhaust manifold heat shield

When you get enough coin together for a chrome-plated header, you'll have the ultimate look. Until then, you can add some color by painting the exhaust manifold heat shield. The only thing you'll need is a can of high-temperature paint in the color of your choice. We chose white because it looks . . . well, it looks white hot!

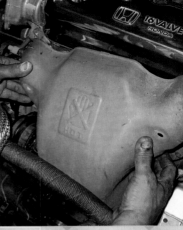

01 First, remove the heat shield fasteners . . .

02 . . . then remove the heat shield

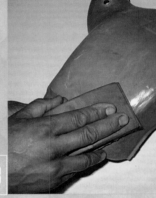

Next, remove all grease and oil with a good solvent or degreaser. Then sand off all rust and any bugs or crud that's baked onto the shield. You're not trying to remove all the original paint, you're just trying to create a nice, roughed up surface so that the paint will adhere to it **03**

04 The surface of the heat shield is one of the hottest places on the engine when it's running, so make sure that you use a high-temperature paint.

05 Apply the high-temperature paint evenly to the heat shield surface.

06 Install the newly painted heat shield . . .

07 . . . and install and securely tighten the heat shield fasteners. Looks better, doesn't it?

Painting brackets

No matter how pretty your engine compartment might look by now, all those black cast-iron and stamped steel brackets for the engine, transaxle, radiator and other big or heavy components are always going to be an eyesore. Of course, if you have access to a machine shop (or, better yet, own one!), you can swap the stock brackets for one-off pieces custom machined from billet. But until that day comes, why not simply paint some of the more prominent pieces to match your engine compartment color scheme? The only things you'll need are some sandpaper and a can of spray paint. You'll be amazed at the transformation. So, let's start with something that's easy to remove and install, like, oh, how about the radiator brackets? Then we'll let you take it from there.

01 First, remove the radiator brackets

02 Remove any grommets or insulators from the brackets

03 Sand off any rough edges or rust

We used a can of metallic blue Krylon to spray paint the bracket. Make sure that you use a paint that's suitable for painting metal and, if you're going to paint any brackets that contact the engine, make sure it's heat resistant

04

05 When the paint is dry, install the insulator or grommet

06 Place the bracket in position . . .

07 . . . install the bracket mounting bolts and tighten securely

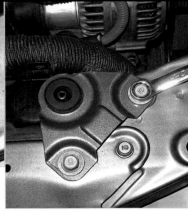

Adjustable hood prop

What happens every time you open the hood and want to prop it up? You grab the hood rod and swing it up into position, which prevents the hood from crashing down onto your head (or, more importantly, your tools!). But what's wrong with this picture? Well, for starters, the hood can only be locked into one opening angle because the hood rod is a fixed length, and its upper end must be inserted into a specific hole in the hood that's there just for that purpose. Okay, fine. But have you ever wished that you could open the hood to the height that you want, and then just leave it there, at that height? Well now you can, with the addition of an adjustable hood prop.

01 Mark the position of the holes you're going to drill in the hood for the upper hood prop mounting bracket

02 Drill the mounting bracket holes in the hood. Be careful - don't let the drill "pop" through and dimple the hood!

03 Clean up the edges of the holes with a reamer.

04 Place the mounting bracket in position and secure it with the screws included in the kit.

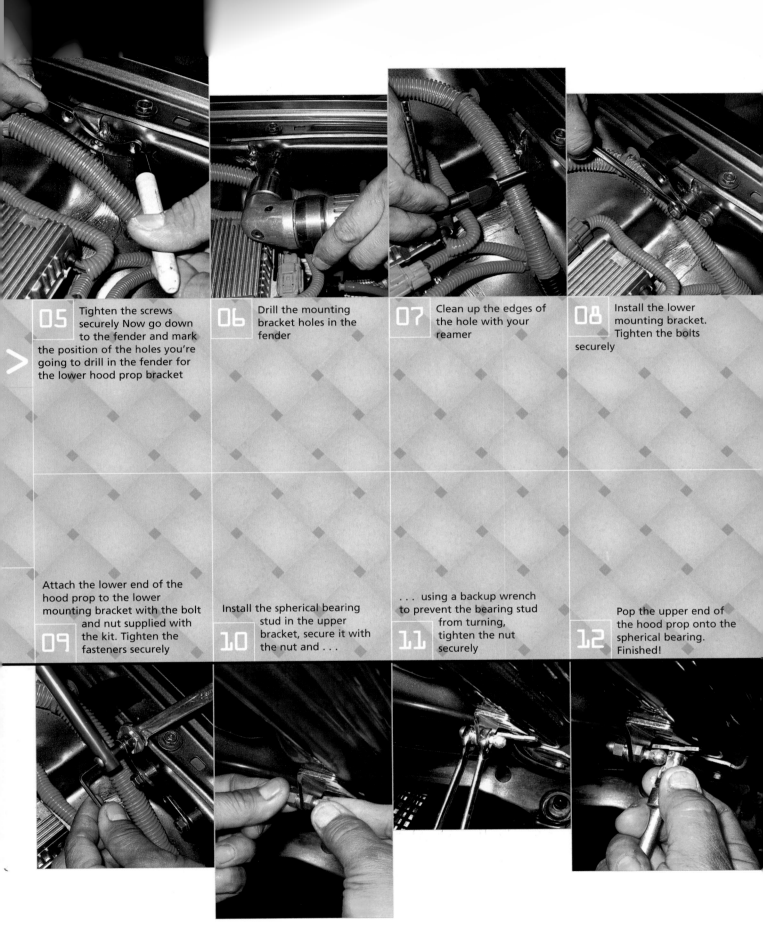

05 Tighten the screws securely Now go down to the fender and mark the position of the holes you're going to drill in the fender for the lower hood prop bracket

06 Drill the mounting bracket holes in the fender

07 Clean up the edges of the hole with your reamer

08 Install the lower mounting bracket. Tighten the bolts securely

09 Attach the lower end of the hood prop to the lower mounting bracket with the bolt and nut supplied with the kit. Tighten the fasteners securely

10 Install the spherical bearing stud in the upper bracket, secure it with the nut and . . .

11 . . . using a backup wrench to prevent the bearing stud from turning, tighten the nut securely

12 Pop the upper end of the hood prop onto the spherical bearing. Finished!

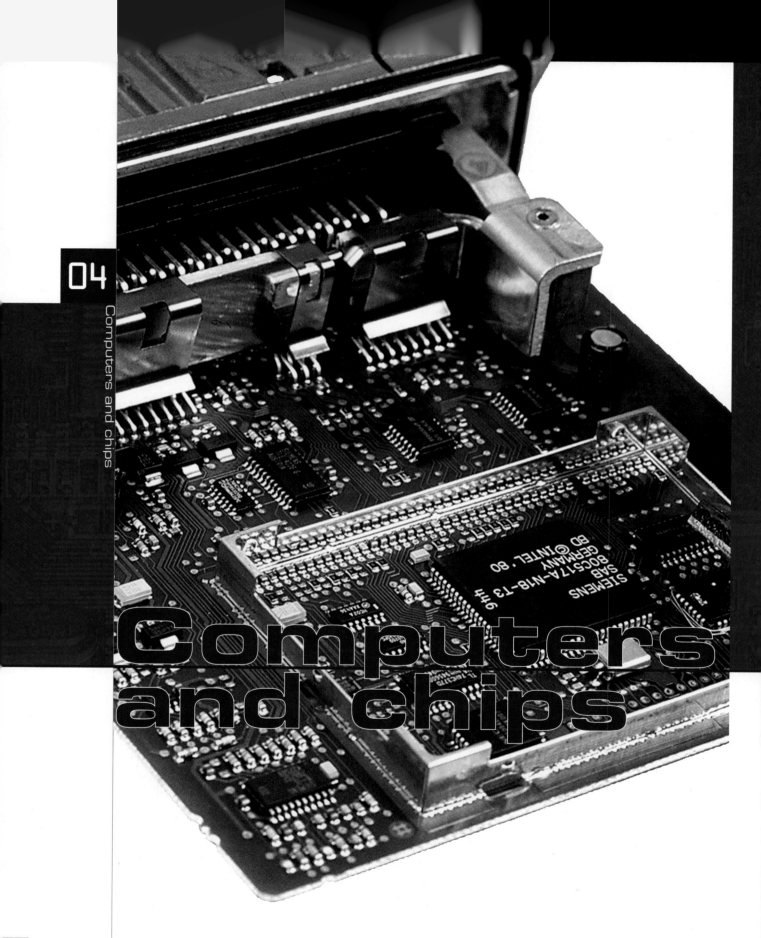

Computers
and chips

The condition of your spark plugs is a good indicator of conditions inside your engine - after each modification inspect the plugs with a magnifier to watch for signs of detonation, which might indicate changes needed in the fuel and/or ignition programming

Understanding your on-board computer means understanding how to get the most out of your engine

Automotive computers began as a means to reduce pollution by controlling numerous fuel and emission-control components. As the sophistication of fuel injection and information sensors increased, so did the power and reliability of the computer running things behind the scenes. In the world of cars, the computer has become a true boon now that the initial bugs have been worked out.

As the engineers really got into it over the years, they kept finding new uses for computer control, taking into account seemingly non-emissions factors such as power steering, air conditioning and transmission performance. Where once there may have been crude information sampling, now cars have higher-performance computers, more sensors, more sensitive sensors, and impressive programming. Some cars have a main computer with one or more "sub-computers" that process data and transfer information between other on-board systems and the main computer. Automatic climate-control systems, where you set the temperature you want in the car and the system provides just the right level of heat or cooling to maintain that temperature, are a perfect application for a sub-computer.

If you're making some basic modifications, and not planning to go all out, a simple chip upgrade for your ECU can improve engine response with increased timing - to go along with this, you may have to upgrade the octane of your fuel to premium, especially if your engine has high compression

Not all ECU's have a customer-serviceable chip, but computer upgrade work can be done by mail - Jet Performance Products can do upgrades for most sport compact ECU's and ship it back to you in 24 hours, all with the special packaging they will supply you

Use your Haynes repair manual to locate and safely remove your stock ECU before sending it out for an upgrade - the ECU may be located in the cowl (here on a German car) or under the dash

By themselves, engine management changes can result in some improvement in power, but each make and model will have varying levels of improvement, depending on how far off the factory programming was from a performance standpoint. As with any aftermarket product, be very careful of power improvement numbers quoted in advertisements and manufacturer literature. Exaggeration by a zealous marketing manager has been known to creep into print. In some cases, the power increase quoted may have been on a worse-case scenario, or on a modified engine that was still using the stock programming. In that case the engine would benefit more than a stock engine would.

That's the thing about chip reprogramming and engine management options; they make only a little improvement by themselves, but should make more improvement when other engine modifications are made. In fact, the mechanical engine changes won't make their advertised power increases either unless you do some reprogramming. A stock vehicle with reprogrammed spark and fuel may gain only 7 or 8 horsepower, although it may affect torque enough at lower rpm to improve the "feel" of the car. Take the same stock vehicle and stock ECU, and add an improved intake air pipe, a bigger throttle body, headers or a new camshaft. Now do the ECU reprogramming and the chip could be worth 20 horsepower this time. The extra airflow, improved breathing and increased fuel flow all need more timing to achieve their best numbers. If there's one lesson to learn about modifying automobile drivetrains, it's that all your modifications must work together in a planned, integrated way to achieve the results you're looking for.

Engine management basics

The on-board computer is called the Powertrain Control Module (PCM), Engine Control Module (ECM) or Electronic Control Unit (ECU), depending on the manufacturer of you car. Apparently, everyone just calling it a "computer" would be too easy. For purposes of this chapter, we'll use the term ECU. The other part of this "engine management system" are information sensors, which monitor various functions of the engine and send data to the ECU. Based on the data and the information programmed into the computer's memory, the ECU generates output signals to control various engine functions via control relays, solenoids and other output actuators.

The ECU is the "brain" of the electronically controlled fuel, ignition and emissions system, and is specifically calibrated to optimize the performance, emissions, fuel economy and driveability of one specific vehicle/engine/transaxle/accessories package in one make/model/year of vehicle.

Performance mods and the computer

The factory programming in your car's ECU is a highly developed, extensively-tested system that works perfectly for your engine in stock condition. Remember that the goal of the factory engineers is maximum fuel economy, driveability, longevity and efficiency. Our goals as enthusiasts are more in the high-performance sphere and our programming needs are slightly different.

Where the factory ECU programming needs some "help" for performance use is in the ignition timing and fuel curves. Virtually all new cars are designed to run on the lowest grade of unleaded pump gas, with an 87-octane rating. To get more performance, the ignition curve can be given more advanced timing and the fuel curve adjusted for more fuel at higher rpms, but the octane rating of the gas now becomes a problem. When timing is advanced, the engine may have more tendency to exhibit detonation or ping (signs of improper burning in the combustion chamber) which is potentially dangerous to the lifespan of the engine. Thus, if you want to alter the timing "map" in your computer for more power, you'll probably have to up the grade of gasoline you buy. In fact, the more serious engine modifications you make, the more you will probably have to "reprogram" your ECU.

While most bolt-on engine modifications will work well with increased timing advance, the serious "power adders" like nitrous oxide, superchargers, turbochargers and even high-compression pistons will require less ignition advance. The big gains in horsepower come from modifications that increase the cylinder pressure in the engine, the force pushing the pistons down. Increases in cylinder pressure really raise the octane requirement in a hurry.

"Non-serviceable" chips must be carefully unsoldered from the board, which is why this is usually done by a specialized company or tuning shop with the proper tools and reprogramming equipment

The upgrade technicians will take into account the engine modifications you have made and "burn" the correct programming into your stock chip

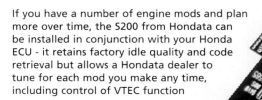

If you have a number of engine mods and plan more over time, the S200 from Hondata can be installed in conjunction with your Honda ECU - it retains factory idle quality and code retrieval but allows a Hondata dealer to tune for each mod you make any time, including control of VTEC function

In many new cars, the programming that affects the areas we want to modify is part of a "chip" on the motherboard of the ECU. The chip is a very small piece of silicon semiconductor material carrying many integrated circuits. These are usually called PROM chips, for Programmable Read Only Memory. In some cases, the chip is a "plug-in" which can be easily removed from the ECU and replaced with a custom chip, other chips are factory-soldered to the board. Cars with plug-in chips are the easiest to modify, but many imports do not have replaceable chips.

It isn't recommended to remove a soldered chip from the motherboard at home. Your factory ECU is very expensive to replace and just a tiny mistake with the solder or the heat source could ruin it. Aftermarket companies offer reprogramming services for these kinds of ECU's, and some tuning shops also have equipment to do this.

Your car is going to be out of service a few days, either parked at the tuning shop that is doing the upgrade, or parked at home while you wait for your modified ECU to come back from a computer upgrade company. How it works in the latter case is that you order and pay for the upgrade service from a reputable company, and they send you instructions, forms to fill out, and special packaging for the ECU. You remove the factory ECU from your car (we recommend, of course, that you use a Haynes repair manual for your make and model to locate and properly disconnect the ECU), and send it via overnight service to the company. There, they will either replace the chip or reprogram it. Based on the information you have given them about your vehicle, driving needs, and modifications you have made to the engine, they will custom-program the timing, fuel and even the transmission shifting information on vehicles with ECU-controlled electronic automatic transaxles. On vehicles so equipped, they can even change the factory-set rev limiter. They ship it back the same or next day and you reinstall it with their instructions.

The modified chip is resoldered to your car's ECU board with just the right amount of heat - too much and the board could be toast, so don't try this at home!

Technicians examine the chip reinstallation with a microscope to make sure it's right

Information sensors

- **Oxygen sensors (O2S)** - The O2S generates a voltage signal that varies with the difference between the oxygen content of the exhaust and the oxygen in the surrounding air.

- **Crankshaft Position (CKP) sensor** - The CKP sensor provides information on crankshaft position and the engine speed signal to the ECU.

- **Camshaft Position (CMP) sensor** - The CMP sensor produces a signal the ECU uses to identify number 1 cylinder and to time the sequential fuel injection.

- **Air/Fuel Sensor (California models)** - Some California models are equipped with an air/fuel ratio sensor mounted upstream of the catalytic converter. These sensors work similar to the O2 sensors.

- **Engine Coolant Temperature (ECT) sensor** - The ECT sensor monitors engine coolant temperature and sends the ECU a voltage signal that affects ECU control of the fuel mixture, ignition timing, and EGR operation.

- **Intake Air Temperature (IAT) sensor** - The IAT provides the ECU with intake air temperature information. The ECU uses this information to control fuel flow, ignition timing, and EGR system operation.

- **Throttle Position Sensor (TPS)** - The TPS senses throttle movement and position, then transmits a voltage signal to the ECU. This signal enables the ECU to determine when the throttle is closed, in a cruise position, or wide open.

- **Mass Airflow (MAF) sensor** - The MAF sensor measures the mass of the intake air by detecting volume and weight of the air from samples passing over a hot wire element.

- **Vehicle Speed Sensor (VSS)** - The vehicle speed sensor provides information to the ECU to indicate vehicle speed.

- **EGR valve position sensor** - The EGR valve position sensor monitors the position of the EGR pintle in relation to the operating conditions of the EGR system.

- **Vapor pressure sensor** - The fuel tank pressure sensor is part of the evaporative emission control system and is used to monitor vapor pressure in the fuel tank. The ECU uses this information to turn on and off the vacuum switching valves (VSV) of the evaporative emission system.

- **Power Steering Pressure (PSP) switch** - The PSP sensor is used to increase engine idle speed during low-speed vehicle maneuvers.

- **Transaxle sensors** - In addition to the vehicle speed sensor, the ECU on models with an automatic transmission/transaxle receives input signals from a direct clutch (or input shaft) speed sensor.

Output actuators

- **EFI main relay** - The EFI main relay activates power to the fuel pump relay (circuit opening relay). It is activated by the ignition switch and supplies battery power to the ECU and the EFI system when the switch is in the Start or Run position.

- **Fuel injectors** - The ECU opens the fuel injectors individually. On most modern engines, the system is called SFI (Sequential Fuel Injection), in which the injectors are fired sequentially according to the firing order of the cylinders. The ECU also controls the time the injector is open, called the "pulse width." The pulse width of the injector (measured in milliseconds) determines the amount of fuel delivered.

- **Igniter** - The igniter triggers the ignition coil and determines proper spark advance based on inputs from the ECU.

- **Idle Air Control (IAC) valve** - The IAC valve controls the amount of air to bypass the throttle plate when the throttle valve is closed or at idle position. The IAC valve opening and the resulting airflow is controlled by the ECU.

- **EVAP vacuum switching valve (VSV)** - The EVAP vacuum switching valve is a solenoid valve, operated by the ECU to purge the fuel vapor canister and route fuel vapor to the intake manifold for combustion.

- **Vapor Pressure Sensor vacuum switching valve (VSV)** - The Vapor Pressure Sensor vacuum switching valve is operated by the ECU during the OBD-II evaporative emission monitor and during an emission test of the evaporative system.

Cracking your computer codes

The ECUs in all vehicles manufactured since the early 80's have the ability to monitor the engine management system's input sensors and output actuators, and detect problems should they occur. This is called the On-board Diagnostic system, or simply OBD.

The diagnostic part of the OBD acronym refers to the ability to retrieve information from the ECU about the performance characteristics and running condition of all the sensors and actuators in the engine management system. This is invaluable information in diagnosing engine problems. The ECU will illuminate the CHECK ENGINE light (also called the Malfunction Indicator Light) on the dash if it recognizes a component fault

The diagnostic codes for the OBD system can be extracted from the ECU by plugging a generic OBD scan tool into the ECU's data link connector (DLC), which is usually located under the left end of the dash. Your Haynes repair manual will show you the location of the data connector and tell you a lot more about the engine management system of your specific make and model.

On some models, the computer will spit out troubleshooting information by flashing lights on the computer itself or by having the Check Engine light blink out a numeric code. On some vehicles you can activate this process by simply jumping certain terminals with a small wire or paper clip (refer to the Haynes manual for your specific vehicle for the proper procedure)

Programmable engine management systems like this one from AEM are ideal for fully modified strip-only vehicles - the stock ECU is replaced by a "plug and play" computer that has tunable fuel and timing maps that can be viewed with Windows®-based software on a laptop computer and features on-board data-logging plus adjustable controls for boost and nitrous

High Performance electronic controls

In the case of some modifications, particularly supercharging and turbocharging, you need a way to control ignition timing and fuel based on a parameter that the factory never considered: boost. Instead of the engine gulping fuel and air under atmospheric pressure like a normally-aspirated engine, a "blown" engine is being force-fed. The more pounds of boost applied to the engine, the more the ignition timing needs to be pulled back, and in some cases the more fuel needs to be injected. The aftermarket companies have a variety of add-on electronic controllers that connect to a manifold vacuum port on your engine and send varying signals to the ECU based on how much boost is being applied. Some even have a dashboard control so that you can select the timing you need based on the quality of fuel available to you. When you have your engine set up for best results on 93-octane and you're stuck somewhere that only has 91 or 89-octane, you'll need to make a timing adjustment or risk engine damage.

If you have a piggyback fuel or timing box, or any other programmable management system, the dyno operator can spot any weaknesses in your overall engine operation much more easily than by unscientific, seat-of-the-pants driving, and he'll know right where your engine needs more/less fuel or spark

When more control is needed, there are aftermarket computers that work in conjunction with the stock ECU. The factory ECU and its programming is retained to do all the closed-loop emissions and efficiency programming (closed-loop means that the ECU is in charge of all functions), while a secondary box attaches next to the stock ECU and handles the functions of controlling timing, fuel and boost. Such boxes are called "piggyback" units. The beauty of these boxes is that they are user-programmable for the functions an enthusiast is interested in. They can be connected to a PC, which will display the fuel and timing maps and let you make changes to suit your level of modification. Some include a fall-back map of basically stock numbers. Once you have dialed-in exactly what you need, you save that map. If you make new modifications to the engine, go back to that map and experiment some more. At least one aftermarket unit allows you to switch, at the dashboard, between any of four maps you have created. You could save your "street use with 93-octane" map, and your "race day with 100-octane" map.

As you might expect, these may or may not be legal for street use where you live. Check with the controller manufacturer and your local authorities before making a large investment.

At the track, pit tuning of a race car is much easier when you can replay a run (from a system with data-logging capability), compare the results with your spark plug examination and make minor tweaks of the system before the next run

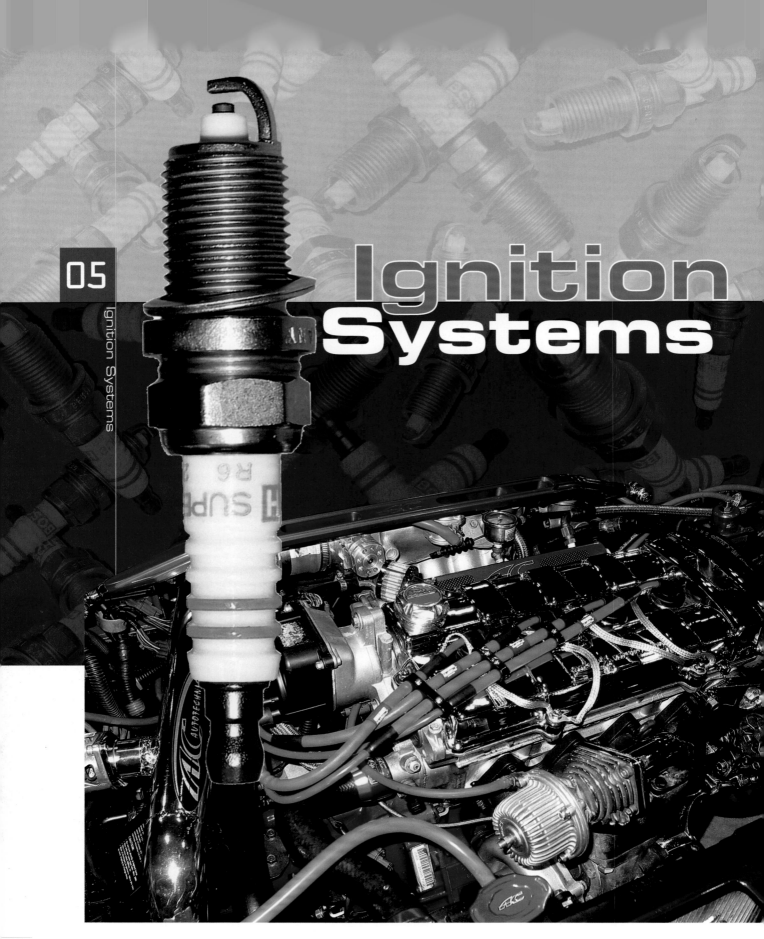

Ignition Systems

Ignition basics

Once you understand the most basic principles of an internal combustion engine, it's easy to see why an ignition system plays a crucial role. For those readers who might need a brief refresher on what happens inside their engine's cylinders, all modern piston-powered automotive engines run in a *four-cycle* (or four-stroke) mode. Let's start with the **intake** stroke. Here the piston is travelling down in the cylinder, creating a suction or draft that draws the fuel/air mixture in through the open intake valve. When the piston reaches the bottom of its stroke, it starts back up again, starting the **compression** stroke, in which the valves close and the piston compresses the fuel/air mixture (which can't escape). This makes the fuel/air mixture very dense and capable of releasing a lot of energy when the mixture is ignited. Just before the piston reaches the top of its stroke,

the spark plug ignites the mixture, beginning the **power** stroke, in which the rapidly expanding gasses from the burning mixture raise the cylinder pressure dramatically and this pushes the piston down the bore. The force imparted to the crankshaft each time a power stroke pushes down is what makes the engine go. By the time the piston reaches the bottom of this stroke, the energy in the cylinder is dissipated and the piston starts back up again, on the **exhaust** stroke. The cylinder contains the mostly-inert residual gasses left from combustion, and when the exhaust valve opens during this stroke, these gasses are pushed out of the cylinder and past the

exhaust valve (to the exhaust system) as the piston rises. This clears the cylinder in preparation for another intake stroke, beginning another intake-compression-power-exhaust four-stroke cycle.

In a nutshell, that's how your engine works. You may be perceptive enough to guess that the exact timing of some of these events in a four-stroke cycle is critical. Chapter 8 will go into much greater detail about how the valves are operated and how valve timing is a major factor in increasing engine performance. This Chapter is concerned with requirements for making and timing that all-important spark that lights off the fireworks.

THE FOUR-STROKE CYCLE

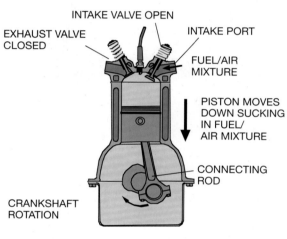

EXHAUST VALVE CLOSED

INTAKE VALVE OPEN

INTAKE PORT

FUEL/AIR MIXTURE

PISTON MOVES DOWN SUCKING IN FUEL/AIR MIXTURE

CONNECTING ROD

CRANKSHAFT ROTATION

INTAKE

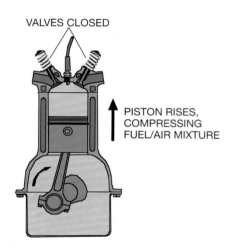

VALVES CLOSED

PISTON RISES, COMPRESSING FUEL/AIR MIXTURE

COMPRESSION

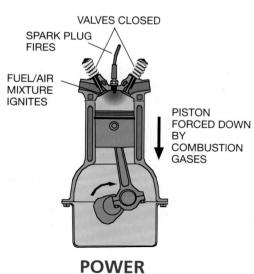

VALVES CLOSED

SPARK PLUG FIRES

FUEL/AIR MIXTURE IGNITES

PISTON FORCED DOWN BY COMBUSTION GASES

POWER

EXHAUST VALVE OPEN

EXHAUST GASES OUT

PISTON RISES, FORCING WASTE GASES OUT OF THE CYLINDER

EXHAUST

Ignition by the numbers

- At 6,000 rpm in a four-cylinder engine, each spark plug is firing 3000 times per minute, or 50 times per second!

- In a basic ignition system, the juice-path starts with battery voltage, which is 12 volts. The ignition coil then steps-up this voltage to 10,000 or more volts.

- An aftermarket coil will typically step up the 12V battery voltage to as much as 60,000 volts

The voltages produced by modern ignition systems are very high, and are potentially lethal in some cases. Extreme care must be taken when working on or around ignition systems. Never disconnect or even touch a spark plug wire or ignition coil when the engine is running!

Computerized ignitions

What they are and how to tell if you have one

On modern, fuel-injected and computer-controlled engines, the distributor only controls the sequence in which the cylinders are fired, while all other timing functions are handled by the computer.

In some modern cars, the distributor has been eliminated entirely. Called **DIS (Distributorless Ignition System)**, the function of the distributor is replaced by a **CPS (Crankshaft Position Sensor)** on the engine that gives the computer a reference to where the crankshaft is rotated in relation to **TDC (Top Dead Center)** for number one cylinder. That's when the piston is at it highest point of travel in the cylinder (**BDC** would be **Bottom Dead Center**, the lowest point in the piston's travel). Based on this and other inputs, the computer makes all timing decisions, which are delivered to coilpacks that are in turn connected by plug wires to the spark plugs.

If you're not sure if you have a conventional or DIS system, follow your spark plug wires. If they end at a distributor driven by one of your camshafts, you have a distributor system. If the wires all go to a cluster of coils mounted on a plate somewhere in the engine compartment (and you don't see a distributor on your engine) then you have a DIS system.

Components of the DIS system include the camshaft position sensor, the crankshaft position sensor, coils (one coil for a cluster of cylinders), igniter and the **ECU (Electronic Control Unit)** or "computer".

A further development of the DIS ignition system is the coil-on-plug arrangement. On these models, each spark plug has its own small coil/igniter pack. The coil is mounted directly over the spark plug and bolted to the valve cover. These systems are easy to spot because there are no spark plug wires. The sensors generate signals that allow the ECU to trigger the correct coil/igniter assembly at the right time. Such systems offer the most complete control of spark ignition to date.

High performance ignitions

Your factory ignition system does a perfectly adequate job on a completely stock engine. In stock configuration, the engine runs smooth, has good economy and the spark plugs last a long time. These are all signs of an efficient engine with the right combination of parts and all parts working properly, but factory ignitions aren't well suited for high-rpm driving or engines modified to create increased cylinder pressure.

Higher rpms put an increased load on stock ignitions, and modifications that lead to increased cylinder pressure can really put out the fire. If you install higher-compression pistons, the spark plugs need a lot more zap to light off a mixture that is packed tighter than ever. The denser the mixture, the harder it is for a spark to jump the plug's electrodes, like swimming through wet concrete. Other major power-adders such as nitrous oxide, supercharging or turbocharging also create much high cylinder pressures and require several ignition improvements.

Check it out first!

Before spending your savings, you'd be well advised to make sure every component of your engine is up to the task of accepting high performance equipment

To use a compression gauge, you must have a gauge with an adapter long enough to reach down the spark plug tubes - be sure to disable the fuel pump and ignition system, and open the throttle as far as possible during the compression check

Use a Haynes Repair Manual for your make and model and follow the simple, step-by-step procedures to test engine compression, vacuum readings, ignition performance, fuel pressure, etc. If anything is amiss, take care of it now, before you modify the engine!

It makes no sense to add performance equipment to an engine that is ailing mechanically, though there is a temptation to do so.If your valves or rings are leaking under normal driving conditions and engine speed, just imagine how less effective they will be with an engine putting out more horsepower. The modifications will make the car seem faster, but you're only hastening the demise of the engine, perhaps even doing more damage than if you had corrected the problems first. Read the information about engine management systems and the retrieval of computer "trouble codes" from your car. Have someone with a scan tool check for any existing trouble codes, and it would be great to have your car run on a chassis dyno to check for troubles that may only show up under a load. This would also be a great time to establish the horsepower and torque baselines, which you can compare to later tests after you have made modifications.

A simple vacuum gauge can be very handy in diagnosing engine condition and performance

Aftermarket coils

This aftermarket coil can produce up to 44,000 volts; some can put out upwards of 60,000 volts!

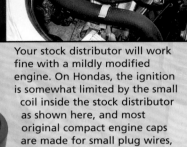

One of the reasons a stock ignition doesn't handle high rpms well is that the stock coil doesn't have time to build the necessary spark energy because of the short time between ignition firings (remember, it's trying to fire 50 times per second). Imagine you are holding your thumb over the end of a slow-running garden hose, blocking the flow of water. You release the water and it blasts out at first, then settles down to a slow flow. If you keep your thumb in place long enough the water pressure builds up, but if you open and close it too often, the pressure never has a chance to build between events.

The typical aftermarket coil is capable of making more secondary voltage than the stock coil, and that's about it. It won't add any horsepower and won't change your mileage, but it could eliminate some misfire problems in the upper rpm range, and that will become more important as you add other modifications to your engine. On most engines with a distributor and separate coil, replacing your stock coil with an aftermarket unit is as simple as modifications get, and inexpensive, too.

Your stock distributor will work fine with a mildly modified engine. On Hondas, the ignition is somewhat limited by the small coil inside the stock distributor as shown here, and most original compact engine caps are made for small plug wires, not the larger aftermarket wires

An aftermarket cap like this MSD "Power Cap" can be used on a Honda to accept an external performance coil, and the posts are made for large silicone-jacketed plugs wires

The stock coil inside a Honda distributor can be removed and an aftermarket external coil utilized, with a modification to the cap

This stock Honda cap has been modified for an external coil by drilling out the coil post and attaching this MSD post adapter to accept an external coil

Timing controls

A multi-spark capacitive-discharge (CD) ignition like the Holley " Quick Strip Annihilator" is especially useful for modified engines - the box is fitted with EEPROM microprocessors that can be overwritten many times and adjust the spark output based on engine rpm

Exactly *when* your spark ignites the cylinder's fuel mix is critical; this is called ignition *timing*. The mix doesn't explode in an instantaneous flash; it actually takes a period of time. The flame front from the point of ignition travels through the mixture, slowly at first and then building speed. This is good, because what is needed is a gradual build of pressure, not a sharp spike, which can be destructive to pistons, rods and crankshafts. Since the mixture takes time to burn, the spark is timed to trigger sometime before the piston reaches the top of its stroke (Top Dead Center). So the initial timing is some degrees BTDC, or Before Top Dead Center.

Firing with too much advance (too far before the piston reaches the top) can cause too much pressure to build in the cylinder before the piston reaches TDC, so that the piston and the rising pressure are fighting each other. On the other hand, if the timing is too late (not enough in advance), the engine can't make the most of the gas expansion, so power and economy are wasted.

To complicate the timing discussion even further, the spark event must have a different timing at different engine speeds. As engine speed goes up, there is less time available for the combustion event, so the spark must occur sooner. Other factors also influence the correct ignition timing, such as engine load, temperature and fuel mixture. If you map out the amount of ignition advance on a graph related to rpm, you have what's called an advance *curve,* an important factor in performance tuning.

Luckily, your factory ignition takes in information from its sensors to provide the optimum ignition timing under all conditions. The system however, is designed for normal driving and stock components. Once you start modifying the engine, you have changed the parameters and you now need to adjust the timing with something other than the factory ECU. Chapter 4 covers modifications to your stock ECU that change the timing parameters. That will help some in power, as long as you use a higher grade of gasoline to compensate for the increased timing, but installing a chip or reprogramming your ECU will not increase the energy level of the spark. For that you need a CD (Capacitive Discharge) aftermarket ignition system.

For racing applications, the Holley ignition system can utilize a "soft-touch" keypad to make instant changes to the ignition programming - it's called the Quickshot Programmer and can change rev limits and has a built-in LED tachometer

MSD's street-and-strip SCI-Plus (Sport Compact Ignition) is a digital ignition control that has dial-in controls for rev-limit and retard functions for single-stage nitrous applications

Jacobs Electronics makes the "Import Car Energy Pak" ignition system, which can be set up either with the factory coil used as a trigger or with an external coil - features include spark output adjusted for engine load (more spark under acceleration) and a 10-degree start-retard that works well for engines with high compression - an optional add-on is a nitrous control

Spark plug wires

The CD ignition usually consists of an electronic box you mount in the engine compartment, and the wiring harness to connect to your vehicle. Your ECU still does the triggering and controls the advance, but in the CD box is a large capacitor, which is an electronic storage device. Juice usually comes into the coil or coilpack as battery voltage (12V) and is bumped up from there to 5,000, 10,000 or 40,000 volts of secondary current. In the CD ignition, the capacitor stores incoming juice until there is more like 450 volts to go to the coil. Now the coil has a much easier time of quickly building up to the required voltage for good spark, regardless of the rpm.

There are different models of CD ignitions, with varying "bells & whistles", but one of the most common side benefits is a "rev control." A single-step control will allow you to set a specific rpm that you don't want the engine to exceed, to prevent engine damage from over-revving during a missed shift or a blown clutch, for instance (such events do happen, even if they're not planned!). Some units are capable of programming-in an adjustable rate of spark retard at high rpms, which is ideal for supercharged or turbocharged applications. Because of the increased cylinder pressure with boosted engines, it is common to retard the spark progressively as the boost level increases. CD ignition systems are available for both distributor engines and DIS engines.

For vehicles that have distributorless ignition systems with coilpacks such as the Mitsubishi Eclipse, MSD makes this digital ignition box that features two-step rev-limit controls and an adjustable high-rpm retard function for engines with power-adders

Aside from making your engine compartment look cool, high performance spark plug wires serve a very useful purpose. If you install a high-voltage coil and keep your stock wires, you are asking for voltage to leak from the wires under load, at high engine speeds, or boosted (blown or turbocharged) conditions. Voltage will try to seek the "path of least resistance" and that could be any engine ground that is close to one of your plug wires.

The typical factory plug wire has a core of carbon-impregnated material surrounded by fiberglass and rubber insulation, which is fine for stock engines.

Most aftermarket performance wires use a very fine spiral wire wound around a magnetic core and wrapped in silicone jacketing, and are available in thicker-than-stock diameters to handle more current flow. Some import cars have stock plug wires as skinny as 5 or 6mm, while aftermarket wires are offered in 8mm, 8.5mm and even 9mm for racing applications. Good aftermarket wires also come with thicker boots, which is important, since the boot-to-plug contact area is a frequent source of voltage leaking to ground. Wires in the 8mm range are big enough to handle the spark of most street-modified cars, and the bigger wires are good for racing, but there's no such thing as having too much insulation on your plug wires.

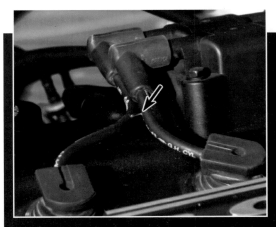

If you want to check for leaking voltage on your plug wires, just watch the engine running at night with the hood open (do this outdoors). If there are breaks in the wires or boots you'll probably be able to see the voltage leaking like tiny bolts of lightning. If the air is damp, the voltage is even more likely to show up, and if you make these observations while your car is on a chassis dyno (with the lights off) you can check for voltage leaks with the engine under load. This is where your stock-based ignition is most likely to break down.

Spark

The final link in the ignition system's chain-of-command is the spark plug. We may have mentioned this before but, as with other ignition modifications, don't expect to make big gains in power or mileage by switching spark plugs. Despite the wild claims dreamed up by advertising copywriters over the last fifty years, the only time spark plugs will make much difference on a street-driven engine is when the engine is really in need of a tune-up and you install fresh plugs. In that instance, the spark plugs could bring back 5 or 10 lost horsepower, but most aftermarket plugs can't really make new horsepower the engine didn't have before.

Nonetheless, there are a wide variety of spark plugs out there to choose from. If your engine is only mildly modified, stick with the factory recommended spark plugs, gapped to factory specs. If you add an increasing number of performance modifications to your engine, you may have to reconsider what type of plugs to run, and even what size electrode gap is best.

Your first key to choosing the right plug is to examine the ones you're running currently. Close examination of spark plugs is the way professional racers fine-tune their engines and detect engine problems in their early stages, before serious damage is done. Even engine builders with sophisticated and fully instrumented dyno facilities still read the plugs with a magnifying glass.

You can read your plugs with an inexpensive tool from the auto parts store. It's like a small flashlight with a magnifying glass on the end. We've included here a color-photo chart of spark plug conditions and what they indicate about the state of the engine. Compare your spark plugs to the ones on the chart. The most important "look" on the spark plugs is that they should all look the same from each cylinder. Any variation in the plug reading indicates a problem specific to that cylinder, and the engine will need a compression test and mechanical examination to find out what's wrong

Assuming you have made modifications, the most common spark plug conditions you might see would indicate them being

Spark plugs play an important role in a performance ignition system and modified engines need better plugs - at left are NGK BCPR7ES-11 plugs, just one range colder than stock Honda plugs and a good application for a hot all-motor car. At right are R7234-10 NGK competition plugs that feature a very fine center electrode; these are really expensive, but are often required for highly-boosted race engines

Plugs

either too cold or too hot. Each plug design is made to operate at a certain temperature, and the final choice is a compromise meant to work well in most operating conditions. In a stock engine, the proper plug has been tested to give good results for many miles. However, once you start modifying an engine and running at higher rpms, with modified ignition timing and perhaps more fuel and more cylinder pressure, that plug is no longer the right choice.

Spark plugs are described as being "hot" or "cold", referring to their heat range. High rpms, high engine temperatures and increased ignition timing or fuel flow at higher rpms can all cause a plug to run hotter. When a spark plug runs too hot, detonation can occur, with subsequent and serious damage to the engine.

The compromise in spark plug heat range is bigger with a modified engine than a stocker. Because we have done everything we could to make more horsepower at high rpms, we need a colder plug to handle this, but at lower rpms our fuel mix may be a little richer than stock and the colder plugs may get sooty fouling on them that interferes with driveability. A few simple mods such as a header, cam and cold-air intake will probably require a plug that is one range colder than the stock plug.

One way to keep the plug compromise of a modified engine less of a problem is to run a performance ignition system, with a better coil and CD box plus improved plug wires. This should allow the engine to run well at higher rpms, and still have enough spark energy to keep the colder plug firing cleanly at lower rpms. It's just another reason the modification of your stock ignition system has to be a complete package approach, with no weak link.

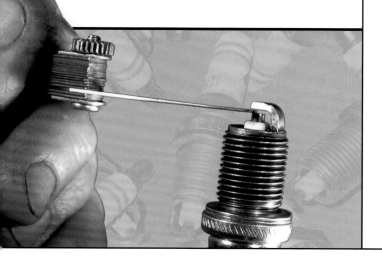

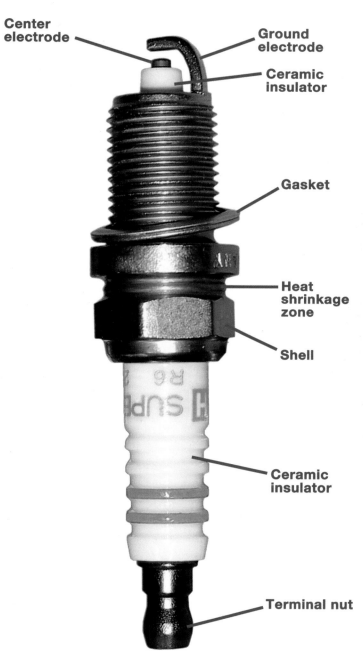

Center electrode

Ground electrode

Ceramic insulator

Gasket

Heat shrinkage zone

Shell

Ceramic insulator

Terminal nut

Common spark plug conditions

Your spark plugs can tell you a story about how your engine is running

Worn

Symptoms: Rounded electrodes with a small amount of deposits on the firing end. Normal color. Causes hard starting in damp or cold weather and poor fuel economy.

Recommendation: Plugs have been left in the engine too long. Replace with new plugs of the same heat range. Follow the recommended maintenance schedule.

Normal

Symptoms: Brown to grayish-tan color and slight electrode wear. Correct heat range for engine and operating conditions.

Recommendation: When new spark plugs are installed, replace with plugs of the same heat range.

Too hot

Symptoms: Blistered, white insulator, eroded electrode and absence of deposits. Results in shortened plug life.

Recommendation: Check for the correct plug heat range, over-advanced ignition timing, lean fuel mixture, intake manifold vacuum leaks, sticking valves and insufficient engine cooling.

Carbon deposits

Symptoms: Dry sooty deposits indicate a rich mixture or weak ignition. Causes misfiring, hard starting and hesitation.

Recommendation: Make sure the plug has the correct heat range. Check for a clogged air filter or problem in the fuel system or engine management system. Also check for ignition system problems.

Ash deposits

Symptoms: Light brown deposits encrusted on the side or center electrodes or both. Derived from oil and/or fuel additives. Excessive amounts may mask the spark, causing misfiring and hesitation during acceleration.

Recommendation: If excessive deposits accumulate over a short time or low mileage, install new valve guide seals to prevent seepage of oil into the combustion chambers. Also try changing gasoline brands.

Oil deposits

Symptoms: Oily coating caused by poor oil control. Oil is leaking past worn valve guides or piston rings into the combustion chamber. Causes hard starting, misfiring and hesitation.

Recommendation: Correct the mechanical condition with necessary repairs and install new plugs.

Gap bridging

Symptoms: Combustion deposits lodge between the electrodes. Heavy deposits accumulate and bridge the electrode gap. The plug ceases to fire, resulting in a dead cylinder.

Recommendation: Locate the faulty plug and remove the deposits from between the electrodes.

Preignition

Symptoms: Melted electrodes. Insulators are white, but may be dirty due to misfiring or flying debris in the combustion chamber. Can lead to engine damage.

Recommendation: Check for the correct plug heat range, over-advanced ignition timing, lean fuel mixture, insufficient engine cooling and lack of lubrication.

High speed glazing

Symptoms: Insulator has yellowish, glazed appearance. Indicates that combustion chamber temperatures have risen suddenly during hard acceleration. Normal deposits melt to form a conductive coating. Causes misfiring at high speeds.

Recommendation: Install new plugs. Consider using a colder plug if driving habits warrant.

Detonation

Symptoms: Insulators may be cracked or chipped. Improper gap setting techniques can also result in a fractured insulator tip. Can lead to piston damage.

Recommendation: Make sure the fuel anti-knock values meet engine requirements. Use care when setting the gaps on new plugs. Avoid lugging the engine.

Mechanical damage

Symptoms: May be caused by a foreign object in the combustion chamber or the piston striking an incorrect reach (too long) plug. Causes a dead cylinder and could result in piston damage.

Recommendation: Repair the mechanical damage. Remove the foreign object from the engine and/or install the correct reach plug.

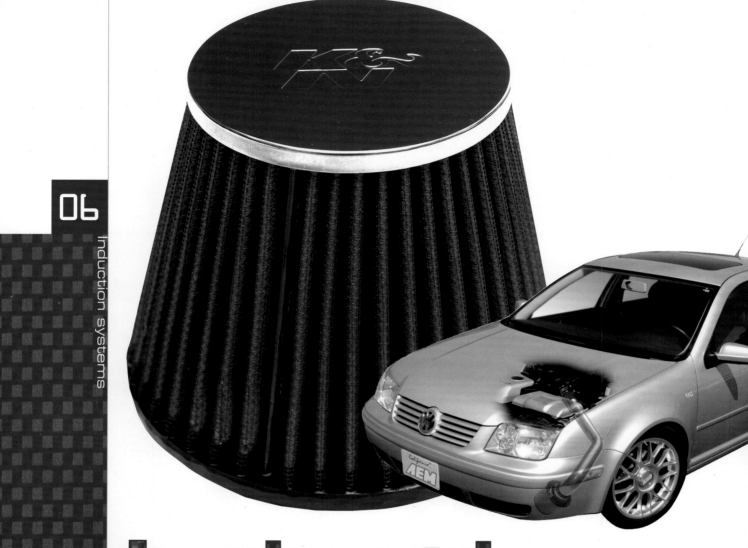

Induction
systems

Your stock intake system is like going through life with a head cold

. . . Let it breathe!

Induction basics

Your engine needs air to mix with the fuel coming into the cylinders. At high rpms, when it's making the most horsepower, it wants more air. If you start adding performance mods, it wants even more air. And if that's not being greedy enough, it would like that air to be as cold as possible, please.

Your stock air filter box is designed for smoothing and quieting the airflow, and represents a considerable restriction, especially at high rpms

Induction systems

One step further away from stock induction would be to eliminate the stock air filter box and flexible hose, then attach an aftermarket cone filter right to the throttle body - in the case of this model, there is no room for an aftermarket intake pipe unless the battery is relocated to the trunk

If you take a close look at most stock air intake systems, it's a wonder the engine gets enough fresh air to run at all! In the intake tract, the engineers have their first priority to develop smooth, reliable power with maximum fuel economy and driveability. Performance is far from their minds.

A further priority faced by factory engineers, and this applies to engineering on all aspects of production car design, is NVH, which stands for Noise, Vibration and Harshness. As most consumers want their cars to be as quiet and smooth as possible, the engineers are increasingly challenged. How does this affect our induction system? Take a look at the stock induction path. If you follow the airflow from outside the car to where the intake manifold bolts to the cylinder head, you'll see a sometimes torturous roadmap full of more twists and turns than a rat maze experiment at the school science fair.

The stock inlet bringing air into the air filter housing (the beginning of the stock airflow system) usually attempts to get some sort of cool air in, but the factory plays it very safe in locating this pipe, hoping to fend off customer problems if any dirt or water were to get into the airbox. Once inside the air filter housing, the air may have to pass by plastic baffles and other devices designed to limit the noise produced by air rushing into the engine. Once past the air filter, the airflow usually goes through a "corrugated" flexible tube and connects to the throttle body. If you're lucky, that tube has only one bend in it on your car, but some vehicles have several. The flexible tubing used is designed more for noise-reduction than smooth, unrestricted airflow. The ribs inside the plastic tubing may dampen noise, but they restrict high-rpm airflow.

To improve the air intake for your engine you have basically three options.

- Your first and simplest improvement to your induction is to step up and pay the price for an aftermarket air filter. If the vehicle has a decent filter box design, just changing to a quality aftermarket air filter can be worth a few horsepower.

- The next step is a performance induction kit that will replace the stock plastic tubing and air filter housing. This kit will come with its own pleated-cotton, high-flow filter. So if you even think you might modify your engine, don't install a replacement aftermarket filter, but put that money towards a new performance intake kit.

- Step three would involve more serious modifications, in addition to the performance filter and induction. If you really need some air, look to improvements in the throttle body and intake manifold on the engine.

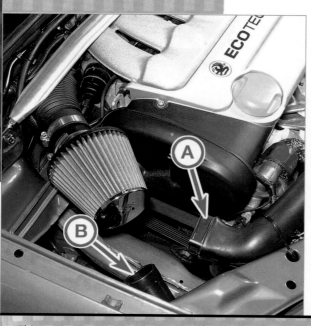

This compact owner removed his stock airbox, then added a cone filter to the stock hose from the throttle body. Ingeniously, he left the stock inlet air pipe (A) to aim cooler air at the filter, plus added another flexible pipe (B) that picks up even cooler air below the bumper - since the pipes aren't connected directly to the filter, there's no danger of water even getting into the engine from driving through a deep puddle

The easiest Power Mod you can make

01 The simplest modification you can make to your stock air induction system is to open the factory airbox, lift out the OEM paper air filter, wipe things down with a damp cloth and drop in a high-flow aftermarket filter with a pleated-cotton lifetime filter - these can be reused over and over by washing them, then treating them with a special oil

02 A replacement air filter is dead easy to fit - release the clips securing the air cleaner top cover . . .

04 Before you fit the new element, if you can, clean out the inside of the filter housing. Use a damp cloth, and make sure that none of the dust and muck goes into the engine.

03 . . . then lift the cover enough to lift out the old element. Take care not to strain the wiring from the airflow meter as the air cleaner cover is lifted up.

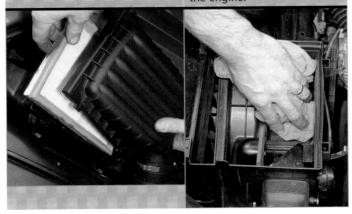

A typical aftermarket bolt-on induction mod is to install a short ram, which is a new, large diameter pipe with an aftermarket filter - these flow much better than stock, though they do make the engine noisier - this installation doesn't allow the best design, since there is a sharp bend near the throttle body that could slow down the airflow

Short ram intakes

Performance air intakes for compact cars are available in two basic forms, the "short ram" and the "cold-air" intake. In each type, the aftermarket manufacturer has tried to design a free-flowing intake without regard to engine noise. Virtually all are made of metal tubing, generally aluminum, with the smoothest possible bends and an interior that has a larger cross-section than the stock system. All types are fitted with a high-flow filter, usually in a conical configuration. The best designs are not only capable of flowing more air volume, but maintain a higher air velocity than a stock system.

The least expensive and easiest intakes to install are the short ram types. You'll spend longer getting the stock air filter box and inlet tube out than installing the short

>

If you do run a short ram, try to find one with a sheetmetal "dam" included in the kit - this can keep hot air radiating from the engine isolated from the filter

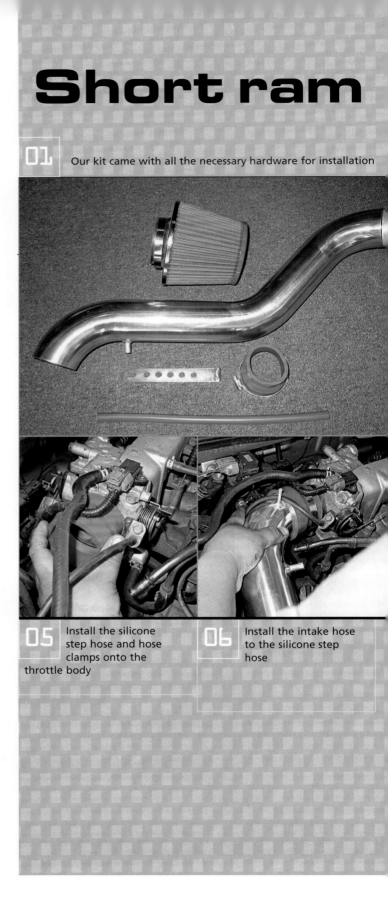

Short ram

01 Our kit came with all the necessary hardware for installation

The Injen short ram installation on this Toyota is good - although not picking up outside air, at least it's far from the hot radiator and safe from any water ingestion

ram. If you have any doubts about removing the stock components, consult the Haynes repair manual for your car. On some vehicles, the MAF sensor is located on the air intake and must be removed, then reinstalled on the aftermarket intake. Most cars also have a hose connecting the crankcase (usually at the valve cover) to the air intake, and the stock hose may need to be shortened to connect to the aftermarket pipe, or a new, longer hose must be used. Short-ram intakes place the new filter relatively close to the engine, and modifications to the engine or body are rarely necessary. Most short-ram installations take only a half-hour to install and may be good for 4 to 8 horsepower, depending on the application.

05 Install the silicone step hose and hose clamps onto the throttle body

06 Install the intake hose to the silicone step hose

Because of the upright mounting of the throttle body on this single-cam application, even a "long" ram pipe stills mounts the filter inside the engine compartment - the sharp bend near the throttle body is the only detriment to airflow here

intake installation

Remove the stock air filter housing. On most vehicles the housing is bolted to the body from the inside. If you can't figure out how to remove it, check the Haynes manual for your vehicle

02

Disconnect the breather hose from the valve cover and loosen the clamp securing the intake hose to the throttle body

03

Remove the intake hose and air filter housing from the vehicle. Keep the duct and housing just in case you intend to sell the vehicle in the future (in stock form)

04

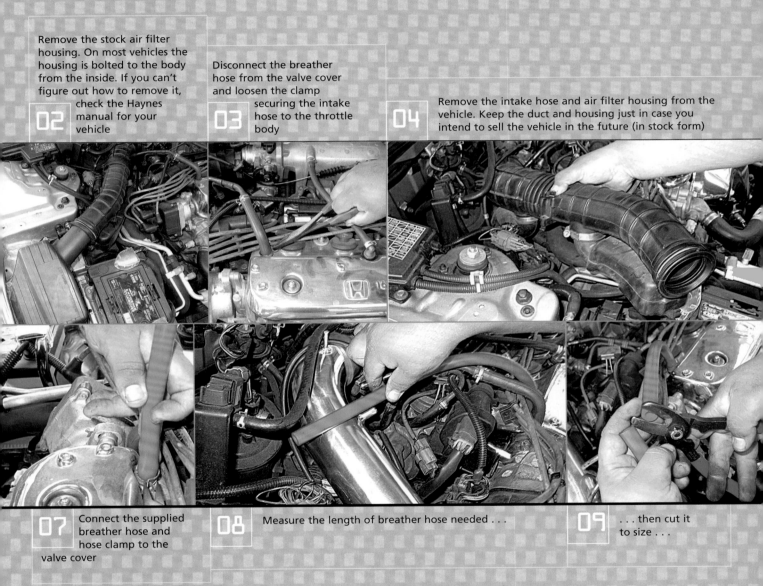

07 Connect the supplied breather hose and hose clamp to the valve cover

08 Measure the length of breather hose needed . . .

09 . . . then cut it to size . . .

10 . . . and attach the hose and hose clamp to the intake tube

11 Attach the filter element to the intake tube . . .

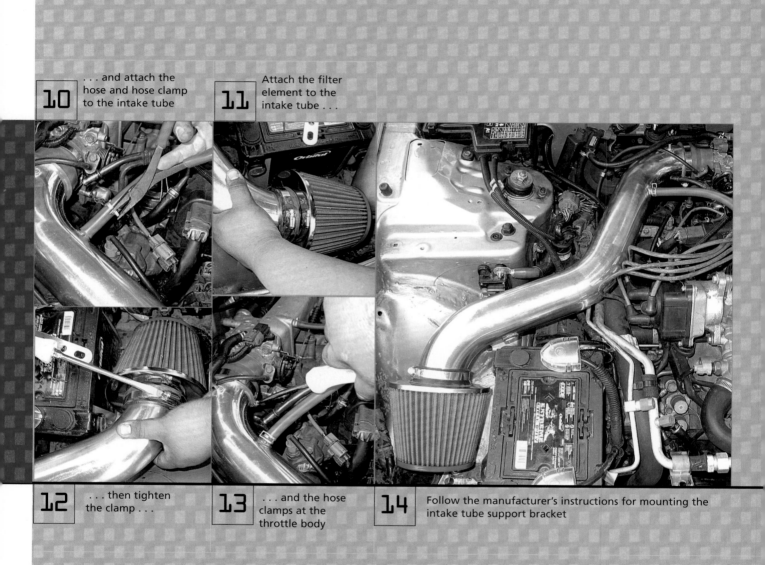

12 . . . then tighten the clamp . . .

13 . . . and the hose clamps at the throttle body

14 Follow the manufacturer's instructions for mounting the intake tube support bracket

Longer rams can pick up colder undercar air - this installation on a Ford Focus looks like a short ram, but the pipe ducks down under the battery box and gets air from under the bumper

Not all cold air intakes are polished metal - this unique system from Comptech is roto-molded plastic and features a radiused entry at the bottom and a quiet filter box that uses a high-flow foam element

When at the track for dragstrip runs, the filter can be removed and a pipe run out to the front of the car to pick up high-speed air - on most Hondas, this means temporarily removing the right headlight, such as on this car where the owner taped a plastic funnel onto the pipe to hopefully pick up even more air

Cold-air intakes

Did we say colder air was important? For purposes of performance, the colder the air the more power you make. For every drop of 10-degrees F in the intake air fed to your engine, your power goes up about 1%. That may not sound like much, but if you have a 150 hp engine now, and you manage to reduce your intake air temperature by 100-degrees, you could gain 15 horsepower!. Air gets denser as it gets colder, so more air is packed into the engine, even with the same volume of airflow.

Aside from the power boost, aftermarket intakes just look cool! Since they are available in a variety of flashy finishes, such as anodizing in blue, red, or purple, a chrome-like high-temperature coating, or a polished finish on the metal tube, they make the most powerful statement that your engine is "modified." When the tube is made of aluminum or stainless steel and is polished, the "wow" factor is upped considerably, and these finishes are easy to take care of.

The cold-air package is important because it is longer, reaching down to pick up colder air from below the grille or in the car's fenderwell, rather than the hotter engine compartment air. Typical engine compartment air temperature could be 30 to 50-degrees F higher than the ambient outside air, even when the vehicle is at speed and cooler ambient air is presumably flowing through the engine compartment.

Aftermarket cold air intake systems can be worth 8 to 20 horsepower, depending on the design and the quality of the air filter included with it. Obviously, a cold air intake is going to need some bends in order to reach the cold air, but if there are too many bends or bends made too sharp, the horsepower gain from the colder air could be offset by a reduction in airflow. The longer the pipe, the more friction there will be for the incoming air, even on a straight length of pipe. A few bends and the air is further restricted.

One additional note about aftermarket air intakes, they are noisier than a stock system (but you already knew that, didn't you). Since you are eliminating the carefully engineered sound baffles and plastic dams in the stock intake tract, you're going to be much more aware of the sound of air rushing through to feed your engine; this is the sound of increased engine power, and that's considered a good thing.

A straight end on a pipe does not pick up air well, even out in front of the car, because the pipe entry is too sharp - a funnel is good, but a tapered round entry like this is much better

This Typhoon ram from K&N is typical of cold air induction systems, shown here with a "rain hood" that slips over the filter for wet weather - the junction of the two pipes is a spot where the lower pipe can be removed to attach the filter there inside the engine compartment, making a short ram out of a long ram, another way of preparing for winter driving

When a gulp of water can be a very bad thing

Don't get too cute about where you put the air filter.

Of course, we want it to be in the cold air stream, but this is usually in the fenderwell where the filter can be at the mercy of dirt and water. In some weather conditions, the filter could become blocked by snow or mud, or water could actually be ingested by the engine. This latter condition is rare but if it happens it could spell the end of your engine! The condition is called hydro-lock, and it means that when water is ingested and gets into the cylinder(s), it doesn't compress like a gas. The pistons are pushing up against something virtually solid, to the detriment of pistons, rods and crankshaft.

There are several ways to avoid the hydro-lock disadvantage of the cold-air intake. The intake and filter companies have wraps and protective plastic or sheetmetal pieces that protect the filter from most water and dirt. Lots of enthusiasts take the front pipe off their cold-air intake off during the winter. There are some models of two-piece cold-air intakes where the fenderwell pipe can be removed and the filter attached to the pipe still on the engine, effectively making a long-ram into a short-ram. Perhaps the best solution if you want to keep the cold-air intake on all year is an air bypass valve. The bypass valve opens if the air filter is submerged in or blocked by water, and lets engine compartment air (filtered by a foam element) feed the engine instead of from the fenderwell air filter.

When a long cold air induction pipe mounts the filter down low on the car, there's possibility water could get into the airflow when driving through a big puddle, causing engine damage - an air bypass valve (arrow) can be installed in the piping to prevent hydro-lock

The AEM bypass valve reroutes air through an external diaphragm to keep dry air flowing, even if the filter is clogged with water - such valves can generally be used only on normally-aspirated (not supercharged or turbocharged) applications

Serious Air

Throttle bodies

Once you have an improved aftermarket intake system installed, there are other improvements you can make to the intake system to flow more air. Everything that is between the cold air pipe and the intake port on your cylinder head also controls the airflow and once you start modifying your engine and need more airflow, these other parts become the still-restricted limitation on how much air you can get into the engine.

If you have changed cams or ported the head, etc., then you may need to increase the airflow allowed by your stock throttle body. As we have mentioned in previous chapters, all of your engine modifications have to be chosen to work with each other as a system. You don't want only one or two parts that make high-rpm horsepower if the rest of the

If you've modified the engine enough, you might need a larger-than-stock throttle body - carefully measure the inside diameter of the stock throttle bore before shopping for a new one, and don't make a big leap in bore size unless the manufacturer of the power-adder you're using recommends it

Free horsepower

An old trick is to "port-match" the manifold to the cylinder head. If you look at the cylinder head mounting surface of the manifold and compare its ports to that of the intake manifold gasket, you'll invariably see that the ports in the gasket are slightly bigger than the ports in the manifold or the head. Remove your intake manifold and mount it in a vise with the ports facing up. Clamp a new gasket on the manifold, with the gasket perfectly aligned over the mounting bolt holes. Now scribe a line inside the gasket ports onto the manifold.

Take the gasket off and use a small electric or air-powered die grinder to grind out the manifold ports to the scribed line. Take your time and don't go beyond the scribed line or you could hinder the gasket's job of making a good seal. Try to gently blend the new port size back up into the ports on the manifold as far as you can, to improve the transition for the incoming air. Ideally, the cylinder head should be treated similarly to match the gasket, but you can wait until you have some other reason to pull the head. Performance gains in port-matching aren't large, but it costs you nothing to make the effort.

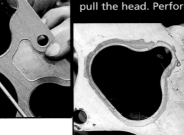

components are going to restrict that effort. Conversely, It does no good to install a high-flow component in one arena of the engine, such as a big throttle body, unless you can run at higher rpms. Don't even think about changing throttle bodies until you have removed all restrictions in the exhaust side of the vehicle.

Throttle bodies are available in various sizes, usually differing from stock units in the main throttle bore diameter.

If yours is a mild engine and there are several steps in throttle body size available, don't just buy the biggest one made, even if it is red-anodized aluminum. Play it safe and buy the smallest increase over stock, unless you install a big throttle body at the same time that you make other major engine changes. If you install a too-big throttle body now, and don't make your other modifications until much later, the interim period will find you with a low-rpm dog, and we don't mean that in a good way.

If you do install a larger throttle body, remove your intake manifold and have the throttle body opening in the manifold enlarged to the same size. It does no good to install an expensive "Type R" throttle body if it's restricted by a smaller, stock-sized hole at the manifold.

Throttle body installation isn't too complicated. A good aftermarket unit will come with clear instructions. Carefully mark all the hoses and wires on your stock throttle body with masking tape and a marking pen so you can connect them all to the right places on the new throttle body. Some cars have hot water hoses connected to the throttle body, in which case you must wait until the engine is completely cool and clamp-off those hoses before disconnecting them. You also have to disconnect the throttle linkage, and on some cars, the cruise control or transmission linkage as well. On most cars, the throttle body is attached to the intake manifold with four bolts, although sometimes it isn't easy to get at all the bolts. Take your time, and if necessary, follow a Haynes repair manual for your car.

Here's a billet-aluminum aftermarket throttle body installed on a thoroughly modified Honda VTEC application

This Holley billet-aluminum throttle body for Hondas accepts all the stock wiring and plumbing and is available in 62mm and 68mm bores, said to be good for 5-10 hp

If you have modified the fuel system or added nitrous, you might need more volume in your intake plenum - for some applications, AEM makes these spacers that mount between the throttle body and the stock intake manifold, to add a little more plenum volume without having to buy a new manifold

This aftermarket Honda intake manifold from Edelbrock (Performer-X model for SOHC D16Y8 VTEC engines) is said to be good for the 3,000 to 7,500 rpm range, and has a larger plenum, nine-inch-long passages, extra injector bosses and 50-state legality

Intake Manifolds

The final component in your intake system is the intake manifold that connects the throttle body to the cylinder head. This is that last section of the exterior intake path. If you have made the kind of modifications that necessitate a larger throttle body, then an improved intake is probably on the agenda also.

Intake manifolds are designed for specific levels of engine performance and rpm range. Your stock manifold was probably a good design for its intended application, i.e. normal driving. To design a performance intake manifold, increased airflow volume and velocity are the goals, just as with the big throttle bodies. The perfect manifold would be one that combined the right size ports, the right length of runners and the internal shapes to make maximum power. As with throttle bodies, the best manifold for pure high-rpm power is going to be unsuited to normal street driving.

Another race-only setup is this engine with individual throttle bodies for each cylinder, and tuned-entry velocity stacks on each throttle body - when ready to make a run, an airbox mounts over these stacks to feed them cold air

Fuel system

It's all about getting the right amount of fuel, at the right time, into your engine

With a stock engine, or one that is only mildly modified, the computer that came with your car will work with your engine management system and fuel system components to do an adequate job of delivering fuel to the engine. But if you become a bit more aggressive with your modifications, your engine will begin starving for more fuel to keep it happy.

This can be achieved in several ways. If you add more pressure, each time the injector opens more fuel will be delivered. If you control the length of time that the injector stays open, you have also added more fuel, even at the same pressure. The final way to inject more is to install fuel system components (injectors, fuel pump, etc.) that physically flow more fuel.

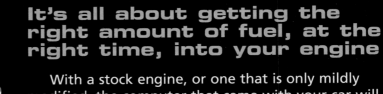

If you're adjusting fuel pressure, you need a convenient gauge to monitor the pressure - many enthusiasts mount theirs on top of the stock fuel filter at the firewall on Honda applications

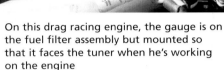

On this drag racing engine, the gauge is on the fuel filter assembly but mounted so that it faces the tuner when he's working on the engine

Fuel pressure

An adjustable fuel pressure regulator is probably the first modification for your fuel system. The aftermarket units are a direct bolt-on for the stock regulator, with the same vacuum connection, but feature an adjuster screw on top. Loosening or tightening the adjuster will change the fuel system pressure. Once you start playing with your fuel system, you must have a reliable way to measure the fuel pressure, which usually means installing a quality fuel pressure gauge. Most enthusiasts mount theirs in the engine compartment, where they do most of their tuning work. Some aftermarket gauges are designed to be screwed right into the stock fuel rail in place of the Schrader valve. An aftermarket fuel rail will usually have a threaded hole just for adding a gauge. It would be nice to have the gauge inside the car to watch it under different driving conditions without having to use a dyno, but a fuel gauge and fuel line inside the cockpit is potentially dangerous. A problem with the gauge or the pressurized line supplying it could leave you with a faceful of flammable fuel.

When you increase the fuel pressure in your fuel injection system, you are putting a greater load on the injectors themselves. Too much fuel pressure will shorten the life of the injectors. Experts tell us that for street cars with mild bolt-on modifications, you shouldn't raise the factory fuel pressure much more than 10%. On a vehicle with 45 psi as the stock pressure, you could safely raise it with an adjustable regulator to 49.5 psi, assuming that your modifications require an increase.

If you assemble a high-pressure fuel system for a boosted or nitrous application, you must use a bypass-type fuel-pressure regulator with a separate return line back to the fuel tank. Too much pressure without a bypass regulator could cause the pump(s) to fail. Also, use only high-pressure-rated metal or AN braided hoses in a high-pressure system to avoid possible fuel line rupture.

Without your own dynamometer to examine your engine under all conditions, especially under load at WOT, you have to tune somewhat by feel and by ear. If you have an experienced tuning shop near you, they can help a lot because they know what has worked on engines like yours. If you have too much fuel, your engine will be "doggy" at the bottom end and initial takeoff will be rough unless you're always leaving an intersection at higher rpms. With a minor increase in fuel system pressure, you can have your stock ECU or chip reprogrammed to handle higher fuel pressure, and this is recommended, but there is a finite limit to how much the stock ECU can handle. An exhaust gas analyzer at a tuning shop is a big help, especially if you can run the car on a chassis dyno (driven by the car's wheels under load). You can also learn something from your friends; see what they have done and learn from their mistakes.

01 On our Honda we relieved fuel pressure by loosening this small bolt on the fuel filter. Each model is a little different, so buy a manual to do it right

02 Tag and disconnect the vacuum line and fuel hoses from the stock regulator – on this Honda the regulator is attached to the stock fuel rail with two bolts

03 We're using a B&M kit that modifies the stock regulator - carefully cut off the top section of the regulator "can" with a hacksaw, then remove the stock spring and file the edges of the regulator body smooth

Fuel pressure regulator modification

04 Here the cut-apart stock regulator and spring (left) is compared to the pieces in the B&M kit, which includes a new spring, adjuster screw, anodized aluminum housing and an O-ring

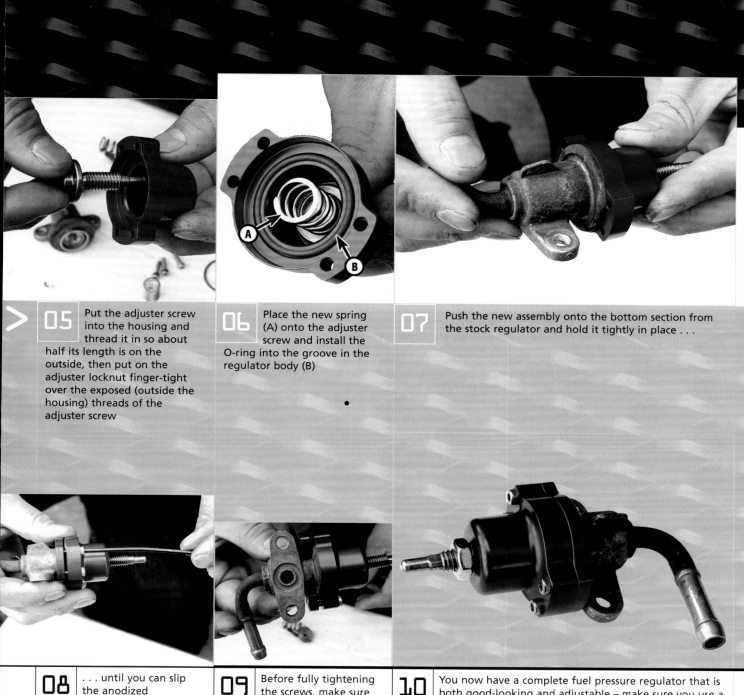

> **05** Put the adjuster screw into the housing and thread it in so about half its length is on the outside, then put on the adjuster locknut finger-tight over the exposed (outside the housing) threads of the adjuster screw

06 Place the new spring (A) onto the adjuster screw and install the O-ring into the groove in the regulator body (B)

07 Push the new assembly onto the bottom section from the stock regulator and hold it tightly in place . . .

08 . . . until you can slip the anodized aluminum bottom piece under the top and start the two screws – Loctite is provided with the kit to use on the screws, which are tightened with an Allen wrench

09 Before fully tightening the screws, make sure the two flat sections of the aluminum bottom piece align with the mounting flange of the regulator, otherwise the assembly won't bolt up to your fuel rail

10 You now have a complete fuel pressure regulator that is both good-looking and adjustable – make sure you use a new factory O-ring at the fuel rail side when reinstalling the regulator

For engines with 400 or more horsepower, you'll need a large fuel pump and fuel filter with large lines, preferably in braided-stainless-covered AN hose that can take plenty of pressure

Your stock black fuel filter can be replaced with a more attractive anodized aluminum filter housing like this one from AEM, which accepts a standard filter element (available at auto parts stores) and has enough fuel flow for high-horsepower engines

Fuel system volume

If you make more serious engine modifications, either internal mods like a ported head and bigger cams, or install a nitrous system, supercharger or turbocharger, you will have to address the fuel volume needs of your engine. This is where fuel system tuning can get tricky, but remember that you are not a pioneer here, many other enthusiasts have done just what you are doing and probably to the exact same vehicle. The manufacturer of the power-adder kit you buy should be able to tell pretty much just what is needed to compensate for the extra fuel needs of the nitrous, turbo or supercharger. How much boost or nitrous you employ has a lot to do with it.

For the typical compact engine modified with bolt-on equipment, your stock fuel pump should be able to handle the fuel supply. Where you might want to make a change is the fuel rail that holds all your injectors. An aftermarket fuel rail is usually machined of billet aluminum and available polished or anodized in cool colors. They look great sitting on your engine as a visual signal that you have a modified engine, even if your particular combination doesn't really need a bigger fuel rail yet.

There is a practical reason to install a fuel rail, especially if you contemplate more modifications in the future. Horsepower can be addictive! The typical aftermarket fuel rail is machined to bolt onto your stock engine with minimal trouble. The advantages, beside looks, are that it can deliver more volume of fuel because the main internal passage is bigger.

Another feature of a custom fuel rail is an extra pressure port that can be used to mount a fuel

An aftermarket rail such as on this race engine can carry the fuel volume to steadily feed larger injectors, and is more easily adapted to braided stainless hoses than a stock fuel rail

Holley offers billet fuel rails in four colors – they are available for either stock injectors or larger performance injectors

pressure gauge. The port can also be used as a convenient source of pressurized fuel if you install a nitrous system and add a separate fuel/nitrous nozzle to your intake tract. The fuel rail is also adaptable to accept aftermarket AN fittings (sometimes called "aircraft" fittings) for tuners who want to plumb their fuel system with colorful, custom lines. For bigger modifications, this will become important, because you may need to increase the fuel line diameter all the way back to the gas tank to assure adequate supply, and the billet fuel rail accepts bigger-than-stock fuel lines easily.

An aftermarket fuel rail is a common fuel system modification, for good looks and the ability to flow more fuel volume for modified engines – the typical billet-aluminum rail accepts a fuel gauge and a stock or aftermarket fuel pressure regulator

Fuel pumps

With the bigger engine modifications, your stock fuel pump may not be able to supply enough volume or pressure. In most modern cars, the electric fuel pump is mounted in the fuel tank, usually in an assembly that includes a filter and the fuel level sending unit. With these other components connected to the fuel pump, and the number of hoses and electrical connectors attached there at the top of the tank, not everyone wants to substitute another pump for the in-tank unit.

Most tuners in need of extra fuel pressure use an extra fuel pump as a booster, leaving the stock pump in the tank. Racers often use two big aftermarket electric pumps just outside the fuel tank. Electric fuel pumps are designed to push fuel rather than pull it, so generally they should be mounted near the rear of the car, close to the fuel tank, but as long as your in-tank pump is in good shape, an aftermarket booster pump can be installed almost anywhere in the line up to the engine, and is more than enough fuel supply for a street-driven ride. It can be installed on the underside of the chassis as long as it's safely away from hot exhaust components or moving suspension parts and is tucked up high enough that it can't be damaged by road debris. Some modified applications install the extra pump in the engine compartment.

When you have fuel pressure needs that go up with high rpms and boost, you can increase flow with MSD's fuel pump booster – it adds more voltage to your in-tank pump as needed and can be varied from 1.5 to 22 extra volts over a range of 5 to 30 psi

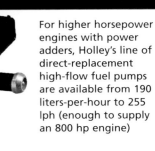

For higher horsepower engines with power adders, Holley's line of direct-replacement high-flow fuel pumps are available from 190 liters-per-hour to 255 lph (enough to supply an 800 hp engine)

Electric pumps are noisy, another reason manufacturers stick them down in the fuel tank where the sound is dampened. Wherever you mount the pump, make sure you utilize the rubber isolation mounts that should come with the pump. A chassis-mounted pump without rubber mounts can make an annoying hum, audible inside the car if you don't have your stereo on.

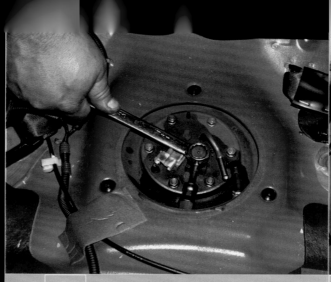

01 On most vehicles, the stock in-tank fuel pump is accessible once the rear seat bottom or trunk floor mat is removed, then an access plate is unbolted and removed. Consult a Haynes Manual for specifics on your car. Higher flowing fuel pumps can be exchanged for the stock pump for supercharger or turbocharger power-adders

02 Relieve the fuel system pressure, tag and disconnect the fuel lines, wires and hoses, then remove the fuel pump assembly mounting screws or nuts

If you don't want to change out the in-tank pump, extra fuel volume can be added with an aftermarket performance pump like this one from MSD added in-line to your fuel system

Typical fuel pump replacement

Lift the pump/fuel level sending unit assembly from the tank and use a large rag to catch any fuel drips **03**

Pull the "sock" filter from the bottom of the pump, then release the protective cover over the main electrical connector at the pump and pull the pump out of the assembly – install the high-flow replacement pump and replace the sock filter **04**

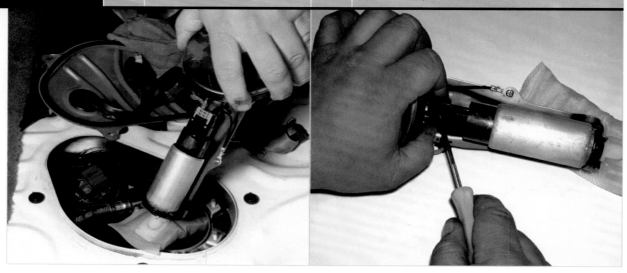

Test and tune

The oxygen sensor in your car has a limited range of air/fuel ratios it can act upon, since it is designed to be sensitive only in the range of the stock vehicle, with all original equipment in place. Once you start modifying your engine, especially the fuel system, the oxygen sensor isn't going to be able to act properly and keep the engine in the "normal" air/fuel ratio range.

Highly accurate air/fuel meters are used by pro racers, but are extremely expensive. A few more-affordable aftermarket sensors and dash-mounted meters are available that can be used to study your fuel needs. They feature a row of LED lights that correspond to different air/fuel ratios, and while you drive you can see what range you're in under different conditions.

If you do go to a piggyback engine-management box added to your stock ECU, or go all the way and have a stand-alone aftermarket system, a laptop PC can be used to monitor your engine as you drive (with a buddy along to hold and watch the computer while you focus on driving), and you can make changes to various parts of the fuel curve.

As mentioned in previous Chapters, you have to learn to "read" your car's driveability and performance. When you know your engine inside and out, you can better evaluate each new modification and how the car behaves differently than before the modification. We always recommend keeping track of your engine by checking the spark plugs as an indication of what's going on inside the combustion chamber. Compare your plugs with the spark plug condition chart in the *Ignition Chapter* to evaluate your engine conditions. It's vitally important to catch the early signs of detonation before engine internal parts are damaged.

An air/fuel ratio monitor can tell you what's going on inside your engine in both economy and power modes - this one from K&N has ten LED lights in different colors that correspond to different A/F ratios and comes with its own oxygen sensor that can be used with almost any fuel (including alcohol) except diesel, nitromethane or leaded fuels

A fuel computer can be added to your system to display air/fuel ratios and make adjustments - the VAFC fuel computer from A'PEXi can adjust fuel ratio for both the low-lobe and high-lobe modes of a Honda VTEC engine

Fuel injectors

A discussion of the parameters of selecting higher-flow fuel injectors could occupy a large book chapter by itself. There's a lot of science to choosing the right set, and a little bit of mystery as well. We'll give you some of the basics, but don't expect that all of your questions can be answered here. It'll take an experienced tuner working with a dyno and plenty of instrumentation to really make a good selection for you.

An electronic fuel injector performs an amazing job when you think about it. Under considerable fuel pressure, it must open, squirt and close in a matter of milliseconds. At high rpms, the injector is working really hard to keep up with the engine's demands. How much fuel gets into the engine depends on the physical size of the injector, how quick it can respond, and how long it stays open. Big injectors obviously flow more fuel, and an injector that is told to stay open longer will also flow more fuel.

The parts of your engine management system that controls the injector operation are called "drivers". Your stock drivers are designed for the stock fuel system, and raising the fuel pressure or changing to larger injectors can leave the computer out of calibration. You car may have the top-end power you need, but fuel economy is going to go down and the air/fuel ratio at lower speeds is going to be too rich, causing sluggish performance. Injector selection is always a compromise, unless it's a perfectly stock vehicle, or a perfectly race-only vehicle that has been tuned and tested with a stand-alone fuel management system that is concerned with high-rpm operation only. In some ways, it's easier to find the combination for a race vehicle because idling, cold-starts and low or mid-range performance or efficiency aren't important.

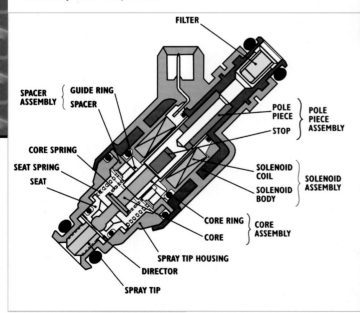

An electronic fuel injector is more complicated than you might think, so aftermarket performance injectors can be expensive - if you know you don't actually need bigger injectors, you can send your stock injectors to a company like RC Engineering and have them flow tested and balanced, protecting your engine from a burned piston due to one bad injector

Fuel injector replacement

After relieving the fuel pressure and disconnecting the battery, disconnect the electrical connectors from the injectors. Most vehicles use connectors like these, with a wire bail that must be released to unplug the connector, replacing your injectors with new ones **01**

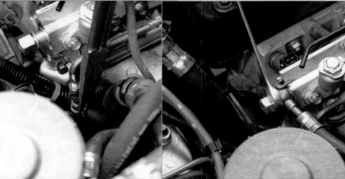

02 Detach the fuel return line from the pressure regulator

03 Unscrew the banjo fitting and detach the fuel feed line from the fuel rail

Whether you're simply re-sealing your stock injectors or installing high-flow performance injectors, the procedure is essentially the same. Furthermore, the injector removal and installation procedure is very similar from one vehicle to the next. The procedure that follows was performed on a mid-'90s Honda Accord with a 2.2L VTEC four-cylinder (F22B1).

04 Remove the fuel rail mounting nuts or bolts . . .

05 . . . then carefully wiggle and pull on the rail until the injectors are freed

06 Remove the injectors from the fuel rail; on most vehicles they pull straight out, but on some they are secured by clips

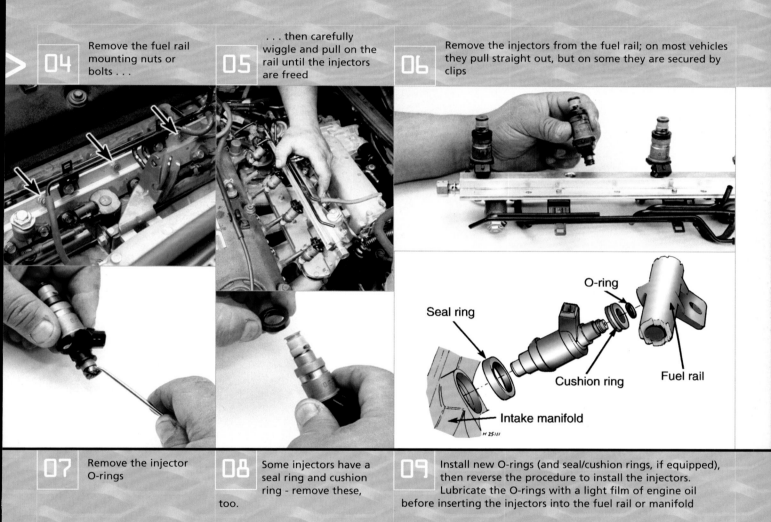

O-ring

Seal ring

Cushion ring

Fuel rail

Intake manifold

H 25III

07 Remove the injector O-rings

08 Some injectors have a seal ring and cushion ring - remove these, too.

09 Install new O-rings (and seal/cushion rings, if equipped), then reverse the procedure to install the injectors. Lubricate the O-rings with a light film of engine oil before inserting the injectors into the fuel rail or manifold

Valvetrain

Valvetrain

Deep breathing

When you run fast, you breathe harder - so does your engine. To make more power, an engine must "inhale" more air and "exhale" more exhaust. To make this happen, you can open the intake and exhaust valves more, leave them open longer and enlarge the "ports" (passages in the cylinder head where the air and exhaust flow). These cylinder head and valvetrain modifications can seem complicated, but understanding them is essential. Mistakes here can cost you power or even an engine overhaul.

Adjustable cam gears like these from AEM allow you to adjust camshaft timing to suit the other tuning modifications you have made or plan to - SOHC engines would use one gear, most DOHC'ers use a pair (some DOHC engines have only one gear - the other cam being driven by a gear or chain from the camshaft with the sprocket)

Cam gears (a.k.a. cam *sprockets*)

Aftermarket cam gears are generally made of aluminum, with color anodizing in red, blue, purple or silver, and can certainly add to the show-worthiness of an engine compartment, especially when you're going for a "theme" of coordinated colors on the accessories. Unfortunately, in order for anyone to see your cool cam gears you have to leave off the timing belt cover (at least the upper cover). The people can not only see the gears, but, when the engine is running and you see them spinning, it gives at least the impression of an extra 30 horsepower!

The only problem with leaving the timing belt cover off is that debris can get into the "beltway" and cause serious problems. If you happen to drop a socket or something else down there when working on the engine and then start the engine up, you could toast the whole motor.

Anything that gets caught up in the belt can cause it to shred or come off the sprockets or tensioner, and either situation on a running engine means that some of the valves are going to be open when the piston comes up. When this happens in a split second, valves and/or pistons are going to be destroyed. This little "lecture" probably will have no affect on most readers, who will leave the cover off anyway. Just be careful.

Aftermarket cam gears look cool and racy, but the only potential power gain by installing them is if an adjustment in camshaft timing is necessary on your engine. The mounting holes for the gears are slotted on the aftermarket units, and a scale is usually engraved there to indicate whether the timing is straight up (normal), advanced or retarded. The range of adjustment is usually 5-10 degrees. Engines that have forced induction (supercharger or turbocharger), high compression pistons or non-stock camshafts are especially candidates for the cam gears, although almost any engine can benefit from a little cam tuning. If your cylinder head

You'll find that cam gears are one of the most popular engine modifications there is

The adjustable gear is two-piece, so the bolts can be loosened and the relationship between the inner section on the camshaft and the outer section connected to the timing belt can be advanced or retarded. Good ones like this AEM "Tru-Time" gear are machined of billet aluminum and feature very clearly engraved timing marks

has been milled at a machine shop, either to gain extra compression or because the head was warped from overheating, you may need adjustable cam gears because milling the head brings the camshafts closer to the crankshaft and retards the cam timing slightly.

If you have a single overhead cam engine (SOHC), you'll only need one cam gear, and on SOHC engines, the phasing between the exhaust and intake lobes can't be adjusted, since exhaust and intake lobes are all on one hunk of iron. You can experiment with your camshaft advanced two degrees and see how it performs, then try it with two degrees retarded. You may find that advancing the cam helps top-end performance but hurts low-end, and vice-versa. You can't get improvement at both ends.

On DOHC (double overhead cam) engines that utilize a separate gear for each camshaft, you have more to play with. By adjusting the intake and exhaust camshafts separately, you are in effect altering the overlap (the period where both valves are open at the same time on the exhaust stroke). This is one of the factors that makes a cam design "street" or "race." The more overlap there is, the better the engine will run at higher rpm, but the bottom-end will suffer some. Most Honda enthusiasts with DOHC engines start out with their exhaust camshaft retarded a few degrees and the intake camshaft advanced a few degrees, which is like having a slightly hotter camshaft. Note that on DOHC engines that only have one cam gear, you can't do this (it's the same situation that was described for SOHC engines).

The exact amount of camshaft advance or retard that's best depends on a host of factors, including the efficiency of the intake and exhaust systems you're using. What works for your buddy's car isn't necessarily what your engine needs. Follow the instructions that come with your aftermarket cam gears and/or camshaft to determine how to set your camshaft timing to "straight-up," then test or drive the car before making any further adjustments to advance or retard.

Most tuners like to show off their modifications, and that means leaving off the upper timing belt cover to show the anodized cam gears - this makes them easy to access for making timing changes, but be careful nothing drops down behind the lower belt cover - it could cost you an engine

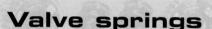

Probably no valvetrain modification is as important as good aftermarket valve springs that are strong enough not to "float" the valves at high engine speeds - these "Ultra-Rev" springs from REV are designed specifically for high-rpm and high-boost forced-induction engines

Valve springs

As mentioned above, proper aftermarket valve springs are a critical component of your modified engine if you hope to run higher rpm and have the engine survive. The valve springs themselves don't make any horsepower but can be considered insurance. At high rpm, the camshafts are spinning at a high speed, forcing the valves to open really fast. The only things that keep the valves following the camshaft are the springs.

Valves: more is better

To oversimplify, more valves mean more usable street power. The standard for modern high-performance engines is four valves per cylinder. But why can't you just use two valves per cylinder, but make them really big? This is where nerds will tell you about fluid dynamics and port velocity. Boiling it down, small ports and valves keep air flowing faster through the heads at low engine speeds, which makes a street car drive smoothly. Many super-fast drag-race engines use only two (huge) valves per cylinder; on these cars, low-rpm driveability isn't very important!

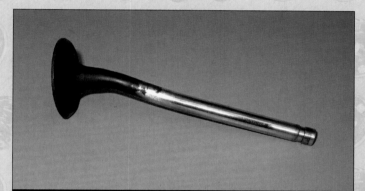

Valve float

Valve float occurs when, at high rpm, the valves are trying to move so fast that they momentarily "float" away from the camshaft or rocker arm lobes. If they float away when the piston is up, damage to something is inevitable. Two factors can keep the valves from floating, the strength of the valve springs and the weight of items in the valvetrain, such as the valves, keepers and retainers. Stronger, aftermarket valve springs are an important upgrade for any sport compact engine. The stronger springs keep the valves following the camshaft, even at high rpm.

Reducing the weight of the valve train items (such as with titanium retainers) is another way to lessen the onset of valve float.

You could install new springs in your engine and use the stock valve spring retainers, but most tuners install new lightweight retainers at the same time as the springs - these Crane titanium alloy retainers are stronger than the stock ones and their light weight allows the engine to rev quicker

Everything we do to make power in an engine is eventually limited by the camshaft(s) - aftermarket profiles are available from mild to wild, but the bigger you go, the more the low end performance may suffer, which is why cams are offered in "stages" so you can pick the design that suits your driving style

Camshafts

The camshaft is one of the key players in the operation of an engine, kind of like a bandleader directing the timing of all the other components. It determines the what, when and how much of anything that goes into and out of the engine. This is another subject a great deal can and has been written about, and we're not going to bore you with heavy theory and formulas. What you need to know for now is that a stock camshaft is designed as a compromise to consider economy, emissions, low-end torque and good idling and driveability. The performance camshaft lifts the valves higher (lift), keeps them open longer (duration) and is designed mainly to produce more horsepower. A performance camshaft usually makes its gains at mid-to-higher rpm and sacrifices some low-rpm torque. The hotter the cam, the more pronounced these attributes become. A really strong cam may not be suitable for the street at all, exhibiting really low engine vacuum and not idling below 1000 rpm.

When you do get the camshaft specs right for your engine and your kind of driving, it's a thrill to hear and feel the engine get up "on the cam" and just take off. A cam design that is advertised for power between 3000 and

One cam or two?

All engines have at least one camshaft to actuate the valves. On Single Overhead Camshaft (SOHC) engines, the camshaft does double-duty in opening both the intake and exhaust valves. Double OverHead Camshaft (DOHC) engines use one camshaft for the intake valves and one for the exhaust valves. The general rule is that SOHC engines use two valves per cylinder (one intake, one exhaust) and DOHC engines have four valves per cylinder (two of each). There are many exceptions to this rule, and some modern engines have four valves per cylinder with only one camshaft.

8000 rpm won't start feeling really good until that band is reached. Aftermarket cams for sport compact vehicles are usually offered in "Stages" of performance. A typical Stage 1 cam might have a little higher valve lift than stock, a little longer duration, and perhaps slightly more overlap. It should retain an excellent idle and work from idle or 1000 rpm up. A Stage II cam would be hotter in all specs (with a band from 3000 to 7000 rpm) and have a slightly

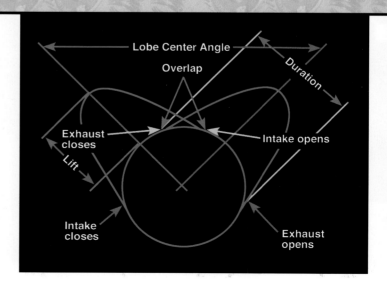

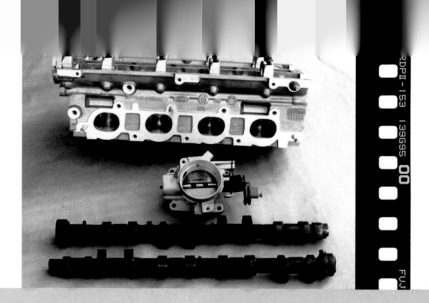

A valvetrain package from Gude that the manufacturer calls the "turbo beater at half the price" includes a ported cylinder head with performance cam(s) - this kit for the Ford Focus also includes a tweaked ECU and a bigger throttle body

rough idle (maybe at 750 rpm), while a Stage III cam would feature serious lift, duration and overlap and make its power from 5000 to 8000 rpm. The hotter the cam specs the worse the idle, low-end performance and fuel economy is going to be, but the more top-end horsepower you'll make. After the Stage III cam, which is usually a serious street/strip grind, the cam profiles are strictly for racing.

One exception to the "can't have your cake and eat it too" philosophy is the VTEC system offered by Honda. Ideally, an engine would have a continuously variable valvetrain, always with the exact right profile for the rpm range. Someday, engines will have such a system, but Honda was on the right track. Basically, the VTEC valvetrain is like three cam profiles in one. There are three lobes on the cam for each cylinder's intake or exhaust: primary, secondary and the "mid" or middle lobe. These lobes with different profiles are actuated at different rpm ranges to provide the cam profile that's best for the engine speed.

When tuners tell you they have put in a "VTEC controller," they mean they have an electronic box that alters the signal to the factory ECU, to allow the VTEC high-rpm profile to come in sooner. You can watch your dyno sheets and if there's a lull at about 5000

rpm, it may be that you could use slightly quicker engagement of the VTEC to take a soft spot out of your modified engine.

When buying a performance camshaft and kit, there is always a tendency to think "bigger is better," since the hotter cam doesn't necessarily cost any more. Look at the technical literature provided by the camshaft manufacturers, in their catalogs and on their websites, and compare the specs of the cams and the comments that describe the cam's idle, driving and power characteristics. Going overboard can mean you have a miserable car to drive in normal traffic. Relate the cam choice to the modifications you have made. Some profiles are designed specifically to work well with nitrous, turbocharging or high compression.

Another consideration in choosing a camshaft profile is will it physically work in your engine without modifications. With a certain amount of lift, there can be interference between the valve and the pistons, especially if you have milled the cylinder head or installed aftermarket pistons. Usually the Stage I or II cams are OK for a stock engine, but check the manufacturer's recommendations. If there is any question, have your tuning shop check valve-to-piston clearance.

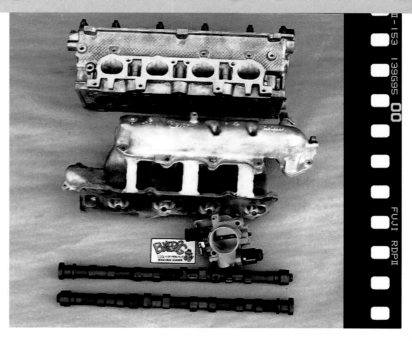

The breathing package Gude offers for the Mitsubishi Eclipse includes a ported head, performance cams, bigger throttle body and a matched intake manifold

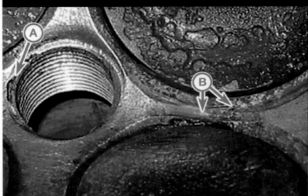

Your engine should be in good shape before doing any modifications, so if you pull off the car's head, check it carefully before reassembling the engine - this engine's tuner didn't monitor his engine and heat and detonation have taken their toll - you can see where the spark plug hole threads are starting to erode (A), and between the two valves at the right there are two expensive-to-repair cracks in the head (B)

Cylinder heads and pistons

With the intake and exhaust system modified and a performance camshaft in place, your next step in improving your engine's breathing should be the cylinder head. Except for port-matching, most cylinder head work is not for the do-it-yourself modifier. Too much experience and expensive equipment is required, so find a well-recommended machine shop in your area that has experience with sport compact cylinder heads for street and racing.

What you do want to do, especially if you have the head off anyway for a camshaft installation, is to have a performance valve job done. In the performance valve job, the valve face and valve seat angles in the head are changed from just one angle to three or more. In a three-angle valve job, the center angle is the one where the valve meets the seat, and the upper and lower angles are designed to smooth the flow path from the port, around the valve head, and into the combustion chamber. This improves the flow

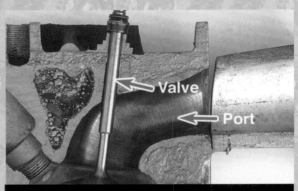

What's a "head?

The cylinder head, or simply "head," is on top of the engine. The head seals the area above the pistons so that compression is created when the pistons travel up. The head is also where the air/fuel mixture enters the engine and exhaust exits. To do this, the intake and exhaust valves in the head open at precise times, controlled by the camshaft(s).

If your engine has 130,000 miles on it, chances are your valve guides are worn and you can't get a good tight valve seal if the guide allows the valve to wobble. When your head is rebuilt at the machine shop, they may suggest installing bronze-alloy guides that keep the valves cooler and reduce valve-to-guide friction

When you are rebuilding your cylinder head, if you discover some bad valves, why not replace the whole set with performance valves like these from REV that are lightweight and made of high-temp alloys to handle boosted and nitrous-equipped applications

GM Performance Parts has quite a list of go-fast equipment for the 2.2L ECOTEC four-cylinder, including this cylinder head that is CNC (computer) ported, has a three-angle performance valve job and comes with a flowbench tech sheet - the head accepts stock or aftermarket valvetrain parts

Back to basics

If your car's got some miles on it, your valves are probably not operating as well as they should. On a worn engine, the valves don't "seat" properly because they wobble in their guides and don't sit properly against their seats in the head. Worn valve parts cost you power and can cause engine damage, since they are more likely to hit a piston. Any valvetrain build-up should include a good valve job to re-seat the valves, and a thorough check of the valve guides and springs.

Notice the "eyebrow" looking recesses in these pistons. They allow more clearance for the valves to open more. Sometimes special pistons are necessary for your hopped-up valvetrain

at low-lift and is not as expensive as porting.

Bigger changes to the cylinder head may be detrimental to street performance, yet critical to a racer in an all-motor class. If you are planning headwork, talk to the machinist first and thoroughly explain everything you've done to the engine so far, and any future mods you plan. He'll make specific recommendations for your particular set-up.

Sometimes swapping cylinder heads is the path to more power - the most common swap in Honda circles is the B16 VTEC head onto a larger-displacement non-VTEC block - when pros prepare the head, some holes in the head have to be modified by TIG-welding, then the head is surfaced

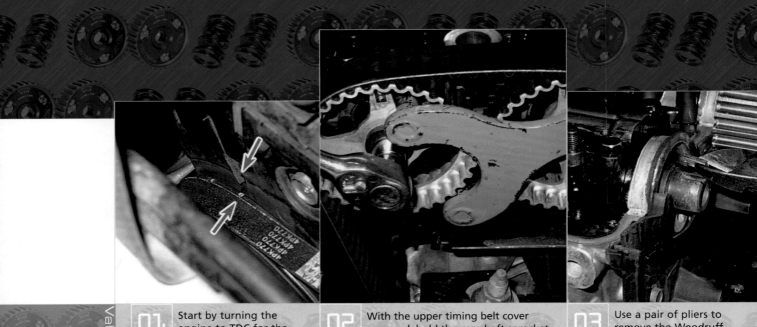

01 Start by turning the engine to TDC for the number 1 piston, aligning the mark on the crankshaft pulley with the mark on the timing cover

02 With the upper timing belt cover removed, hold the camshaft sprocket with a two-pin spanner like this or with a large screwdriver jammed in one of the sprocket holes, while you use a wrench or socket to remove the sprocket-to-camshaft bolt

03 Use a pair of pliers to remove the Woodruff key from the slot in each stock camshaft - save them to re-use on the new cams

HOW-TO: Camshafts, valve springs and timing gears

Our Haynes repair manual for your particular vehicle covers the removal and installation of camshafts and the alignment of timing marks, but this procedure includes some details that are different in performance tuning applications. Our subject car was a typical Honda with a B16 DOHC VTEC engine, already equipped with a header and intake tube. We installed a pair of Crane cams (part #253-0010) along with their performance valve springs, spring seats and lightweight spring retainers, all very important if we want to go fast and yet keep from floating valves at high rpm.

Two procedures used here are not covered in repair manuals, finding true Top Dead Center (TDC) for an engine, and "degreeing in" the camshaft. For all ordinary purposes, the factory timing marks are valid, but in a performance application, precision is important. If your head has been surfaced, your camshaft timing may be off slightly, or your crankshaft pulley may be off a degree or so. So we check with a dial indicator.

To find true TDC, we use the dial indicator on the top of the piston, with the engine at the stock TDC marks and the indicator reading zero. Rotate the engine 10 degrees or so clockwise from TDC and read the indicator. Now rotate the engine counterclockwise the other direction until the pointer on the crank pulley is 10 degrees the other side of TDC and read the indicator again. Take the range of movement on the indicator and divide it by half, then rotate the engine clockwise until the indicator shows that exact amount, which puts the engine at true TDC. Now you can make the temporary timing pointer and marks we illustrate in the photos.

The point of degreeing the camshafts is to find where they are in relation to the crankshaft. Aftermarket cams come with a card that indicates the opening and closing times of the valves. There can be variations in your timing due to milling the head or other tolerances in the engine. Tuners use adjustable cam gears to try different timing settings to seek out a few more horsepower. This is not a fixed thing, you have to experiment with your combination, but Honda VTEC tuners often retard their stock exhaust cam a few degrees and advance the intake a few, which usually gives more performance from the stock cams.

In degreeing, you set the number 1 cylinder at TDC on our "new" temporary marks, then attach a dial indicator to rest on the rocker tip (or retainer or cam follower, whatever the case may be) of the number 1 intake valve, and zero the indicator at TDC. Our Crane timing card for the Stage 1 cams said the intake valve starts to open at 8 degrees after TDC. We rotated the engine very slowly past TDC while someone watched the dial indicator. When the indicator said the valve had opened 0.050-inch, we stopped.

When a cam "starts to open" is a relative thing to describe, so most cam manufacturers use the figure of 0.050-inch as a standard point of reference. Our timing marks showed we were at 6 degrees, which means that our intake cam was advanced slightly, which is what we wanted. If you wanted to advance it more, or have it 'straight-up' to be exactly as the card described, you can adjust the timing gears to get what you want. On the alignment marks on most two-piece adjustable cam gears, one mark equals two degrees at the crankshaft, and the gears should have markings that indicate which direction is advance and which is retard. Once you have degreed-in your cams, you won't have to go through this procedure again, you just go by the marks on your adjustable gears. When you have the settings that seem to make the most power, leave it there and enjoy!

04 Loosen all of the bolts for the camshaft caps and the reinforcement plates, in the opposite of the tightening sequence (see Step 31) - loosen all bolts a quarter-turn first, then loosen again in sequence and remove the bolts

05 Use a plastic-faced hammer to lightly tap the sides of the camshaft caps to separate them from the cylinder head. Make sure the caps are numbered from front-to-rear, and have an I for the intake cam caps and an E for the exhaust cam caps. If there aren't any marks, make your own

06 Lift out both of the camshafts, taking the front seals with them

Note:
The procedure shown here was performed on a Honda with a B16 DOHC VTEC engine. If you're working on something different you can use this as a guide, but be sure to consult your Haynes manual for the specifics.

07 Loosen the locknuts at each rocker arm, then use a screwdriver to back off the valve adjustments all the way, then tilt the rocker arms up for access to the valve springs and retainers

08 The valve spring tool is a pair of stands that mount each end of the cylinder head and a shaft that runs between the two brackets - when you push down on the lever the spring is compressed at the retainer - you can rent one these tools

09 To hold the valves in place while the springs are compressed, put the cylinder you're working on at TDC and insert an air hose that has a spark-plug threaded adapter at one end into the spark plug hole for that cylinder

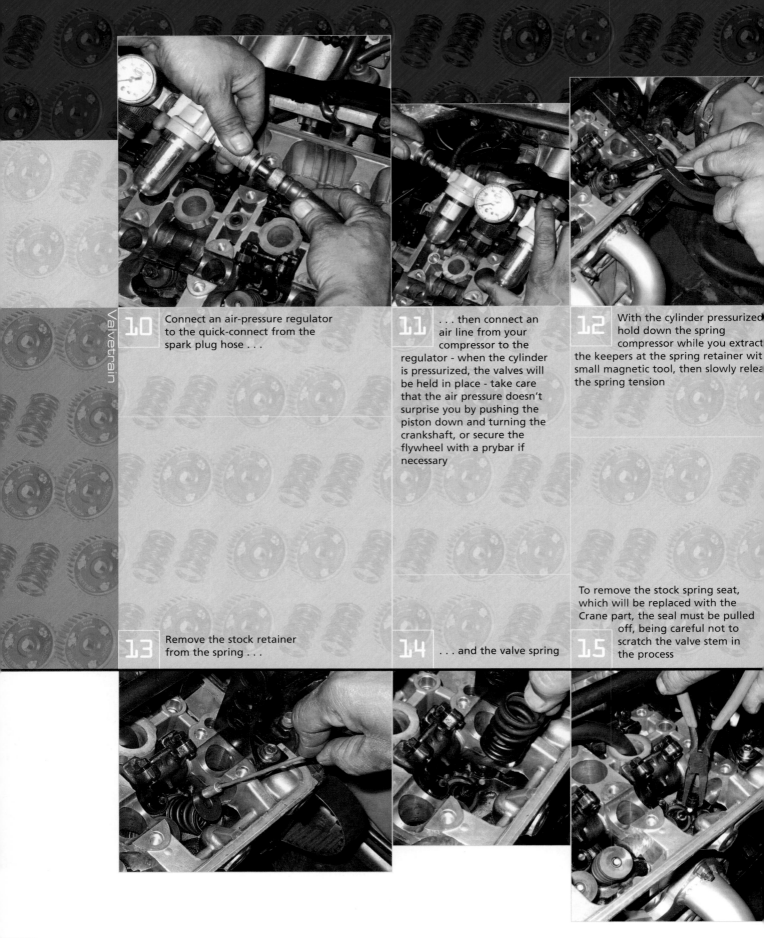

10 Connect an air-pressure regulator to the quick-connect from the spark plug hose . . .

11 . . . then connect an air line from your compressor to the regulator - when the cylinder is pressurized, the valves will be held in place - take care that the air pressure doesn't surprise you by pushing the piston down and turning the crankshaft, or secure the flywheel with a prybar if necessary

12 With the cylinder pressurized, hold down the spring compressor while you extract the keepers at the spring retainer with small magnetic tool, then slowly release the spring tension

13 Remove the stock retainer from the spring . . .

14 . . . and the valve spring

15 To remove the stock spring seat, which will be replaced with the Crane part, the seal must be pulled off, being careful not to scratch the valve stem in the process

16 Remove the stock spring seat from the pocket in the cylinder head

17 Clean the valve spring pocket in the head with a degreaser, then lubricate the new Crane spring seat with engine oil and set it in place, making sure it is located properly

18 Lubricate the valve stem with engine oil, then push a new valve seal onto the valve - push down evenly and no further than the stock seal went - the seal should hit a machined stop near the bottom of the valve guide - the seal package in your gasket set (not furnished with the camshafts) should say if the seal is for the intake or exhaust, which are different on some engines

Place the new high-performance Crane spring in, making sure that it sits flat and is centered on the new **19** spring seat

Now you can install the Crane lightweight retainer - notice the stepped area on the underside of the retainer; this self-centers the retainer and **20** spring

Apply a little white grease to one of the valve keepers and insert it while you have the retainer and spring held down with the valve spring **21** compressor - the grease will hold it in place

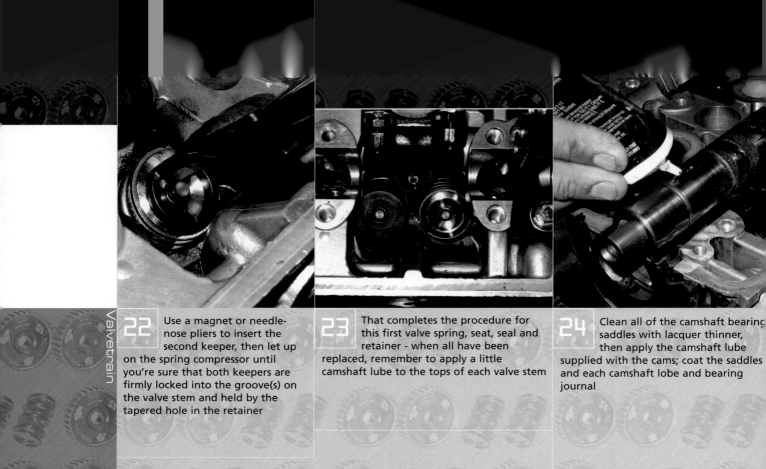

22 Use a magnet or needle-nose pliers to insert the second keeper, then let up on the spring compressor until you're sure that both keepers are firmly locked into the groove(s) on the valve stem and held by the tapered hole in the retainer

23 That completes the procedure for this first valve spring, seat, seal and retainer - when all have been replaced, remember to apply a little camshaft lube to the tops of each valve stem

24 Clean all of the camshaft bearing saddles with lacquer thinner, then apply the camshaft lube supplied with the cams; coat the saddles and each camshaft lobe and bearing journal

25 Lay out all the camshaft caps you removed from the head and clean them thoroughly - they are numbered from front to back - then apply a small amount of camshaft lube to the saddles of each one (the lube has been applied to these saddles, but still needs to be spread out over the bearing surfaces)

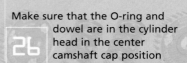

26 Make sure that the O-ring and dowel are in the cylinder head in the center camshaft cap position

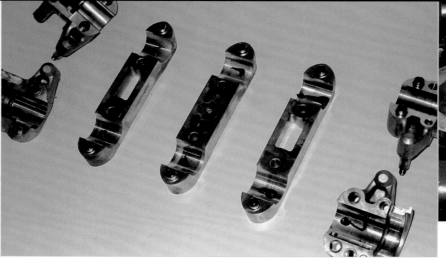

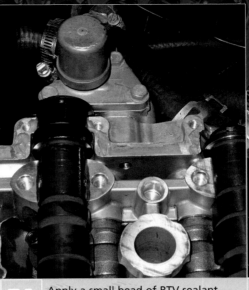

27 Grease the inner lip of the camshaft seals with white grease, then carefully push them squarely over the end of each camshaft

28 Apply a small bead of RTV sealant to the areas indicated, just before placing the camshaft caps back onto the cylinder head

29 Install all of the caps in their proper positions, tapping them squarely and lightly to seat them

30 With all the camshaft caps in place, lay the two camshaft cap stiffener plates in position and hand-tighten all the bolts

31 Torque all of the bolts in several stages and in the proper sequence, with the engine at TDC . See the Haynes manual for the correct specification and sequence (this is the proper sequence for our Honda B16 VTEC)

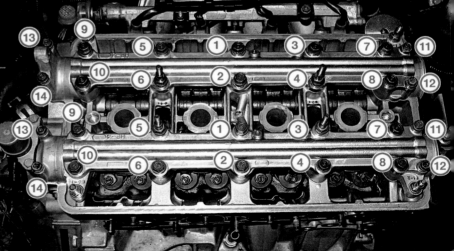

32 With the Woodruff keys tapped all the way into the keyways on the new Crane cams, you can now install the cam gears (technically they're "sprockets") - we're using a pair of adjustable Crane gears

33 With a tool through one of the holes in the cam gear, tighten the gear-to-camshaft bolt - note that all of the adjuster nuts on the gear must be tight before using this method to install the gear - the nuts can be loosened later if your need to advance or retard the cam timing

34 With the crankshaft at TDC for number 1 cylinder, all the timing marks must align properly. Now install the belt and release the belt tensioner - rotate the engine a few times by hand and check that the gear marks still line up at TDC - now follow the valve adjustment procedure in your Haynes repair manual, and install the distributor at TDC

If you don't have a degree wheel to attach to the crank, measure the circumference of the puller and divide by 360 (as in 360 degrees in a rotation) - in our case, this worked out to 1/16-inch for each degree of crank rotation - we epoxied a temporary pointer to the pan rail and made tiny punch marks on either side of the "new" TDC mark at 1/16-inch intervals (see intro text for procedure to find true TDC) - this location was used because it's much easier to see than where the stock marks line up at the timing belt cover

For precise performance, we'll check to see if the TDC mark at the crankshaft pulley is accurate enough for us - we bent a large washer, drilled a hole in it and bolted it to the head as a stand for the magnetic-base dial indicator

35

With an extension, we have the dial indicator on the top of the number 1 piston

36

37

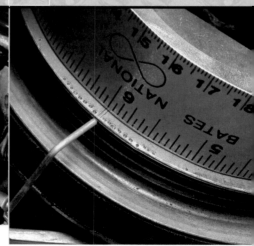

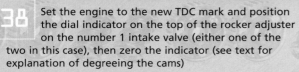

38 Set the engine to the new TDC mark and position the dial indicator on the top of the rocker adjuster on the number 1 intake valve (either one of the two in this case), then zero the indicator (see text for explanation of degreeing the cams)

39 When we rotate the crank and watch the dial indicator, we stop just as the indicator shows the valve has moved 0.050-inch, which is the point most cam manufacturers give you a timing spec for - our cam timing card said we should be at 8 degrees ATDC (after TDC) at the crank with the valve down 0.050-inch

40 If you look at your "new" timing marks at the crank, it should show the 8-degree ATDC mark lined up, this means our cam is 'straight-up' to the engine - if it isn't, or we want to experiment with advancing or retarding the cams, we loosen the nuts on the Crane gear, rotate the alignment marks the direction we want and tighten the nuts again

41 All timed and ready to go, we were anxious to put the valve cover and other pieces back on - our engine already had a header and cold air intake, so the new cams were just what we need to add a little more "bite to our bark" - midrange was good and the VTEC was even better

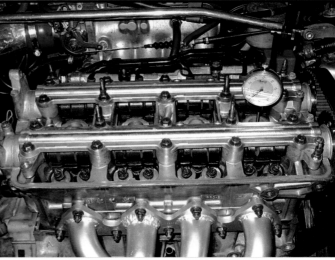

Nitrous Oxide

Nitrous oxide as a horsepower source can appear to be a miracle or a curse, depending on your experience. It's a fact that nitrous oxide (N2O) is the simplest, quickest and cheapest way to gain serious horsepower boost in your car. But, just like in children's fairy tales, you court disaster if you don't follow the rules that come with the magic potion.

Carefully used and tuned, a nitrous oxide system is the biggest power-per-dollar performance enhancement you can make on your sport compact

Nitrous oxide is an odorless, colorless gas that doesn't actually burn. It carries oxygen that allows your engine to burn extra fuel. When you inject nitrous oxide and gasoline at the same time and in the proper proportions at full throttle, you'll get a kick in the butt as if you were instantly driving a car with an engine twice as big!

Nitrous kits

Done right, a nitrous kit is one of the best horsepower-per-dollar investments you can make, and is the most popular power-adder for small engines. The smallest nitrous kits offer at least a 50-horsepower shot for an investment of $500. In other engine bolt-on speed budgeting, that same $500 wouldn't even cover a really nice cat-back exhaust system that may only net you 15 horsepower.

Kits are available that add up to 300hp, because the more nitrous and fuel you add, the more power the engine makes, right up to the point where the engine comes apart. And that's the other side of adding nitrous. In the end, it is the durability of the engine itself, that determines how much nitrous you can run. As tempting as it is to just keep putting bigger nitrous jets in your engine for more power, you need to do your research first to see what are the limits of your engine and what can be done to protect against damage done by detonation. You may have heard horror stories about engine disasters caused by nitrous oxide, but in most cases the cause is usually a fault in tuning the application. Serious racers have done everything possible to their engines to strengthen them to handle big loads of nitrous.

The basic street-use nitrous kit consists of: a nitrous bottle, usually one that holds 10 pounds of liquid nitrous oxide; bottle mounting brackets and hardware; fuel and nitrous jets; high pressure lines, usually braided-stainless covered AN–type with a Teflon inner liner for the high nitrous pressure; nitrous filter; solenoids, switch and electrical connectors. Kits are always sold without the nitrous in the bottle; you'll have to go to a local speed shop to have the bottle filled.

There are two basic types of nitrous kits that differ in how the nitrous and fuel are delivered. The "dry" system has a nozzle and solenoid only for the nitrous, and this nozzle may

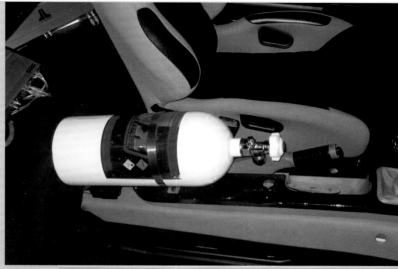

The basic nitrous oxide installation kit includes everything you'll need, including the 10-pound bottle to hold the N2O - this kit from NOS includes brackets to mount the bottle in the trunk at the proper angle

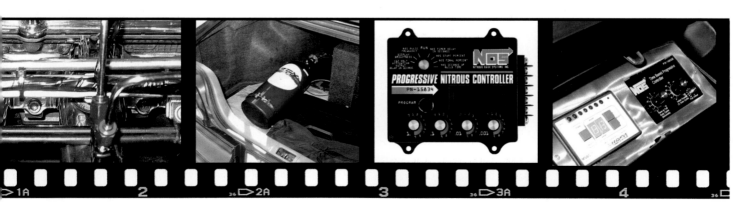

be almost anywhere in the intake system; behind the MAF sensor (if equipped) and ahead of the throttle body is typical. The dry systems are designed for factory fuel-injected engines. To deliver the extra fuel to go with the nitrous, the stock system fuel pressure is raised during the WOT (wide-open throttle) period of nitrous usage, and reverts back to the stock fuel pressure in all other driving conditions.

The "wet" system of nitrous will have solenoids for nitrous *and* fuel, both of which are turned on when the nitrous system is activated. The fuel and nitrous in a simple system are plumbed into a single injector that merges the two, the gasoline and its oxidizer, as they enter the engine. More sophisticated wet systems may have an N2O nozzle for each cylinder of the engine, and one or more fuel nozzles mounted separately. In high-output racing applications, individually feeding each cylinder allows for tuning each cylinder separately for fine control. The extra nozzles also mean there is ample supply of nitrous and fuel for very high-horsepower installations.

There are all sorts of "bells and whistles" available as extra features on most of the nitrous kits on the market today. There are varying designs of nozzles, different electronic controls that work with your factory ECU to control timing and fuel delivery, optional bottle covers, bottle warmers, remote shut-off valves for the bottle, ECU piggybacks (see Chapters 4 and 5) that pull back the ignition timing under nitrous use, and "staged" nitrous kits that deliver a certain amount during launch, then a little more, and the full blast for the top end.

On this Nitrous Express setup there is an inline filter in both the fuel (A) and nitrous (B) lines leading to the solenoids, a good idea to prevent clogged injectors or N2O nozzles

In "wet" systems, the nitrous nozzle (arrow) can mix and spray both gasoline and nitrous into the intake

No laughing matter

Nitrous can be intoxicating, but confine your high to the feeling you get from gobs of extra horsepower, not from inhaling the nitrous. Yes, it was once called "laughing gas" and used by dentists as an anaesthetic, but that is medical-grade nitrous, which is a controlled substance. What you're going to buy at your local tuner or speed shop is industrial-grade nitrous, which has a serious irritant added to it. If you try to inhale this stuff, you'll be sorry. Your engine, on the other hand, will love it.

The N2O solenoids and controls should be mounted in the engine compartment, close to the intake system - this Zex installation is 'dry" meaning that only nitrous is injected through the nozzle on the intake (the extra fuel comes through the stock injectors based on an altered vacuum signal to the fuel pressure regulator under "juice")

Model-specific kits are available in addition to the more universal nitrous packages - NOS offers this kit for the Ford Focus with a unique plate-style injection and an rpm "window" switch to prevent rpm-induced backfires from the factory rev-limiter

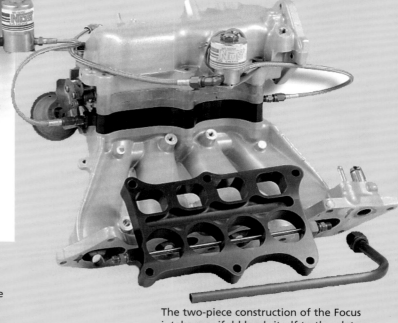

The two-piece construction of the Focus intake manifold lends itself to the plate system; the plate sandwiches between the two manifold sections

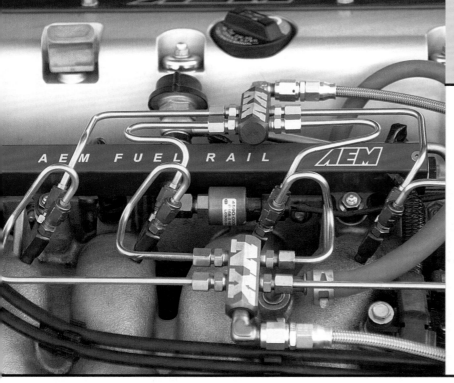

In the really 'serious' nitrous installations, there may be a nozzle for each cylinder, installed in the intake runners - this clean setup uses fuel (blue) and nitrous (red) distribution blocks and individual stainless-steel hard lines to connect to the four nozzles

The most universal sport compact kit from Nitrous Express is this one that is adjustable from 35-50-75 horsepower levels - this wet-style kit needs no electronics for timing retard and uses the stock fuel pump

How does it work?

In basic terms for a simple nitrous system, the tank or bottle of nitrous oxide is mounted in the trunk and plumbed up to the engine compartment with a high-pressure line. This is connected to an electric solenoid, from which nitrous (still a liquid at this point) can flow to the nozzle attached to your intake system. If you turn on an "arming" switch in the car, battery voltage is available to another switch that is a button-type located on the steering wheel, dash or shifter. Push that button when you're hard on the throttle and the solenoid releases nitrous oxide which passes through a sized jet or orifice and turns into a vapor, to mix with your vaporized fuel in the engine. The extra fuel admitted at the same time as the N2O is easily oxidized and creates enough cylinder pressure to add 50, 75, 100 or more horsepower in an instant.

That's the basics, but there is a lot more to the science that's behind having this much fun. To start with, most systems today are not activated by a hand button. There are dangers associated with having the nitrous come on at any time other than WOT (Wide Open Throttle), not the least of which is the chance of a puddle left in the manifold. Anytime there is nitrous hanging around in the intake tract at other than WOT, a backfire could cause an explosion that could violently separate the intake system from the engine. Not a good thing. Thus, since you can't always trust yourself as the driver to only push a button during WOT, manufacturers have several methods to ensure that nitrous is delivered only at the right time. The most common system uses a momentary-contact electrical switch that is mounted to your throttle body and is turned on only when the throttle is wide open. Other nitrous kits use a controller that taps into the signal wire from your stock throttle position sensor (which changes voltage with the amount of throttle opening).

Your nitrous is generally stored in a 10-pound metal bottle mounted in the trunk - it should be kept out of direct sun and mounted with the knob end forward, the label up and the bottle tilted slightly up at the front as shown here

The way adjustable kits can vary the horsepower levels is through small jets that control just how much fuel and nitrous are delivered to the engine - here's a handy kit that stores jets and a spare nozzle, and comes with a billet jet wrench

Installations
balancing function with style

Here are some of the things you'll be doing in a typical installation. Obviously, you should follow the instructions that came with the kit for specific steps. The bottle of nitrous oxide is usually mounted in the trunk of the car as the first step. Your kit manufacturer's instructions will tell you how to mount the bottle, which must be oriented a certain way to supply nitrous under acceleration. The high-pressure hose is run from the bottle up to the engine compartment, either through the interior under the carpeting and through a hole (always have a grommet around the hose) in the firewall, or routed under the car. If you take the latter route, secure the hose all the way along with tie-wraps and keep the nitrous line away from hot or moving components and where it won't be subject to abrasion or rock damage. Whatever the route, tape off both ends of the hose before routing it through the car, and if you have any nitrous related wires (such as for a bottle warmer, remote gauge or remote bottle opener), route them along with the hose.

Next, the solenoid(s) are mounted to the firewall, then the nitrous line for the tank is connected to the nitrous solenoid. If it is a "wet" system, the stock high-pressure fuel line must be tapped with a "T" and a fuel line run to the gasoline solenoid. Remember, never disconnect any fuel line without first relieving the system pressure safely (see a Haynes repair manual for your vehicle and Chapter 7).

Your kit's instructions will be very specific about these safety-related connections. Now find the manufacturer-recommended location for the nozzle and install it (usually on the intake

On a cool day at the track, competitors often remove the bottle and keep it in the sun until it's warmed up enough to provide the necessary pressure, too low a pressure and you'll run rich and not make as much power - too much pressure and you run lean and perhaps hurt the engine

You have to open the bottle before you can use your nitrous, and you should shut the bottle off after use - a convenient way to do that without going to the trunk every time is a remote bottle opener like this Nitrous Express Next Generation kit

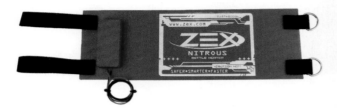

A more dependable and civilized way to keep your baby's bottle warm on a cold day is an electrically-heated warmer like this Zex unit - it wraps around the tank and you can turn it on at the dash.

tube) with the nozzle oriented towards the throttle body, and install the jet(s) for the horsepower level you've selected. If have an adjustable system , like 55-65-75 horsepower, start your first usage with the jets for the lowest HP level until you have learned more about how it works on your particular engine. Connect a nitrous line from the solenoid to the nozzle, then do the same with the gasoline (if yours is a wet system) from the fuel solenoid to the nozzle. Wet system kits generally have different-colored hose for the fuel and nitrous lines so there is no mix-up.

Follow your kit's instructions carefully about wiring the solenoid(s) and switch(es), and about purging the fuel and nitrous lines. Having the fuel line empty on your first shot of nitrous will get you off to a bad start. When everything checks out, take your car out to a track or safe location and put "the squeeze" on your engine (give it N2O)! Sweet!

If everything is working well you will soon discover your nitrous thrill will be tempered with the realization that "horsepower isn't free." The cost of a nitrous oxide refill varies in different areas but ranges from $35.00 to $50.00 to fill a standard 10-pound bottle. Just as an example of how long this can last you, a "100 hp" system will use 0.8 pounds in a ten-second blast. Actually, you may find that ten seconds is a long time at WOT unless you're on a dragstrip with no other traffic. One final tip: when you are not using your nitrous, you should shut off the bottle, just in case there could be a tiny leak somewhere in the system.

Detonation

If a detective were investigating all the horror stories about engine damage when using nitrous, he'd find that detonation was the culprit in almost every case. Detonation is when the pressure and temperature in the combustion chamber spike up enough to create uncontrolled burning of the fuel/air mix.

More than one flame front causes the detonation that burns up valves and pistons, and hammers at the rods and bearings. The use of nitrous oxide does not automatically mean you'll experience detonation, but even when using reasonable amounts of "juice" all conditions in the engine must be right to take full advantage of this power-adder without engine damage.

Improper setup of a nitrous system (otherwise known as "pilot error"), is one of the leading causes of detonation damage. Even mild street kits require the highest-octane pump gasoline you can get. If you're in a situation where you're forced to buy a lower-octane gas, either don't use your nitrous until you use up all that gas and get premium again, or carry a few bottles of octane booster in your trunk. Just make sure the booster absolutely does not contain lead.

Octane requirement is critical to successfully using "laughing gas." If you have installed high-compression pistons or swapped in a Japanese Domestic Market (JDM) engine, then you will need octane higher than the usual pump premium. In Japan, pump gasoline has much higher octane than here in the US, and because they have less-stringent emissions laws, their engines have higher compression than ours. With a 10:1 compression ratio or higher, you can get by on the street with 93 octane, but if you add a nitrous kit on top of that compression, you should be using premium plus an octane booster. In some areas of the country, you can buy 100-octane unleaded at certain stations. Tuners and speed shops also may carry sealed 5-gallon cans of 100 octane unleaded.

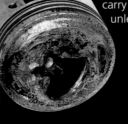

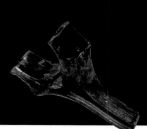

Prepping for Nitrous

The ignition system is especially important in a juiced engine. Very high cylinder pressure, as is created when nitrous and extra fuel are ignited in the combustion chamber, make it more difficult for the spark to jump the electrodes in your spark plugs, and misfiring is like throwing out an anchor behind you. In the typical 50hp street kit, a stock ignition is probably all right as long as all components are in perfect shape. You'll need good plug wires, good cap and rotor, and the right spark plugs. For most street applications you should go one range colder on the spark plugs. In setups using more than 50hp jets, plugs two steps colder may be required and an aftermarket ignition with high-output coil, fat wires and ignition amplifier box will be more helpful, as will a header and cat-back exhaust system.

If you have previously added a chip or had your ECU reprogrammed to make a few more horsepower, then you should revert back to stock specs, since most computer "upgrades" increase ignition timing. The nitrous more than makes up for a few horsepower and going back to stock specs can help avoid detonation. In engines that have 10:1 compression or that use higher doses of nitrous, you'll want to install an aftermarket timing control that will actually retard timing while the juice is on. Some companies include with their N2O kits an electronic controller that gives you two programs, one for standard performance with increased timing for normal driving, and another that retards timing and automatically switches on when the nitrous is engaged.

Your engine should be in top condition before adding a nitrous kit. The extra cylinder pressure can cause blow-by on worn piston rings and any oil that sneaks into the combustion chamber can create immediate detonation. Even in a good engine, you should change the engine oil and filter after using a lot of nitrous, because some gasoline has probably gotten past the rings and into your oil. Other engine conditions that could induce detonation under nitrous use include a dirty or poor performing cooling system, fuel pump not up to spec, restricted exhaust system, or dirty fuel injector(s).

Running the engine lean, meaning not enough fuel was added to go along with the nitrous, is one of the biggest tuning mistakes that result in detonation. After you have made your first few runs on your newly-installed nitrous system, you should do what any good race tuner would do, pull all of your spark plugs for a very close examination. Refer to Chapter 5 for inspection of spark plugs, looking for discoloration or any of the other signs of overheating that signal detonation. When you make any other modifications or changes to your engine, you should do another plug reading. When you see the early signs of detonation on the spark plugs, you have time to examine the engine and find the cause before any parts are destroyed. If you have a factory or aftermarket rev limiter and it interrupts the ignition system as a way to limit the rpms, then you may want to invest in an aftermarket "window switch" that can disengage the nitrous system just before your rev limiter cuts in.

The pressure in your N2O bottle has a definite effect on the richness/leanness of your combination on nitrous. Consistent bottle pressure is important. Your kit manufacturer will probably give you a recommended bottle pressure or range to work within. Below this pressure will induce a rich condition, which will hurt power some but won't damage the engine,

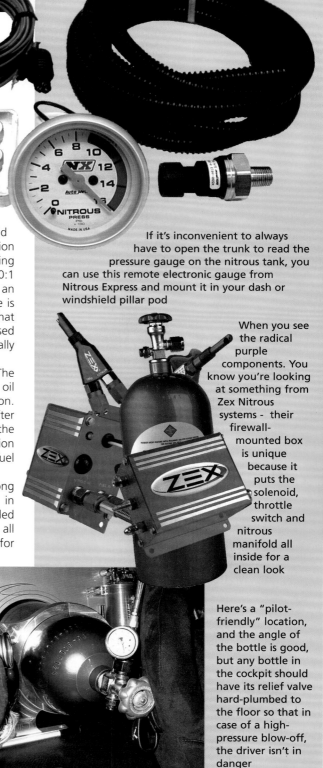

If it's inconvenient to always have to open the trunk to read the pressure gauge on the nitrous tank, you can use this remote electronic gauge from Nitrous Express and mount it in your dash or windshield pillar pod

When you see the radical purple components. You know you're looking at something from Zex Nitrous systems - their firewall-mounted box is unique because it puts the solenoid, throttle switch and nitrous manifold all inside for a clean look

Here's a "pilot-friendly" location, and the angle of the bottle is good, but any bottle in the cockpit should have its relief valve hard-plumbed to the floor so that in case of a high-pressure blow-off, the driver isn't in danger

and too high a bottle pressure will cause a lean condition, and we've established by now what *that* means.

The temperature of the bottle has a lot to do with the internal pressure, which is why on a cold day at the races, you may see people in the pits with their nitrous bottle out of the car, trying to warm it in the sun. To raise the pressure in a bottle, many tuners use an electric bottle warmer, which is a plastic wrap that goes around the bottle and has a heating element in it. When the tank pressure is right, you can turn off the warmer, and a bottle cover (like an insulated blanket) can be put over the bottle to retain the warmth.

An additional option to avoid detonation is an adjustable low-fuel-pressure switch, which taps into your fuel system. If your fuel pump slows down or there is a leak that cause the fuel

You've seen the pro racers squirting a blast of fog from the engine just before takeoff? - that's called purging and it ensures that the solenoid gets only liquid nitrous, no spots of gaseous N2O - this is an NOS purge kit operated by a dash button

On a show car, there's nothing like the appeal of a nitrous bottle, especially when it's a polished one

In an unusual mid-engined application, this one gets the nod for "most interesting nitrous layout" - three bottles feed into a Nitrous Express rail with a single gauge, while two solenoids at each end of the rail feed the engine

If yours is a race car and every pound counts, consider a composite bottle like this one from Nitrous Express - it's half the weight of a metal bottle and holds two extra pounds of N2O, for 12 total

Sometimes the trunk becomes the scene of a competition for space between two passions, music and performance - this owner laid things out right . . .

pressure to fall below a threshold you set, the nitrous is shut off to save the engine from a lean burndown. That's good insurance.

The bottom line for avoiding detonation is regular checks of your spark plugs. If you start to see any signs of detonation, then use a slightly smaller jet in your nitrous nozzle to richen up the fuel/nitrous ratio. Most systems are set up rich to start with to be safe, but once you're more familiar with the use of nitrous and you're brave enough to try leaning it out a little for more power, make sure you jet in tiny increments and keep checking those plugs!

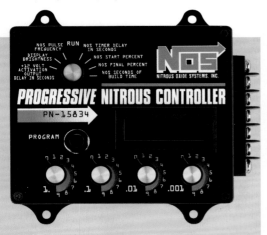

Nitrous controls have become very sophisticated compared to controls of even five years ago - this box from NOS can set a variety of tasks, especially multi-stage application of the nitrous for drag racing

. . . while here the speakers got the best of the situation and the bottle is mounted all wrong - the sideways location means the system could go way rich under acceleration (not enough nitrous)

Nitrous and turbocharging

As we'll discuss in the next Chapter, turbocharging and nitrous can work well together, especially on a race car. Turbos can add tremendous horsepower to an engine, but it's not a simple bolt-on. The turbocharger itself must be sized exactly right for the application to work well in a variety of conditions. When a turbo is large enough to flow really well at high rpms, it will usually be too big to start up quickly at the low end, thus exhibiting what most enthusiasts call "turbo lag."

Racers have found that they can have the best of both ends by using nitrous and turbocharging together. They design a turbo system that works great at the top end for maximum horsepower, but add a carefully calculated dose of nitrous, which is just what is needed down at the low end. When it's coordinated properly, the car has a great launch from the nitrous and the juice is cut off just when the boost is up and the turbo takes over for the rest of the ride, with no lag! Some nitrous kits can be optioned with a control that shuts off the "go-juice" when a preset level of boost is achieved.

Obviously, when you have two such amazing power-adders on your engine at once, there's a giant step up in the cylinder pressures. Some of the things we may have mentioned as "options" for a mild N2O system are suddenly mandatory, like free-flowing intake and exhaust components, an all-out ignition system with racing plugs, a pumped-up fuel system with an extra pump, bigger injectors and a fuel management box, and a few items to prolong the life of the engine. Forged pistons, good connecting rods, strong crankshaft and cylinder head studs may all be necessary. Your car is going to have a serious problem getting all this new-found power to the ground, so you might also look at aftermarket driveaxles. Once you put on the slicks you need to get traction, the high loads are going to take their toll on your economy-car driveline components.

One final note on nitrous oxide; you will start off your "adventure in chemistry" with a manufactured kit for your car that is designed for safe operation when installed and used as directed. If you start altering the engine in other ways or you're having some problems, contact the tech people at your kit's manufacturer. A few minutes on the phone getting their advice could save you an engine!

A number of companies offer a switch that cuts off the nitrous system in the event of the vehicle's fuel pressure running low and also prevents nitrous application when you're flipping the throttle body when the engine's not running

Turbochargers

Show, go, race, street, aftermarket or factory-installed, there's something special about a turbo car - equipped with all the right goodies, its like having a big monster motor under the hood, just waiting to come out and play.

Left - This layout of Edelbrock's 1996 to 2000 Civic SOHC VTEC turbo kit shows the kinds of components to expect in a good kit - there should be good instructions, turbo, turbo manifold, pipes hoses, hardware, oiling components and air filter - the Edelbrock kit makes 5-7 psi of boost with a Garrett T28 turbo, and includes an intercooler and their Performer-X intake manifold

Below - If you're planning on making a show-and-go ride out of your Ford Focus, Gude has this turbo kit with intercooler and all the other hardware you need, plus the pipes are all chromed

Boost, the increased pressure inside your engine when the turbocharger is working, pumps up both the engine and your heart rate. Unlike nitrous oxide, which only comes on when you arm a switch and hit full throttle, the turbocharger lies under your hood ready and waiting for any opportunity to rocket you forward with a smooth whoosh and a high-speed whine like a small jet engine. The sound and the performance are both addictive. You find yourself looking for opportunities to see some psi on your gauge, and let the guy you passed know what kind of magic science gave you that mid-range/top-end advantage.

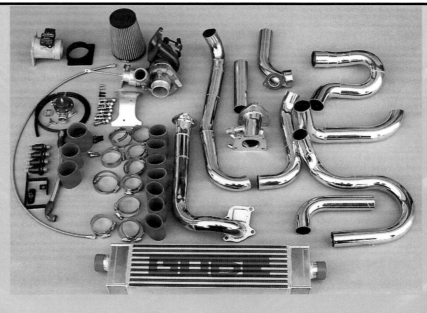

In a typical turbo installation, in this case a GReddy kit on a Honda Prelude, the main components of a non-intercooled system include: the exhaust-driven turbocharger (1); the exhaust downpipe from the turbine to the exhaust system (2); the compressor side of the turbo (3); the piping to duct the pressurized air to the intake manifold (4); and the intake piping that brings air into the compressor (5)

How it works

There are basically three main elements to a turbocharger: the exhaust turbine; the intake air compressor; and the housing/shaft/bearing assembly that ties the two pressure-related sections together. The job of the turbine is to spin the shaft of the turbocharger. The turbine is composed of an iron housing in which rotates a wheel covered with curved vanes or blades. These blades fit precisely within the turbine housing. When the turbine housing is mounted to an engine's exhaust manifold, the escaping hot exhaust gasses flow through the housing and over the vanes, causing the shaft to spin rapidly. After the exhaust has passed through the turbine it exits through a large pipe, called a downpipe, to the rest of the vehicle's exhaust system.

Within the compressor housing is another wheel with vanes. Since both wheels

Before and after

This typical complete turbocharger kit (GReddy for Civic SI) has all the good stuff, plus a set of performance fuel injectors and a computer upgrade, and . . .

. . . this is what that same kit looks like after installation on a Civic SI in the real world

are connected to a common shaft, the intake wheel spins at the same speed as the turbine, so the compressor draws intake air in where the rapidly spinning wheel blows the air into the engine's intake side. The more load there is on the engine, the more the turbocharger works to give the engine horsepower. As the engine goes faster, it makes more exhaust, which drives the turbocharger faster, which makes the engine produce more power.

The unit in the center of this turbo "sandwich" has the important function of reliably passing the power between the two housings. What makes this so difficult is the tremendous heat involved and the high speeds the shaft must turn.

Millions of turbochargers have been manufactured using a sleeve-type bearing that relies on a high volume of engine oil to keep it and the shaft cool enough to continue without seizing, but many of today's performance turbochargers feature ball-bearings. The technical name for the center portion of the turbo is the CHRA, for "center housing and rotating assembly." Some turbos are fitted with a water-cooled CHRA, where engine coolant is circulated through the bearing housing to carry away extra heat beyond what the oil can do. The CHRA is also sometimes called a "cartridge".

Turbochargers
by the numbers

- You like high engine speeds, like 8,000 or 9,000 rpm? At speed, a turbocharger is rotating at 100,000 rpm or more!

- Some turbo tuners speak of boost in "inches" instead of psi because it's a finer measurement. If you need to mentally convert, the inches are about double, i.e. 20 inches of boost is about 10 psi.

- A good intercooler will reduce the intake air temperature by at least 50%. If this is a difference of 100°, that translates to a 10% increase in horsepower.

- After a period of "spirited driving", parts of the turbocharger can heat to 1800°.

Here are two show-winning efforts on the same kind of car, the Toyota Supra inline six-cylinder - this one uses HKS turbo components to blow through an up-front intercooler (not seen here) then into a Veilside "surge-tank" intake plenum with huge 100mm throttle body - there's some serious flow here . . .

Consider the turbocharger like the six-gun "equalizer" of the old west - the SOHC applications are a good candidate for boost because it allows them to compete in performance with the more-talked-about DOHC VTEC motors

Advantages and

This cycle of the engine driving the turbine is why some say the turbocharger makes "free" horsepower. What they mean is that the engine's exhaust is making the turbo go, unlike a supercharger that is driven mechanically by the engine, through belts/pulleys, a chain or direct gearing to the crankshaft. With a supercharger, driving the blower takes some engine horsepower away because it must operate at all times, from idle on up. A turbocharger imposes very little load until called upon to do some power-making.

The "not at all times" boost of the turbocharger is an advantage for fuel economy, operating noise level and driveability, but in some cases may be a drawback when compared to the mechanical supercharger. Elsewhere in this book, we'll get more into supercharger design, but while a supercharger adds boost in relation to rpm (i.e. the faster the engine goes, the faster the blower pumps)

. . . but look at this setup - two turbochargers, in fact two of almost everything and nitrous oxide for the bottom-end punch until those big turbos start spoolin'

disadvantages of the turbocharger

it runs up against physical limitations eventually and can't pump any more. In order to make any more boost with a supercharger, you have to change the pulleys or gearing that drives it, and there is generally nothing you can do to the inside of it to make more boost. The good side of the supercharger is that the positive-displacement type blower gives an engine more bottom-end torque because the blower is working right from idle on up.

The limitation for the blower-equipped car is in top end performance, and this is where the turbocharger has the distinct advantage. The turbocharger is much more customizable, with various wheels and housings available to suit whatever the intended engine or purpose. Boost can be made to come in early, or come in later at a higher boost level. The same basic turbocharger can be used for street use or modified to make more boost than your engine

can live with! Such customizing, called sizing, should be done by an experienced turbo shop that can select the exact components for your engine size and power requirements. A turbo expert can take your information on the engine modifications, bottom-end strength and projected horsepower goal, figure the airflow required to meet those parameters, and come up with the right-sized turbocharger with the right compressor and turbine. Too big or too small and you and your engine will be unhappy.

One of the more serious disadvantages of the turbocharger is the heat it will put into the intake air charge. Actually, superchargers also heat up the intake air, but the hot-exhaust-driven turbocharger definitely warms the air charge most, which is why most successful turbo systems utilize an intercooler to combat this.

While trying to make and keep heat in the exhaust to make boost, you also need to protect other components in the engine compartment from heat - in this very professionally-done turbo Supra installation, the turbine has a heat shield, but also a metal heat dam was placed to protect the ABS brake components from turbo heat

Turbochargers and heat

Anytime air is compressed and made to move very quickly, it gets hotter. For example, run your hand slowly across the carpeting in your house and you can feel slight friction from the carpet. Now move your hand more rapidly across the carpet at the same hand pressure and you'll feel warmth in your hand, go too fast and you'll have "rug burn." The same thing happens to the air inducted into your engine. Just travelling through your air intake, throttle body and intake manifold in non - turbo mode, air incurs a certain amount of friction between it and the surfaces its touches, especially cast surfaces that aren't perfectly smooth like the inside of an intake manifold. Now induct that air under the pressure of a turbocharger making 10 pounds or more of boost and the high-speed air tends to really heat up.

Beyond the frictional heating of the air, the turbocharger itself adds extra heat because it's mounted on the exhaust. If you've ever seen a performance turbo on an engine operating under a load on the dyno, you can turn out the lights and see the turbine housing and exhaust manifold start to glow red-hot! It's making serious power at this point but obviously the air compressor side of the turbocharger is going to get some of that heat.

This heat is perhaps the biggest downside to turbocharging, but a number of excellent fixes have been developed over the years. First, improper turbo selection can worsen the heat problem. If the chosen turbo is not running at its proper efficiency, it can overspeed (over 100,000 rpm), a condition in which the air is moving too fast for the capacity of the engine and "backs up" in the pipeline, so to speak. This hurts the turbocharger and your performance. The proper initial choice of turbocharger and the match of its turbine and compressor to your exact needs should keep you out of that range and make the right amount of boost without excessive shaft speeds.

Next up, everything should be done to keep the turbine's heat isolated from the compressor. It's true that heat on the exhaust side is what makes the turbine work, but that heat should be kept "inside" as much as possible and not transferred to the engine compartment air and the compressor/intake side. This is perhaps more critical on engines that have the exhaust side of the head facing the radiator, like most Hondas. Extra hot air from the radiator is flowing right over your turbo, which is usually mounted in very close proximity to the radiator, probably the hottest spot in the engine compartment.

Custom-fabricated tubing headers for turbocharger installations make sense in terms of equal-length flow or if there is no cast manifold available for the application, but they tend to develop weld cracks and don't keep as much heat in unless the header is thick stainless steel or ceramic-coated

This racer used a cast-iron manifold with wastegate mount, and had the manifold high-temp-coated to retain even more heat in the turbine for more boost - heat is good on the turbine side, bad for the intake side

An efficiently-designed cast-iron manifold, here with a Turbonetics wastegate directly mounted, is ideal for street applications that see constant heating and cooling cycles, but regular "high-temp" header paint will come off in no time - temperatures here get into the red-hot range under a full load

One of the best ways to keep the exhaust heat inside the turbine tract where it's needed is the right manifold. Though it may not look as trick as a custom-fabbed bundle of tubular pipes, a cast-iron turbo exhaust manifold is the most durable choice for the exhaust, especially on a street-driven application. It's thick enough to retain the heat inside and can withstand repeated heating/cooling cycles without cracking, which is a problem with exhausts made from tubing. This heat can be further isolated by having the cast manifold treated to a high-temperature coating. The standard "high-temp" coatings used on headers will probably fail on a turbo manifold, but some of the coating companies have a ceramic-based coating that can withstand very high temperatures (up to 2000 degrees F). The equal-length tubular exhausts you may see on turbocharged race cars can extract that last little bit of extra horsepower, but a good one is expensive and if it isn't made of thick-walled tubing, preferably stainless steel, it may not retain all the heat, and all the weld joints along the route may even slow the exhaust gasses down.

Further isolation of the exhaust side heat can be realized by using a shield over the turbine housing. Shields are available that are a formed sandwich of thin stainless steel sheetmetal with a core of high-temperature insulation. Some have an exterior that looks like formed tinfoil, but others have a smooth-shaped stainless exterior that has the added benefit of making the whole installation look as cool as it acts.

Proximity of the exhaust and the turbocharger to the radiator in most Honda applications led this tuner to have his tubular header ceramic-coated and also used a large, aftermarket aluminum radiator

You say your need for speed exceeds - then top off your turbocharging installation with a full-on nitrous package that pours on the juice until the turbo is pumping - this installation uses four Nitrous Express nozzles and stainless-steel hard line plumbing for both the fuel and N2O

When you add an intercooler to the mix, you have additional plumbing - here on a GReddy turbo installation on a VW Golf (shown here with the front bumper cover off for clarification), the hot, boosted air leaves the compressor on the engine, travels out to the front where it enters the intercooler, exits the intercooler in "refreshed" mode and finally enters the intake manifold

The Subaru WRX also has its factory intercooler located on top of the engine - when some tuners do a turbo upgrade on the WRX they install a much larger aftermarket cooler in place of the stock one

Intercoolers

The most effective and most common method of dealing with air temperature in the intact tract on a turbocharged car is an intercooler. This is a honeycomb affair much like a radiator, usually mounted out in front in an opening below the bumper, where cooler air is found. The boosted air from the compressor is ducted through pipes and into the intercooler, and then to the intake of the engine. Thus, the cooler is between the compressor and the engine, so it's called an *inter*-cooler.

Most intercoolers for street-driven machines are of the air-to-air type. Intake air flows through the end tanks, through the tubes and fins of the cooler just like engine coolant does through a conventional radiator. The outside air, especially at vehicle speeds where the turbo is really working, flows over the intercooler and cools off what's passing inside. Although the longer piping of the intercooler system does add more frictional area for the air to pass over, the cooling effect makes enough change in horsepower to more than make up for that. In some cases, a good intercooler is taking out more than half of the intake heat, and for every drop of 10 degrees F in the intake air fed to your engine, your power goes up about 1%. If the intake air from your compressor is up to 200-300 degrees F (depending on the boost level), the intercooler can drop that to 100-140 degrees F. Do the math and the intercooler's effectiveness is a no-brainer! The same engine and turbocharger combination may make one pound or so more boost without all that piping to travel through, but the temperature improvement is worth more than that slight drop in boost.

Of course, you can run a turbo setup without an intercooler, but you can't make optimal horse-power and the dreaded specter of detonation will be haunting you unless you're using *high*-octane gasoline and a few other tricks. Even factory-built turbocharged cars, like the Subaru WRX and others, have intercoolers designed into the car, both to make more power at a safe level of boost and to cope with the poor quality of gasoline available to us at most pumps.

If you want the maximum airflow over the intercooler, and you want everyone to know you're packin' forced induction, the area below the bumper provides the space for a wide intercooler installation

Boost Controls

The main boost control device on a turbocharger is an exhaust wastegate - the more the turbo system is designed to flow, the bigger the wastegate must be to be effective

As wonderful as boost can be, it's a dangerous animal that needs certain controls to harness its power. Too much boost for the octane rating of your fuel and you have serious detonation, and even without detonation, high boost can and will destroy your engine if it isn't sufficiently reinforced to handle the increased cylinder pressure.

The primary "leash" on the turbo beast is an exhaust wastegate. The wastegate is a device that senses boost pressure in the engine and releases some exhaust to the atmosphere when needed. If the boost is too high, releasing the exhaust pressure built up causes the turbine wheel to slow down, reducing the boost to a safe level. On most production turbocharged cars, the wastegate is integral to the turbocharger and dumps excess exhaust back into the exhaust system downstream of the turbine. In most of these applications, the system is designed for a relatively-low level of boost to maintain OEM reliability and when the wastegate actuates, the driver never even notices it. The power simply doesn't increase.

If you make more boost than the factory intended, the engine will need more fuel and probably less ignition timing advance. You may be able to do both with an aftermarket electronic "piggyback" controller. There are boost-regulated mechanical fuel pressure regulators that raise the fuel delivery pressure to meet the boost conditions, more fuel for more boost. Depending on the make of your car and turbo, even higher boost levels can be obtained if you're careful. As always, our advice is to make changes in incremental steps up, listening to your engine signs of detonation, and always keep checking your spark plugs for signs impending problems.

The efficiency of your exhaust system has a lot to do with the boost level you can achieve. Sometimes the OEM engineers design an exhaust with just enough backpressure to keep the turbo from making too much boost. A really free-flowing aftermarket downpipe and larger-diameter cat-back exhaust system will probably increase your boost and still be within acceptable levels.

Really high-performance turbocharging applications will use a wastegate that is not integral to the turbocharger, but rather mounts on the exhaust manifold ahead of the turbine. These are generally much larger than the factory type and are adjustable for

boost level with the simple turn of a screw on top of the wastegate. They can also be regulated by on-dash controls that alter the vacuum/boost signal to the wastegate. To operate efficiently, the wastegate must be sized to the horsepower level of the application. Too small a wastegate can't keep up with a powerful turbo, and you could overboost beyond what the wastegate is set to. While factory wastegates dump their excess exhaust downstream into the system, the aftermarket wastegate is usually allowed to vent into the atmosphere, though they all have a mounting flange that can permit a pipe to be installed that routes the gasses away from the engine compartment. Given the nature of import tuners, most enthusiasts don't put on a pipe, they like the loud "braaakkkkk" noise when the wastegate opens!

A second type of control used in most aftermarket turbo installations is a blow-off valve. Unlike the wastegate, this type installs on the intake system. When a turbocharger is spinning at high speeds and making boost, it can't stop or even slow very easily or quickly. If you happen to quickly back off the throttle when you've been under boost, the intake system is still filled with pressurized air. The blade in your throttle body is closed but the turbo's compressor is still packing in air behind it. Since the pressure has no place to go, a pressure wave backs up into the compressor and tries to make the wheel go the other way, causing a pressure surge that is damaging to the compressor. Another negative effect of the pressure backwave is that the compressor starts to slow down, so when you get back on the throttle again it has to work to catch up to the pressure it had before. These two problems can happen to any turbo car if the throttle is closed, but is particularly prevalent on manual-transaxle cars where you are on-off-on the throttle for every shift.

The solution is the blow-off valve. Mounted on the intake pipe, the valve contains a spring-loaded diaphragm or piston that lifts when it senses a surge. As soon as the air is released for a split-second, you're through with your shift and the boost resumes with hardly a noticeable lapse. Aftermarket blow-off and bypass valves are available for any turbo application, but the most common is the blow-off valve because it makes a sharp and loud hiss when it opens. As with the wastegate, tuners like to hear the sound, except the blowoff valve makes its music every time you shift.

Wastegates mount in the exhaust stream ahead of the turbine; when the boost limit is exceeded the wastegate releases some exhaust to slow down the turbo - in this installation with a very tall wastegate, the installer used an elbow to mount the wastegate for hood clearance - note how they wrapped the downpipe with header wrap to keep the heat from passing over to the engine's oil pan

To be a little more subtle and quiet, the installer of this wastegate plumbed a pipe down to the exhaust system - he also wrapped that pipe with header-wrap to keep the extra heat away from the radiator

The other type of boost control is a blow-off valve, which is designed to be mounted on the intake side and prevents pressure surges if you close the throttle very quickly, like when shifting, while the turbo is working hard

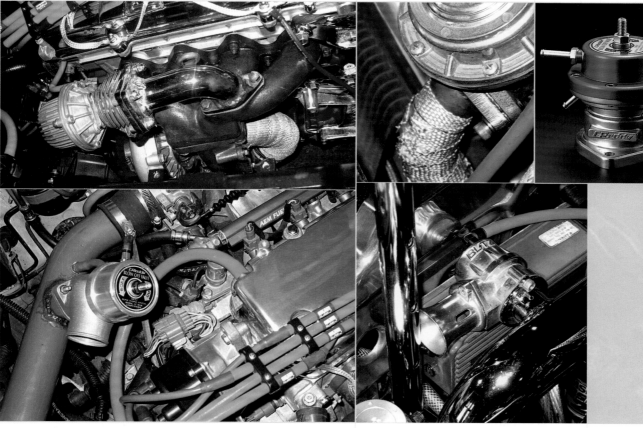

In this SOHC installation, a flange was welded to the intake tube just before the intake manifold to mount the blow-off valve - as in most sport compact setups, the valve's release port is left open to the atmosphere rather than plumbed back into the intake ahead of the turbo (the idea here is to make more noise)

When you really want everyone to know you're boosted, blow-off valves like this are available that have horn-shaped exits to make a real blast sound that marks every shift you make under boost

Preparing your car for turbocharging

Of all the accessories you can get to go along with a forced induction system, none is more important than the boost gauge

Although most turbocharging kits have everything you need to actually install the turbo, there are a number of considerations beyond the supplied parts. Is your engine ready for boost? The kit instructions, if they're good ones, will give you recommendations for other modifications you can make to allow the turbo setup to work even better on your engine.

Perhaps no other "accessory" is more important for a turbo'd car than an accurate boost gauge. Unless you have a way to keep track of actual boost in the engine, you'll never know if the turbo is working at its potential or if the wastegate is adjusted where you want it and working. The gauge is also helpful to troubleshoot your system. If you see a lesser amount of boost than normal (under the same conditions of throttle, rpm and load), you should inspect the piping and hoses in your intercooler plumbing to see if there is a minor leak. The best boost gauges are dampened to give steady needle readings and indicate both vacuum (negative side, in inches of mercury) and boost (positive side, in inches of mercury or psi).

A strong aftermarket ignition system will be very helpful to fire the plug gaps in the dense atmosphere in the combustion chamber when the turbo is cramming all that air in. The manufacturer may also recommend different spark plugs to use or a different plug gap for the stock plugs you're using.

Heat is always a critical factor in a turbocharged application. The turbo kit you use

This import pilot has the controls and data equipment he needs to watch over his boost-accumulating engine - one is a piggyback fuel controller and the other an electronic boost controller, both from A'PEXi

should include or recommend what's needed in the way of fuel management and timing controls to prevent detonation, but there is also the matter of engine heat. A really good radiator is going to be more important than ever, and you may want to consider an aftermarket heavy-duty radiator with more rows of tubes than stock. Aftermarket companies also make some really excellent fan/shroud combinations that flow more air through the radiator than a stock fan. If you don't opt for a new radiator or fan, then at least consult in the Haynes repair manual for your car to learn about cleaning and troubleshooting your stock cooling system.

Oil is a big issue with a turbo because the oil not only lubricates this very precisely machined and balanced assembly, the oil also is the cooling system for a device that gets really, really hot. Keeping the turbo alive and cool means that there must be a steady flow of clean oil, in and out. The supply line should be free of sharp bends or kinks, but this is even more critical on the much larger drain hose that comes from the bottom of the CHRA. The hose doesn't carry a great deal of pressure like the supply hose, but it must be capable of carrying away an unrestricted volume of oil back to your oil pan. Plumb the drain hose without kinks and when the drainback hose fitting is welded to your oil pan, have it come into the pan at a slight downward angle and above the normal oil level. If there is any restriction in this drainback system, oil will back up into the CHRA and slow the cooling/lubricating action.

Most kits don't include this, but you may want to consider a turbo timer as an option. This is an electronic unit that will run your engine for a specified period, say five minutes, after you shut it off with the key. This is a cooling cycle for the turbocharger, and some OEM turbo cars have one. The reason for this is a problem called coking. It occurs when you have been running your turbo hard and then shut off the engine. Tremendous heat-soak occurs in the CHRA because oil is no longer flowing through to cool the bearing. The coking happens because the oil that remains sitting in the turbo's bearing area may carmelize into coke, the kind of coal-like material used in steel foundries. These little particles of now-crunchy oil get circulated in the turbo and the rest of your oiling system. The turbo timer gives the turbo a chance to cool down after a run.

A final for your good-to-do list in terms of oiling is using an engine oil cooler. Many import engines have a factory oil cooler sandwiched between the oil filter and the block, with coolant lines connected to the cooling system. If your car doesn't have one, there are a number of aftermarket oil coolers available. An oil cooler is a good thing for any high-revving small engine, but particularly appropriate insurance for a turbocharged one.

As we have mentioned in other Chapters, your engine should be thoroughly checked out and in top shape before any mods are undertaken, but especially for a power-adder like a turbocharger. Boost is going to hasten the demise of any engine with weak valve springs, worn rings or loose bearings. Depending on the level of boost, there may be other steps to take to give your engine a longer life under pressure. If you're running a 5-7 psi setup and you have adequate controls against detonation like good octane and fuel/timing controls, you should be fine unless your driving style is to be under boost for five minutes of every ten-minute trip to the grocery store. Higher levels of boost require more safeguards, starting with your pistons. New forged pistons with a lower-than-stock compression ratio will help deal with the pressure much better. Once you get to the 8-10 psi range you should lower the static compression to 9:1, and if you venture to higher boost levels, you'll need to get pistons for 8:1 compression. In the higher ranges of boost for serious street or drag racing horsepower, you'll have to do a lot more to strengthen your engine, and these kinds of insurance mods are covered elsewhere in this book..

Above - The GReddy "Profec EO-1" is a multi-tasker for the boost-minded - it can manage your boost, has several warning functions, can log three hours worth of data, and the LED screen can display boost, rpm and another channel all at once

Left - In some boosted applications the fuel pressure is raised under boost or larger injectors are used to supply additional fuel - using one or more additional injectors that are only used under boost is a way to keep the engine happy without affecting normal driving air/fuel ratios, and a controller for the additional injector(s) makes this possible

The 300ZX may be old now, but you can't tell by how it runs - the JWT-upgraded twin turbos do their thing, and the engine's never had the heads off for work in 200,000 miles

Turbos and durability

It looks like a plain, white, older Nissan, despite it being in great shape and having a nice set of wheels. The 1990 Nissan 300ZX owned by Alfred Torres is actually a fine-handling sports car that is driven daily and turns dangerously close to 11-second times at the dragstrip.

Alfred bought the car when it was two years old, and has put 200,000 miles on it (under boost most of the time) and it is a great example of what you can do by buying a factory turbo car and upgrading it.

The performance work on the twin-turbo car was done over a period of time, as the owner could afford the changes, and included a pair of upgraded turbos from the Nissan specialists at Jim Wolf Technology, a computer from that same firm, and a number of aftermarket control devices. The automatic transmission was upgraded during a rebuild after several years of flogging the car, and it has some handling additions and nice wheels and tires. The electronics include: a GReddy exhaust gas temperature gauge, A'PEXi multi-checker, GReddy boost controller, two boost gauges (one for each turbo bank), and a steering wheel button (wireless) that operates the boost controller without Alfred's hands leaving the wheel. The EGT is hooked to the number six cylinder, because Alfred says that one usually runs the hottest and leanest so that's the one to watch. He uses iridium plugs, one range colder than stock.

The happy owner controls the boost setting mainly depending on the fuel available on any one day. In everyday driving, the control is set for 15-16 psi for basic 91-octane gas. When Alfred can get a little high

Two boost gauges, several electronic aftermarket control devices, and an ominous-looking pushbutton on the steering wheel all contribute to putting the driver in control of when and how much power he wants to make

Turbo ultra-performance

There couldn't be a better example of the power potential of turbocharging when dealing with small engines than the car seen here. The Summit mail-order performance company of course is a familiar name to any performance enthusiast, whether a fan of domestic muscle cars or high-strung imports. They campaigned this "2002 Chevrolet Cavalier" in the NHRA/Summit Sport Compact drag series, where it won the 2002 Modified Championship.

It ran a best of 7.665 E.T. at just shy of 180 mph in the quarter, and what makes that a phenomenon is the engine that accomplished it, a 2.2L Ecotec four-cylinder. While the car was built by Jerry Haas and driven by Matt Hartford, our real interest here is in the compact engine that runs like a blown hemi V-8.

John Lingenfelter Performance Engineering, famous builders of Chevrolet engines, took a quite basic Ecotec engine that originally squeezed out 130 horsepower, and turned it into a fire-breathing race motor with 1080 horsepower on the dyno!

We don't have all the proprietary specs on the engine's internals, but it's safe to say that considerable work was done to make the reciprocating parts stronger and lighter, to reinforce the block to withstand the huge increase in cylinder pressure, and to do everything possible to the cylinder head in port work, valves, and cams to achieve high-rpm flow on the highest order.

Obviously, the star player in the engine compartment has to be the big Garrett ball-bearing turbocharger, and most of the power increase is from the serious amount of boost it pumps. We do know that the engine sucks air in through a large intake duct, and that the compressor output travels through a liquid-to-air intercooler before entering the fabricated Hogan intake manifold with big throttle body. The engine also features an MSD 8 ignition, an Autoverdi dry-sump oiling system and a Big Stuff 3 engine management system.

This race car was built by some of the top people in the country, and we're not suggesting that this kind of power level is available to you simply by bolting on a turbocharger, but it is a remarkable example of what can be done in small-engine turbocharging. Probably no other technology would have permitted such performance from a couple of liters.

Owners of Ecotec-powered Cavaliers and Sunfires (and Saturns with the same engine) should be very encouraged by the variety of performance equipment offered for these engines by GM Performance Parts Division of General Motors. Their catalog includes a heavy-duty block with steel sleeves, bigger head and main studs, and it's machined for metal O-ring type head gaskets. They also have available billet crankshafts and rods, a fabricated intake manifold and a CNC-ported cylinder head.

These DOHC engines have balance shafts in stock form, but most engine builders feel these are a limitation in high-rpm race engines, so GM even offers a pair of balance shafts with "neutral" balance for use in performance engines.

performance unleaded (93-octane) he clicks the control and runs 18 psi, and when he's at the track and can get racing gas, he's got his "phasers on stun" at 23 pounds of boost! That's when he runs right around 12 seconds or less in the quarter.

What's the moral of the story? Just that, contrary to most street talk, you can have a performance daily driver that is smooth, dependable and you can keep it for years. Do careful research on the right car and the right components for it, learn what you need to know to take care of it (of course, you would buy a Haynes repair manual for it) and know the car's limits, and yours.

Superchargers

If you have read Chapter 6, you know that an internal-combustion engine operates like a compressor. It sucks in a combustible mixture of air and fuel, ignites it and uses the resulting pressure to push the piston up and down and make the crankshaft deliver the power to the transaxle. For purposes of this Chapter, the key word in that very simplistic explanation is "sucks."

Your engine relies on the down stroke of the pistons to draw the air/fuel mix through the air filter, intake pipe, throttle body, intake manifold, cylinder and finally, past the valves to the combustion chamber where the action is. That's a long tortuous journey when you think about it! Many

Atmospheric pressure -

or why your car runs better at the beach than in the Rockies

Our atmospheric pressure is 14.7 pounds per square inch (psi) at sea level. At high elevations this pressure is less, of course, because there's that much less atmosphere "stacked up" over us. So 14.7 pounds is all that we have to urge a mixture to enter out engine. When the piston goes down and creates a vacuum, he atmospheric pressure is higher than the "negative pressure" of the vacuum, so stuff goes in.

Boost, that intoxicating elixir of performance, is any pressure beyond 14.7. If you have a turbo or supercharger that is making 14.7 psi of boost, then you have effectively added another "atmosphere" of pressure. Twice that amount of boost and you've added two atmospheres, and you command the bridge of a rocket ship!

methods have been tried to "help out" the engine so it didn't have to work so hard just to get a breath of freshly vaporized gasoline and air. Forcing air in by some external device has been the project of engineers almost since the automobile was invented. Superchargers have been used on piston-driven warplanes and racecars since the Twenties and the technology and marketplace have narrowed this field called "forced induction" down to two basic devices we are concerned with in this book: turbochargers and superchargers.

This Toyota V6 features a belt-driven, roots-type blower. The entire bolt-on kit is available from Toyota Racing

Our last Chapter dealt exclusively with the turbocharger. It is similar in function to the supercharger, but differs in that the turbo is driven by exhaust gasses, rather than by mechanical means. A supercharger is driven by the engine, either with gears, chains or belts, so there is direct correlation between the engine speed and the boost produced by the supercharger. While the turbocharger may have the upper hand when you're talking about all-out high-rpm performance on the track, the supercharger shines at improving street performance almost from idle speed on up.

Since the supercharger is directly linked to the crankshaft, it starts making its boost right from "the basement". This gives you the kind of low-end power you get to enjoy in most normal driving circumstances without hammering the right pedal to the floor all the time. Driving a supercharged car gives you the sensation that you have a much bigger engine, without the nose-heavy weight and less-acceptable fuel economy.

Low-end torque is what we need and that's what a mechanical supercharger does best. By packing in more air, the engine ingests a denser mixture of air and fuel without the effort of having to suck it in with nothing but normal atmospheric pressure.

Boost

You must have a boost gauge to monitor the performance of any forced-induction engine. The best gauges indicate both the full range of vacuum (negative pressure, usually in inches of mercury) on one side of the Zero mark, and the positive pressure (boost) side goes from that Zero mark to 10, 20, or more psi of boost. In a typical vehicle in good condition, your engine may be idling at 600-700 rpm and vacuum is high, maybe 17-20 inches unless you have an aftermarket camshaft, which would lower the idle vacuum. This vacuum will drop rapidly when the engine is accelerated quickly, but then smooth out at most speeds; when you're in top gear and cruising, your gauge may again read something like your idle vacuum, indicating that you are driving at good efficiency.

Put a supercharger on that same vehicle and your gauge readings are quite different. The idle might be close to stock, but once you first start to push down the pedal and the rpm raises, you'll see the vacuum reading go down and stay down as you increase rpm. At a certain rpm under power, say 1500 to 2500 rpm, you start to go right onto the boost side of the gauge. What many newcomers to boost-gauge watching don't realize is that the section of the vacuum/boost gauge that is from your idle vacuum reading all the way up to Zero on the gauge can't be discounted. Anytime your forced induction system is "taking away" vacuum, it is making performance, so you don't have to be showing 6 pounds of boost to feel like your engine is bigger than it used to be. The more your gauge goes clockwise, the more you have to hang on!

As heady as all this is, we must be realistic about boost levels. As with a turbocharger, the mere installation of a supercharger doesn't mean the ruination of your engine. Nonetheless, there is a finite limit to the boost your blower can make, and probably a much lower limit of how much boost your engine can take, regardless of how the boost was generated. You'll find most street supercharger kits are limited to 5-7 psi, to make some

Above left - This shot of the JR Focus kit outside the car shows how the long belt arrangement works the blower drive in with all the factory accessories

Once the kit is installed, the underhood view of the completed Focus installation by Jackson Racing looks almost stock, until you spot the Eaton supercharger near the firewall

power while working well on a basically stock engine that sips pump gasoline. Some kits on the market have optional pulleys that will spin the blower faster for more boost, but, as with any power adder, you can only go so far in increasing cylinder pressure before you have to make serious modifications to strengthen the engine (see Chapter 13 for more on engine durability mods).

Your engine's existing compression ratio has an important effect on the boost level you can hope to utilize with any forced induction system. The higher the static compression ratio, the less boost you can run without detonation. If your compression ratio is too high, the small amount of boost you can reliably use may not be worth the effort and expense of the supercharger system.

Our sport compact engines generally have higher compression ratios than other vehicles on the road, and that's a good thing for all-motor performance, but not so good for supercharging. If you have a swapped-in JDM (Japanese) engine, the compression could be 10:1 or even higher because of Japan's 100-octane gas and less stringent emissions laws, and in that case, your engine is not a candidate for forced induction unless you change to much lower compression pistons. Just as a guideline, you should be able to use 5-7 psi of boost if your engine's compression ratio is 9:1 or lower. If you are rebuilding your engine before installing the forced induction, it's a good idea to equip it with new forged pistons of 8:1 compression. This will allow (all others factors being equal) 8-12 psi of boost, which is a big difference in performance when your big right foot goes down. This is just a general guideline, and the design and efficiency of the supercharger you choose will also be a factor.

Most us only dream about riding in a true sports car like the Acura NSX, but if you've got one, the Acura experts at Comptech have this screw-type blower package you'll want - it fits under the stock engine cover and doesn't void your warranty (most of these kits are installed by Acura dealerships)

With the top cover off the Whipple twin-screw blower used on the Comptech NSX kit, you can see how the two screws squish and compress the incoming air between them for good mechanical efficiency - such precision-built superchargers are more expensive than most other types for sport compact engines

Heat and detonation

We discussed the demon that is detonation in the turbocharging Chapter, but it bears repeating here because the problem is the same with all power adders. The octane rating of a fuel is an indication of its anti-knock resistance. In the Sixties, you could buy 100-octane gasoline right from the pumps (like you still can in Japan) for 35 cents a gallon, and those were the glory days for hot rodders, who ran around the streets with 12:1 pistons. But once that nasty lead was removed from the gas for environmental reasons, what we are left with at the pumps today is not so conducive to modified engines. Knock, ping, pre-ignition and detonation are all terms that describe abnormal combustion in an engine. What it boils down to is when the combustion chamber pressure and temperature rise to a certain point, hot spots develop in the chamber and instead of one steady flame front across the mixture, you have more than one fire burning or burning takes place before it's supposed to.

The two main factors in detonation and its control are heat and timing. Octane is also a factor, but once you have stepped up to using the "premium" pump gas, there isn't much you can do to get more octane unless you resort to using a can of aftermarket octane booster with every tank of gas. That can get both

Intercoolers help make more power and stave off detonation by cooling the incoming air and making it more dense

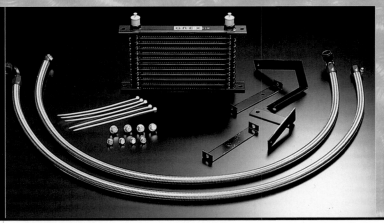

Heat is the enemy of your engine, and the more you can reduce that the more boost you can run - an aftermarket oil cooler kit will help keep temperatures down

annoying and expensive. Ignition timing does offer some ways to deal with detonation. Supercharged engines generally "like" more timing, especially initial advance, but once you are making full boost and the vehicle is under load, too much ignition advance can bring on the "death rattle" you don't want to hear. Your computer-controlled engine management system incorporates a knock sensor on the block that signals the ECU to pull back ignition timing if knock begins. However, things happen more rapidly in a boosted car under heavy acceleration than in a stock application that is just reacting to a bad tank of gas. How much advance your application can handle is a trial-error-experience thing, but if you are using a production blower kit from a known manufacturer, these tests have already been made and some kind of timing control program should be included.

Note: *When you do pull back ignition timing, you are also reducing your power, so there is a point of diminishing return.*

Heat, in the blower and intake tract, has a major effect on detonation control. A boosted application that can take 8 psi on a cool morning may need some kind of controls to counter detonation on a hot afternoon. Although a supercharger does not put as much heat into the intake tract as does an exhaust-driven turbocharger, plenty of heat we don't want is still added to the intake tract. When you compress air and force it through the whole intake tract, the friction of these parts against the airflow heats the air. Hot air is less dense, and remember that the reason for using a supercharger is to make the intake charge denser. A mechanical supercharger may add 100-200 degrees F to whatever the ambient air is, so on a 100-degree day, the intake air could be 300 degrees!

As we discussed in the turbocharging chapter, one really effective way to lower the temperature of the intake side is with an intercooler. This is a heat exchanger, usually an air-to-air cooler, which mounts in the intake tract. When boosted air is forced to travel through a cooler (like a small radiator) that is exposed to outside air, the intake charge temperature drops and power goes up. That's the beauty of intercooling; it not only helps avoid detonation, it makes more power. Normally-aspirated or forced-induction, every 10 degrees F you drop the intake temperature, you gain one percent in power. Drop the temperature by 100 degrees and you gain 10%, which is substantial when we're talking about already efficient small engines.

The bad news is that most bolt-on supercharger kits don't include an intercooler. In some cases, small mechanical superchargers don't make high levels of boost, and plumbing the whole thing through more pipes and an intercooler may slow down the air enough to almost negate the positive effect of the cooling.

Blower kits

There are several types of small superchargers used in kits designed for compact-car engines. Of course, each manufacturer will tell you that their design is the best, but you should do plenty of research on your own before making a decision to buy a kit that may cost $3000 or more. The two main types of supercharger design you will see are the roots type or "positive displacement," and the centrifugal design.

The roots-type mechanical blower uses a pair of rotors that turn inside a housing. Some may have straight rotors with two or three lobes, and as the rotors turn, they capture a certain amount of air and propel it to the inner circumference of the case and out to the intake manifold. Each time they turn around, they capture air, hence the "positive" description. The benefit of this type is that it starts making boost at very low rpm, but some roots-type blowers are noisier than other designs, induce more heat into the intake tract and take a little more crankshaft horsepower to drive. Most of the smaller blowers used on sport compact kits have very proven designs that have been around for years, and in the case of the Eaton blower, have been used by major car manufacturers on OEM-supercharged installations.

A variation of this type of blower is the screw-type. These have two rotors with helically-wound vanes that, as the name implies, look like two giant screws. When the two screws mesh together (there is a male and

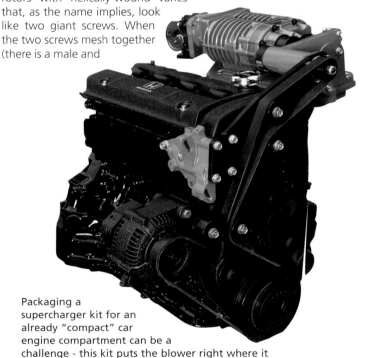

Packaging a supercharger kit for an already "compact" car engine compartment can be a challenge - this kit puts the blower right where it needs to be by using a long-belt drive system

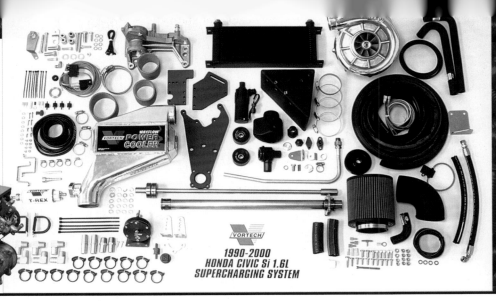

This well-engineered Civic SI kit from Vortech includes a shaft that is belt-driven at the drivebelt end of the engine, and place the centrifugal blower at the transaxle end where there's room - the kit includes a blowoff valve and a liquid-to-air intercooler not often seen on street-driven compact

This very complete package includes wiring, hoses, fuel pump, FMU, supercharger and drive, and the compete water system for the Maxiflow Power Cooler

a female rotor), the air is actually compressed between the screws.

The other major type of bolt-on supercharger is the centrifugal design. From a quick examination, the centrifugal blower looks just like the compressor half of a turbocharger, being a multi-vaned wheel within a scroll-type housing. Unlike a turbocharger, this type of blower isn't driven by exhaust but by a mechanical drive from the engine, usually a belt. On the back of the compressor is a gearbox that speeds the compressor wheel up compared to engine rpm. Now you have some of the boost potential of a turbocharger without the added intake heat from the exhaust-driven turbine. These types of blowers are not "positive-displacement", and thus do not necessarily make their boost down on the low end, but have plenty of air-movement potential when they are spinning rapidly. The centrifugals also do not take as much horsepower to drive as some other mechanical blowers that are positive-displacement. In general, centrifugal superchargers will make more power (all other conditions being equal) than a positive displacement type, but the power will come at higher rpm. You have to decide what your own performance needs are to decide on the right kit for your application.

Unlike a turbocharger kit, the supercharger kit for the average import includes a whole new intake manifold, since the intake must match the outlet configuration of the blower. On most centrifugal blower kits, however, a new intake manifold isn't needed, because the boost can be plumbed to your existing intake as is done with a

This Honda is equipped with an Eaton blower from Jackson Racing - note how neatly the blower drive tucks in under the stock power steering pump, like it was made to be there

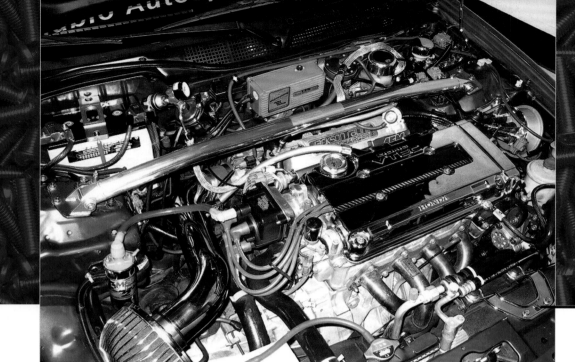

The well-thought out installation that takes maximum advantage of the supercharger will include other modifications - in addition to the JR blower, this showy Honda has an intake pipe, header, high-output ignition and a revamped fuel system with custom fuel rail, FMU, fuel pressure gauge and big fuel filter

turbo install.

Most reputable blower kits have everything you need to install the system and use it reliably. Contents include the blower, intake manifold (if needed), belt, mounting hardware, instructions and some type of electronic gear to control fuel delivery and/or ignition timing. Some kits use a larger-than-stock fuel pump that replaces your in-tank pump, and a special fuel-pressure regulator that may be boost-sensitive. Other components could be hoses, wire harnesses, air intake, an intercooler, and parts that relocate items in the engine compartment to provide room for the blower. Some installations may include an oil filter relocation kit that allows for easier oil changes after the supercharger kit is installed. These kinds of extras are installation-specific.

Most kits can be installed by a competent mechanic, provided he reads the manufacturer's instructions before ripping out the stock parts and slapping new parts in. The quality of the instructions varies among manufacturers, but all companies have tech lines to answer your questions about installation or tuning, as well as web sites that explain the typical FAQ's (frequently-asked questions). A Haynes repair manual for your specific vehicle will be a big help, especially when dealing with "where did this gasket go or what wire went here?" If you are new at this kind of engine work, you may want to have a tuner shop do the install for you, or at least have a friend who has more experience provide a helping hand. Most manufacturers claim their kits can be installed in 8-10 hours, but some installations are more complicated because of engine compartment and engine layout, and you may need to spend the weekend working on it. Just take your time and you'll have a successful conversion to forced induction!

Not all supercharger kits are street-legal in every locality. You should check with the manufacturer of the kit and also your local authorities, especially if you have periodic emissions inspections.

Good for any forced-induction application, Holley makes this boost-compensating adjustable fuel pressure regulator - adjustment range is from 20 to 75 psi and it will raise fuel pressure four psi for each psi of boost the engine sees

Making your engine suit the supercharger

The manufacturer of the kit you utilize has done their homework to make their blower right for your car, but it's your responsibility to see that your engine is ready for the blower. At the relatively-low boost levels of most kits, a stock engine in good condition should work fine. The supercharger should not have any serious effect on the engine's longevity, but of course that assumes your engine is in perfect condition to start with. There is an extra load on the crankshaft to drive a mechanical blower, and the boost is not going to be all that effective if your valves are leaky and piston rings really worn. Leaking valve guides or rings can permit some engine oil to enter the combustion chamber, and this is an invitation to detonation under boost, even if everything else in your installation is done right.

Start your "boost-suitability-check" by giving the engine a thorough tune-up, then check the engine's compression and take vacuum readings. Both of these important diagnostic checks are covered

If you need to have a stronger head gasket to handle boost, this GReddy metal-reinforced piece is what your need - some are available in a thick version to reduce static compression so you can apply more boost

In race applications with lots of boost, you may need an extra injector to provide enough fuel - bosses like this GReddy can be welded to an intake tube and accept stock or aftermarket injectors

in Chapter 2 of the Haynes repair manual for your vehicle. Your car is most likely computer-controlled, which means that the engine management system stores fault information called diagnostic trouble codes. If you experience some idling or driveability problems that your tune-up didn't fix, you may want to visit a good shop that has a diagnostic tool called a scanner that can extract any trouble codes from your car (see Chapter 4 of this book to read more about scanners and DTC's).

Check your Haynes repair manual to learn more about troubleshooting your fuel system, and perform all basic maintenance, such as changing fuel filters and checking fuel pressure. In Chapter 7 of this book, you'll find more information about aftermarket improvements to your fuel system that ensure a steady supply of clean fuel so you aren't going to "lean out" under boost.

By now you're aware of the effect of high temperatures on your engine, and adding a forced induction system will tax your cooling system further than most other mods. You must make sure your radiator and water pump are in perfect order. At the very least, you should have the radiator professionally cleaned and tested at a radiator shop. If you plan on running under boost a lot, or want to upgrade to higher boost levels, you may need a larger aftermarket radiator to keep coolant temps under control.

We have discussed earlier in this Chapter how big a role is played by your existing static compression ratio, and how switching to a low compression piston like an 8:1 will help you make better use of a supercharger by allowing more boost to be used. Aftermarket steel head gaskets are available that are thicker-than-stock, to reduce

Split Second makes several types of programmable electronic controls and software for modified engines - this Additional Injector Controller does just what the name implies, it can control up to four extra injectors and is usually calibrated by forced-induction kit installers

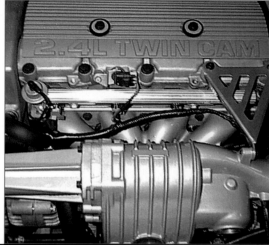

GM Performance Parts is there for the forced induction needs of 2000 to 2002 Cavalier and Sunfire owners with 2.4L twin-cam engines - this Eaton blower package includes a special MAP sensor and a 12,000 mile warranty, you can buy it at your dealership and recalibration of your car's engine management is included (recalibration is done at a dealership)

If your import persuasion swings you to the German side, Neuspeed has this nicely-packaged blower kit for the Volkswagen

compression ratio for power-adder applications. Even if you have a relatively-low compression ratio in your engine already, use of more than 8 psi of boost can compromise engine internals if you learn to love the sensation of boost and are constantly on throttle. In such a case, you may want to switch pistons anyway to install forged aftermarket pistons that can better take the stress. After all, the first components to feel the bad effects of detonation will be the tops of your pistons, and forged pistons can take abuse longer than your cast stock pistons. Hopefully, you won't experience detonation, but the forged pistons are just good insurance. When you get into boost in the double-digit range, further engine modifications may be required.

Boost and detonation both put increased loads on pistons, rods, bearings and crankshaft. For applications where you will be drag racing or running high boost on the street, you might consider aftermarket internals such as improved connecting rods and a high-strength crankshaft if one is available for your engine. At the very least, if you have the engine apart anyway, have a performance machine shop go over the rods by Magnafluxing them for flaws, smoothing the beams, shot-peening, restoring the rod bores, balancing, and fitting them with aftermarket rod bolts.

As with turbocharging, if you're running high levels of boost, you may want to go over your cylinder head by installing stainless steel valves, a three-angle valve job, and even machining the head for metal O-rings to better seal the cylinder bores. Unless you are racing, you don't need to spend money on porting and polishing the cylinder head. While we're talking about the cylinder head, camshaft choice can make a difference in your boosted engine. What works best for an all-motor (no power-adder) engine is not going to be productive for your supercharged engine. Consult with the manufacturer of the kit you're planning to install to see what they recommend. Even if

you leave the stock cams in place, at least install high-performance valve springs and lightweight retainers (see Chapter 8).

The two most important engine modifications that can complement your forced induction (other than a low-restriction air intake, which we'll consider a given) are the exhaust and ignition system. The supercharger is designed to pack more air into the engine, and your stock exhaust system is going to stifle all that from getting out of the engine. A good header and cat-back exhaust will help reduce backpressure, allowing the supercharger to do a better job.

The ignition system will be important because of the extra-dense mixture that the plugs are trying to ignite. All that boost pressure makes it harder for the spark to jump the plug gaps, so an aftermarket coil and plug wires should be considered a minimum investment here. Any of the good CD ignition boxes will also be helpful (see Chapter 5 of this book).

If you've done your homework and picked a good kit, set your engine up properly to take advantage of all the supercharger can provide, installed a good boost gauge on your dash and loaded your fuel tank with premium, then buckle up your belts and get out there and rock 'n' roll! You will love the feeling of boost, and for your first month of driving you'll be using it all the time, but you may eventually settle down to where you only use the boost 5-10% of your driving time, and your fuel economy will come back to something near stock. While a supercharger does have some mechanical noise to it, it's more "stealthy" than a turbocharger, without the sound effects from a blow-off valve or wastegate. You can expect to gain anywhere from 50 to 100 horsepower with a blower, depending on the type of kit and your application, but whatever the improvement, you can bet it will outweigh quite a few other 5-10hp mods, and it can all be installed in one weekend!

Installing a Supercharger

The staff at Comptech deal with precision work and demanding customers all the time. They have a range of intake and exhaust components for most Honda applications, including the common-man models you and I drive, but their greatest involvement has been with the higher-end cars from Honda, like the NSX, the new S2000 and the Acura 3.2L CL Type S and TL Type S. The following is an installation on the 3.2L V6 equipped with an automatic transaxle. While many of their kits have been installed on the six-speed manual transaxle cars, this was the first one on the automatic version.

Comptech's kits are complete and have very detailed photo-filled instructions, but they still like to see their kits installed by professional mechanics. They include an ESM (electronic signal modifier) with every kit, but they need to know your exact year and model to include the right calibration. The ESM interrupts and modifies the signal between the MAP sensor and the ECU to allow the ECU to handle boost.

Certainly each supercharger installation will be unique to the make, model and model year of the vehicle and engine. Before attempting the installation at home, thoroughly research every step of the job.

01 The first order of business (after disconnect the battery negative cable) is to relocate the power steering pump's remote reservoir with a new bracket supplied in the kit - the drive end of the supercharger system has to squeeze in at this end of the engine - also relieve the fuel system pressure (follow your Haynes repair manual)

02 The alternator is unbolted and the alternator pulley swapped for a new Comptech pulley with new grooved section to power the blower- you can remove/install a pulley with two wrenches but an impact gun makes the job way easier

03 When the alternator is reinstalled, the upper bracket is replaced by this billet Comptech mount that will secure one end of the supercharger drive - the wiring harness has to be relocated slightly where it runs by the alternator

04 Once you have the extra air coming into an engine that a forced induction system can supply, headers are highly recommended to allow the engine to exhale better as well

05 Drain the cooling system - clearance is tight in the narrow corridor between the engine and the radiator, but that's where the blower will live, so a new radiator hose is supplied (installed here) that has a tighter radius on the upper bend

06 The fan shroud on the left (stock one on the right) has been modified by Comptech (it's an exchange item) to give clearance to the new radiator hose (notice the cut-down area at the front here) - two ribs are removed also

07 In addition to the shroud modification, the fan motor is moved to the radiator side of the shroud (only on automatic transaxle models), and mounted using these spacers between the motor and the shroud effectively giving more clearance from the fan to the blower and new radiator hose

08 The stock battery and battery tray (big ones at the left) are taken out and replaced with a new battery tray, new "slenderized" coolant overflow bottle and more compact 51R battery - big kid toys are just like little kid toys . . .the battery isn't included

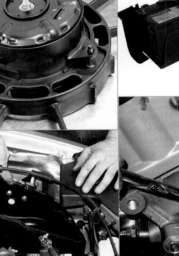

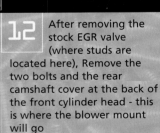

09 Comptech calls their air intake system the "Icebox", and this V6 Icebox is included with each supercharger package

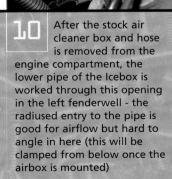

10 After the stock air cleaner box and hose is removed from the engine compartment, the lower pipe of the Icebox is worked through this opening in the left fenderwell - the radiused entry to the pipe is good for airflow but hard to angle in here (this will be clamped from below once the airbox is mounted)

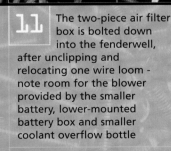

11 The two-piece air filter box is bolted down into the fenderwell, after unclipping and relocating one wire loom - note room for the blower provided by the smaller battery, lower-mounted battery box and smaller coolant overflow bottle

12 After removing the stock EGR valve (where studs are located here), Remove the two bolts and the rear camshaft cover at the back of the front cylinder head - this is where the blower mount will go

13 The aluminum blower mount is fitted with an O-ring and pushed into the camshaft hole (provided for camshaft removal) - lubricate the O-ring with clean motor oil and work the mount into the hole slowly so the O-ring isn't pinched

14 The blower mount is bolted to the cam cover holes and the EGR valve is reinstalled with a new gasket - for further blower support, a third bolt is threaded into the cylinder head, but because of the casting variations in the heads, a threaded collar is adjusted to take up space between the bracket and the head before the bolt is tightened

15 There are two throttle bodies on the automatic cars - here the first TB (for the traction-control system) is unbolted and set aside

16 This cast-aluminum elbow will take the place of the main throttle body (at right) - tag and disconnect all the hoses and electrical connectors at the throttle body, then mount this block-off plate with O-ring to the original MAP sensor location (A) on the throttle body - the MAP sensor (B) is relocated to top of this cast-aluminum elbow which will take the place of the throttle body at the intake manifold

17 The Comptech supercharger package comes assembled as you see it here, with the Eaton blower, the drive and the cast intake and outlet housings in place

18 Tim carefully lowers the package into place onto the two Comptech mounts at the engine, making sure there is no interference with wiring harnesses or coolant hoses

19 At the belt-drive end, the air conditioning hose is moved until it fits between the mount bracket and the pulley - install the two bolts through the mount and into the alternator bracket, but don't tighten them yet

20 The lower four bolts where the drive meets the blower are removed (do NOT loosen the top bolts or the blower's internal oil reservoir could leak) - when the longer Allen bolts are inserted through the mount on the engine to the blower and started, you can tighten the pulley-end mounting bolts to spec, then tighten the four Allen bolts at this end

21 Before mounting the rest of the intake system components, a brace is mounted from the supercharger body to the transaxle - note that the studs from the top of the throttle body mount at the intake manifold were removed (use double-nuts to remove) and installed at the blower intake flange, along with a new gasket

22 Hoses that were attached to the throttle body in its stock location are replaced with longer hoses (mark the end locations before removing the stock hoses, so there's no mix-up) and several wire groups that went to the throttle body sensors (idle air control, MAP, throttle position sensor) must be separated from the corrugated plastic looms, run to the new locations and then any unprotected wires should be covered with loom material or electrical tape

23 Slide the silicone hose and clamps over the intake elbow, bolt the elbow to the intake manifold with a new gasket, then center the hose over the joint and tighten the hose clamps

The fuel pressure regulator mounts to the edge of the cowl (you work through a hole in the cowl once a small access panel is removed) and is plumbed according to the instructions - it's specifically sized for this application with a large diaphragm to respond better than the small stock regulator

24

The stock fuel pressure regulator is removed and replaced with an AN fitting (A) whose braided lines goes to the "IN" fitting on the Comptech FPR, and a new vacuum hose (B) runs from the intake manifold to the FPR - the other fuel side of the FPR connects with a hose to the stock steel fuel return line

25

The main throttle body is rotated until the cables are up and there are no kinks, then its bolted to the intake elbow of the blower and the coolant hose and IAC and TPS connectors are hooked up - This elbow being clamped in place is to mount the other throttle body for the traction-control system

26

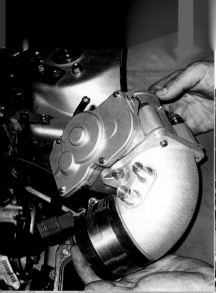

27 The bottom of the elbow (shown here with traction-control throttle body attached) has two fittings for vapor lines, one from the valve cover (A) and one to the air-assist valve (B) for emissions - it's easier to attach the hoses here before mounting the elbow or throttle body - they hook up just as they did stock but here with longer hoses

28 Here both throttle bodies are installed and all linkages, hoses and wires connected

29 Remove the top from the Icebox air filter housing and mount the new air filter and its rubber elbow in place, clamping the elbow to the traction-control throttle body, then reinstall the airbox cover

30 At the belt end of the installation, you can see how the new blower belt goes around the blower drive and the Comptech alternator pulley, while the supplied tensioner keeps it tight - you can also see here how the AC line is routed and why the PS pump reservoir had to be relocated

This is an overall of the six-speed installation - in both manual and automatic applications, there is some minor trimming of the plastic engine covers where they meet the blower and drive -

31 The last step before the car goes back to an anxious owner is a thorough check of everything on the Comptech chassis dyno - a calibration of the electronic signal modifier between the ECU and the MAP sensor and the V6 was running OEM smooth, but with extra horsepower to use - the test automatic car made 40 more hp, but they are looking to greatly improve that with a piggyback fuel/spark controller

32 Just for comparison to our subject car, here's the intake end of the package on a six-speed manual car, where there's only one throttle body

33 the six-speed cars gain up to 70 hp with the Comptech conversion

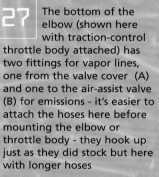

Exhaust systems

It's not all about the sound.
You can gain some horsepower too!

Whether you're a real performance crazy or just content to pose and profile, you car's sound is still important. What's lucky for us is that a good performance exhaust system can satisfy both interests. When you assemble the right package of exhaust components that allow your engine to really breathe, the car's going to sound as good as it performs. It bears repeating here that the exhaust system is one of the few aspects of the car you can modify that gives you the performance you want without any of the drawbacks or compromises that usually come with engine mods. On the contrary, the exhaust work should have no effect on your idling or smooth driveability, and your fuel economy will actually go up, not down! The cool sound is a bonus, too.

Production car exhaust system designers are saddled with a trunkful of considerations, such as emissions testing, vehicle floorpan configuration, bean-counting accountants who want the least expensive part that does the job, and achieving sound levels down to that suitable for the average library. Unfortunately, none of these restrictions contribute to the production of a highly effective performance exhaust but, luckily for us, the aftermarket has been filling that void almost since the car was invented.

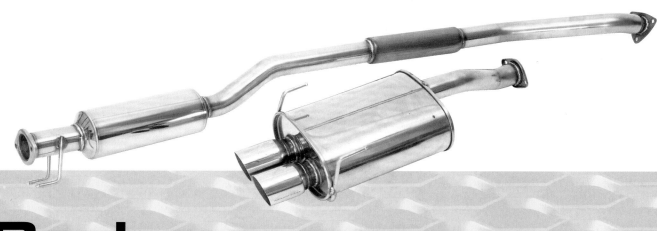

Backpressure and flow

Even a stock engine that operates mostly at lower speeds has to get rid of the byproducts of combustion. If it takes fuel and air in, it has to expel those gasses after the reciprocating components have turned the cylinder pressures into work. The exhaust system needs to allow swift exit of those gasses, and any delay or obstruction to that flow can cause engine efficiency to suffer. If there is an exhaust flow problem somewhere in the system, the pressure waves coming out with the gasses can "back up," which can cause the cylinders to work harder to complete their four-stroke cycle. In exhaust terms, this is called backpressure, and getting rid of it is the chief aim of performance exhaust system designers. An old prank kids used to pull was to take a raw potato and stick it into the end of a car's exhaust pipe. While the kids watched, the owner would start the car and it might run for a second or two, but then quit and not start again. A silly thing, but it demonstrates the important role played by the exhaust.

Almost every type of system has some backpressure. Even a straight length of open pipe adds some frictional delay to the flow. The biggest compromise to having the least backpressure is the muffling of the sound.

The two main sections of the performance exhaust system are the tubular header that lets the exhaust out freely and may even draw it out . . .

. . . and the remainder of the exhaust system, including the muffler and exhaust pipe(s) – even the catalytic converter you choose can be a performance factor

Any vehicle that operates on the streets is going to have some kind of exhaust system that quiets down the engine to an acceptable level. Almost anything you can do to muffle the sound of an exhaust system will incur some backpressure, so the trick of performance tuning the exhaust is to have the best compromise. For instance, there may be dozens of muffler designs that will reduce sound to the desired level in any one application, but the trick is finding the design that accomplishes this with the least backpressure. If a potato created maximum backpressure and caused the engine to quit, what would be the effect of say, half a potato? The engine would run, but its efficiency would be drastically reduced, especially as engine speed went up. A sharp old mechanic we used to know would check many things on the car when a customer came in with a complaint of a sudden power loss when accelerating or on the highway. He always checked the full length of the exhaust system on a hoist, because he knew from experience that a kink or crush in the exhaust pipe from road debris or driving over a curb could cause this sluggishness on an otherwise perfectly-tuned engine.

It would seem that if you improved components to the point where you had no restriction at all then you could do no more for the exhaust, but there is another element of gas flow dynamics we haven't talked about. It is possible for an exhaust to perhaps flow better than a straight piece of pipe, or at least to make more horsepower. Why does an aftermarket intake setup make more power than just having the throttle body open to the air with no filter or entry pipe? Part of it is due to cooler air coming in, but also because the long shiny intake pipe helps build an intake momentum, what used to be called a "ram" effect. Instead of letting air come in, the intake pipe helps the air come in better.

The same type of improved flow is what aftermarket exhaust engineers have been focused on for decades. There are many theories and lots of experiments have been tried, but one thing we know for sure, the right parts can almost suck the exhaust out of the engine. In other words, instead of releasing the gasses, the right system can draw them out. On a multi-cylinder engine, a combination of the right size and shape of pipes, connected in the right order, can take advantage of the engine's timing of its exhaust pulses. Let's say your engine's firing order is 1-3-4-2. If you arranged the header pipes in a way that the pipe carrying the exhaust pulse from cylinder one was meeting the pipe from cylinder four at the right time, it could conceivably create a slight negative pressure that helped the pulse from cylinder four come out faster. If you follow the idea, it's possible for a header to be designed where each cylinder's exhaust pulse helped the next one, in a process called cylinder "scavenging."

Headers

The first major component of your performance exhaust system is the header, a tubular replacement for your stock cast-iron exhaust manifold. In most OEM sport compact applications the stock exhaust manifold isn't too bad, at least for the needs of your stock economy engine. The exhaust flow needs of an engine go up exponentially with the state of performance "tune." The flow and backpressure needs of a stock engine aren't excessive, especially when the engine spends the bulk of its driving life under 4000 rpm. But what happens when you modify the engine and then take advantage of those modifications by using the high end of the rpm scale? The exhaust system that was once adequate is now restrictive to a great degree.

How much power you make with just the header depends on several factors. On a car with a really restrictive stock exhaust system, particularly an exhaust manifold full of tight bends and twists, the header will make a bigger improvement than on a car with a decent system to start with. What's behind the header can make a big difference as well. If the stock exhaust system includes restrictive converter and muffler designs, small-diameter exhaust pipes and lots of "wrinkle bends" to boot, the header isn't going to have much chance of making a big improvement in performance. A good header on a typical sport compact engine with few other modifications can be expected to make only 3-5 horsepower, depending on how good or bad the stock manifold had been. That's with a stock exhaust system from the header back.

That sounds disappointing, but if we take a case where the engine has numerous modifications yet still has a stock exhaust manifold, the same aftermarket header could gain 10 horsepower. Any of the big "power-adder" modifications, including nitrous oxide and supercharging virtually "require' a header and free-flowing exhaust system to take advantage of their power potential.

Installation of a performance header is quite easy.

Header design is an inexact science, most of what we know is through trial and error, but basically the idea is to have the right size and length pipes and arrange them so each pipe complements the others in terms of timing

One of the popular header designs in the sport compact world is the 4-2-1, in which four pipes merge into two pipes which travel back and finally merge into the one collector pipe – this Civic with a swapped-in Japanese VTEC engine has the JDM factory 4-2-1 pipes

Most aftermarket headers are made to use all the factory mounting points and braces. In fact, beware of one that doesn't because the header may sound "tinny" when installed if the proper braces aren't connected. Make sure before buying a header that you give the shop your exact year, model and if it's an engine swap or not, especially if it's an imported, used Japanese engine you have swapped in. The location of the oxygen sensor varies among models, and especially between US and JDM installations.

Other factors to consider when header shopping would be looking for thick flanges that aren't going to warp and leak, and thick-walled tubing that won't rot out (and sounds better than thin tubes). Ground clearance is another issue.

When shopping for a header, look for clean complete welds and thick, flat flange plates for a good seal – note the pairing of cylinders 1 and 4 and 2 and 3 in the four-tube section

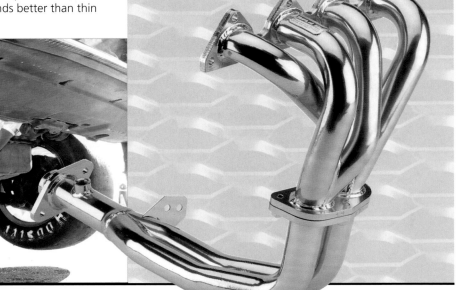

This JDM four-to-one racing header design keeps all four pipes long, for good torque – a four-to-one design may provide less ground clearance on street applications than a 4-2-1 – note that this racer has wrapped all the pipes to keep heat in

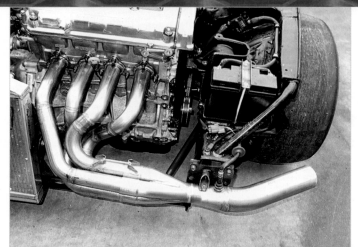

If your ride is stock height and going to stay that way, most any header design is going to work for you, but on a seriously lowered car, you may want to stick with a 4-2-1 header, because the two pipes under the car are side-by-side and take up less room under there than the four tubes on a 4-1 header.

Header finish is a consideration. There are usually a few choices, even within one brand of header. The least expensive finish would be plain steel, which you would paint yourself with spray cans of header paint (lots of colors available). Next would be factory-painted headers, followed by high-temp-coated headers and headers made of stainless-steel. The high-temp coatings and stainless pipes are the longest lasting, and the polished stainless pipes are arguably the coolest looking. Some headers are also available in chrome-plated steel, which is pretty showy, too.

In a race-only application, there's room to build an exhaust without compromises – most designs use larger tubes because they're only concerned with high-rpm operation, and equal-length pipes and collector length are also important when the header is all there is to the exhaust system

Some headers have unusual requirements to satisfy in the application – this Focus header has to work with the existing cat location and flange, so to get some primary-tube length, the tubes have to curve around like this

Racing "improves the breed" they say – Shad Huntley of Comptech poses with his company's stainless-steel four-cylinder Honda header and a pair for a V6

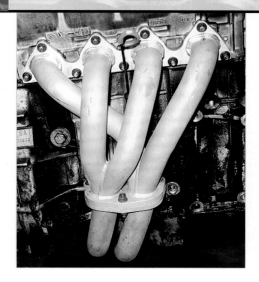

While American models of compacts get cast-iron exhaust manifolds, some JDM models have tubular performance headers as factory equipment - compare to . . .

. . . a typical aftermarket 4-2-1 header like this one

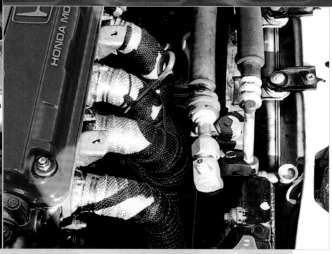

This 4-2-1 by DC Sports has gone a little further in trying to get all four primary pipes to be of equal length - the outside pipes have to be longer, so the inside pipes snake around just a little before joining the others

Keeping the heat in the headers makes the exhaust flow faster, which is what we want – this high-temperature insulating "header wrap" may not look exciting, but it could help you a little on exhaust scavenging

All about exhaust flow

STOCK - "Wrinkle bends" often seen in OEM and mass-produced aftermarket pipes will give some restriction as the exhaust exits

BETTER - A second type of bend, the "crush" bend, is normally seen on pipes bent on hydraulic benders at muffler shops – it's smoother inside than a wrinkle bend, but not ideal. Note how the section at the bend is a smaller diameter

BEST - Good aftermarket performance exhausts have less bends than stock, and where there have to be bends, "mandrel" bends are used that are smooth and as consistent in diameter as the straight sections of pipe

Stock mufflers often have an indirect route for the exhaust, through a "maze" that scrubs off some of the harsh tones (as well as some of your power)

A classic performance muffler is a straight-through design, in which there is a perforated core surrounded by fiberglass sound-dampening material (Airmass Thundermuff shown)

The converter and beyond

Depending on the level of modifications, the exhaust pipe in the cat-back system should be sized for the displacement and state-of-tune – this Warlock system by Airmass features two-inch pipes, which should be good for most any street sport compact application

Once the exhaust gasses leave your efficient new header, they must travel a ways to get out from under your car, and our goal is to make it more of a freeway than a labyrinth. First off, there is the catalytic converter, usually bolted right there to the collector of your header. For most of us, this is not an optional component because we have to have it. That's fine, because the converter does do a great job of cleaning up engine emissions, and the designs of current converters are more free-flowing for legal street use than the older ones, so the converter isn't something to whine about too much. If you have to replace yours due to its age, by all means shop around and try to find as free-flowing a replacement cat as you can. There are a number of "performance" cats on the market that have a stainless-steel shell, which is long-lasting and looks good. If your engine is going to eventually get forced-induction, you might even think about using a slightly larger cat, or at least one with larger inlet and outlet pipes than your stocker. If considering a catalytic converter replacement, check all applicable emissions laws before putting down your money).

If your stock converter is going to stay for the time being, at least have it checked out to make sure it isn't clogged. A clogged converter can choke your engine down like the half-o-potato we talked about earlier. The biggest causes of a clogged catalytic converter is using non-approved fuels or additives, or a worn engine whose rings allow too much oil in the exhaust (you'll be able to tell because people driving behind you will always be coughing).

Comptech has this polished stainless-steel pipe and muffler for the Acura RSX – stainless-steel exhaust parts will probably last the lifetime of the vehicle

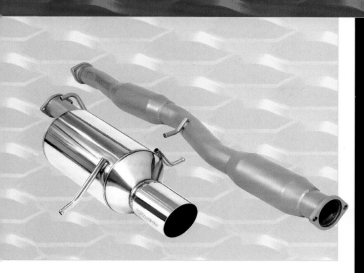

Most of the aftermarket exhaust systems on the market are called "cat-back", because they include everything from the converter back. The system may come in several pieces (see our how-to procedure on installing one) to simplify packaging, shipping and installation, but it should bolt right up to the back flange of your converter and include whatever silencer(s) and muffler(s) are needed. Many of the cat-back systems include the muffler, which on most sport compacts is a part of the car that's very visible, especially when it's a really big one mounted right at the rear bumper. In this case, if you feel the systems out there don't offer the "muffler aesthetics" to suit you, buy a system that doesn't include the muffler and add whatever kind you want.

Changing the exhaust of your vehicle for a performance system is one of the modifications with more perks than almost any other. You get increased power, improved fuel economy, the sound that will complement your performance profile, and parts that make your ride look better, too. All that, and there's no real downside or sacrifice as with most engine mods!

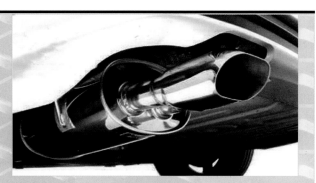

If you have lowered your car quite a bit, you might consider using a system with an oval-shaped muffler rather than round – the oval muffler and oval tip (GReddy G2 here) doesn't hang down as low as a large round muffler, giving you some additional ground clearance at this critical spot

? WHAT IF . . . rusted exhaust bolts and nuts

Exhaust system fasteners can be REALLY tough to remove, especially from older vehicles. The high heat coupled with the exposure to the elements can "weld" the bolts and nuts in place. Do yourself (especially your knuckles) a favor and buy the best penetrating oil you can. Spray it on all the fasteners you need to remove - and don't be shy, use a lot of it. Then let it soak in for a good long time.

When it comes time to remove the fasteners, you may need a long breaker bar to gain some extra leverage. In some cases (like exhaust pipe or hanger bolts) if things go snap, it's not a problem since you will be using new replacement fasteners anyway. But when it comes to exhaust manifold bolts or studs on the engine, be very careful. How 'bout another shot of that penetrating oil!

If the fasteners are rusty, get out the penetrating oil and give them a good soak first. Hopefully, once the clamp nuts are unscrewed, the clamp can be persuaded off, and the joint itself will separate - removing a section like this isn't as bad as a "sleeved" joint, like you get on the muffler

Hold the bolt heads with one wrench, and loosen the nuts with another. If the bolts break, thats okay. If the nuts have rusted away to nothing, you're in trouble - locking pliers or a nut splitter will be needed.

After unscrewing the manifold nuts, inspect the studs - if they're really rusty or damaged, replace them

Cat-back installation

01 Use a long ratchet and six-point socket to loosen the nuts/bolts at the rear of the catalytic converter

For the performance enthusiast, the exhaust system consists of two main ingredients: the exhaust manifold or header, and everything else. The latter makes up much of the system, and on today's cars with emission controls, we call them "cat-back" exhaust because we have to keep the catalytic converter to pass emissions tests. The modern catalytic converter poses less of a restriction than older ones; just make sure yours is not plugged up before you add high-performance exhaust components or you won't get the gains you expect.

The installation of a quality-built cat-back system like this one isn't difficult, and while the use of someone's hoist would be great, it can be done with the car on jackstands if you need to. Just follow common sense practices with the jack and four sturdy jackstands. New performance and the sound to go with it can be yours in one to two hours!

02 This Honda has another bolted joint at the rear of the system, just ahead of the rear suspension – take these fasteners off

03 Use a pointed prybar to get the rubber exhaust hanger "donuts" off the body mounts – be gentle because these are going to be reused (if they're in good shape)

04 There's also a donut near the rear system joint, and another holding up the muffler

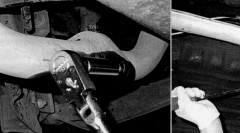

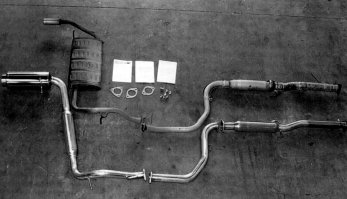

05 Clean the exhaust donuts of grime, then reinstall them on the car – any broken ones must be replaced

06 Here laid out on the shop floor, you can see how the shiny new stainless-steel Tanabe system compares to the stock exhaust (upper in photo) just removed – it fits just the same but is much more free-flowing

07 Before putting the new components on the car, apply a little white grease to the holes where the exhaust hangers have to squeeze in

Clean the threads on the studs at the converter flange, then put the new gasket in place **08**

The exhaust came with stainless-steel fasteners, so stainless nuts were put on at the cat, with a little anti-seize on the threads, so they'll come off easier if needed in the future **09**

The rear section of the exhaust includes the large muffler/silencer – hang this section on the rubber donuts at the front and rear – this holds the pipes so you can bolt them up **10**

11 The system is in three pieces and we have the front and rear hanging there, so now position the middle pipe to the back of the front section, using the new gasket, and start the nuts in place by hand – you still have to support the rear of this piece while doing the front, so you may want a helper

12 When you bolt up the rear of the middle section with a new gasket and bolts, the whole system starts to line up and become more solid – tighten the bolts at both ends of the middle section now

A little tip for your stainless steel

Go over all that polished stainless with alcohol, because any fingerprints or smudges you may have made may stay forever if you heat the new stainless without cleaning it first

The Tanabe muffler at the rear has a "coffee-can" size tip, but it comes with this bolt-in insert – this system has a great sound, not raspy, but with the insert bolted in (one bolt) it gets even more civilized

13

Header Installation

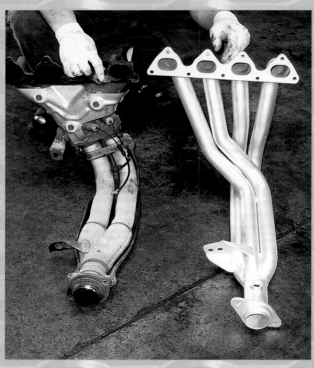

For comparison, you can see the restrictive stock manifold (left) and the new DC Sports 4-1 header – the DC header is much lighter and maintains good exhaust velocity all the way to the collector

Almost everyone with a sport compact has at least two modifications: a long shiny intake pipe with an aftermarket air filter, and an exhaust header. When the onlookers see your engine compartment, they expect at least that, but a good exhaust system is important for more than just cool looks. The right header for the application, a good cat-back system and a few tuning tweaks at the dyno shop and you have the feel and sound of performance along with the looks.

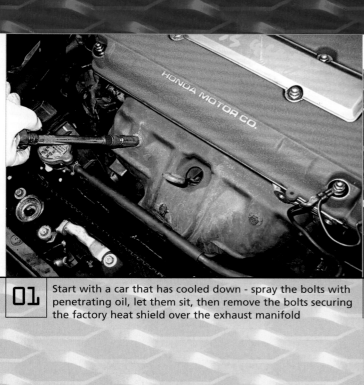

01 Start with a car that has cooled down - spray the bolts with penetrating oil, let them sit, then remove the bolts securing the factory heat shield over the exhaust manifold

02 Soak all of the exhaust manifold retaining nuts with penetrating oil, then remove them

>

Depending on the application, the oxygen sensor may be in the manifold, the collector or the catalytic converter – if it's in the way, disconnect the electrical connector and remove the sensor

03

Remove the nuts/bolts at the collector-to-catalytic converter flange

04

Remove the remaining bolts and brackets securing the forward pipe and manifold

05

Slowly work the exhaust down and out of the car (take care not to damage the radiator in the process). On some vehicles, like this Honda, the front crossmember will have to be removed because it's in the way

06

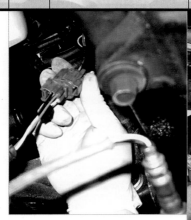

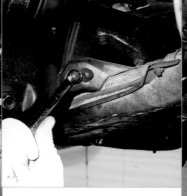
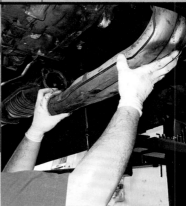

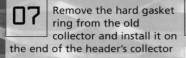

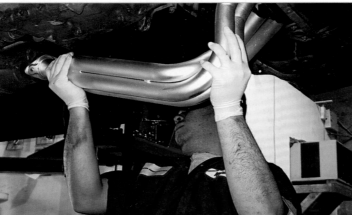

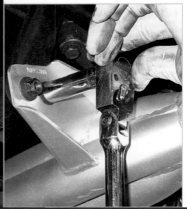

07 Remove the hard gasket ring from the old collector and install it on the end of the header's collector

08 With the old crossmember removed, there is plenty of room to install the new high-temp-coated header

09 Attach the fasteners, but leave them loose at this time

10 If your application uses a header gasket, install a new one and bolt the header to the cylinder head with all of the original nuts

11 Tighten the bolts at the header collector-to-converter flange and the header is completely installed. Don't forget to reinstall the oxygen sensor!

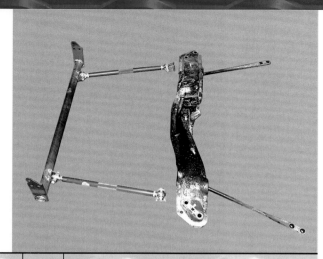

12 Several companies make special crossmembers for such applications, but we used one manufactured by Midnight Performance – compare the cool-looking high-strength steel tubing crossmember and racy anodized radius rods to the ugly stock crossmember

The tubular crossmember bolts into the Honda to the same bolt holes where the original towing bracket used to hang down. The new radius rods bolt to the crossmember and lower control arms with spherical joints at each end, and its length can be adjusted by holding the knurled center, threading one of the joints in or out, then tightening the large jam nuts – an alignment shop should make the final adjustment for you (it affects the front-wheel **13** caster setting)

? WHAT IF . . .
flanges don't line up?

One problem you may encounter, especially with engine swaps or when parts had been previously replaced, is that the "clocking" or arrangement of the flange bolts may be different

We just removed the cat, cut the front flange off with a bandsaw, put the cat back onto the car and moved the flange (now free to rotate) in front where it would line up with the header flange

A minute or two with the MIG-welder and both the header and cat flanges align perfectly

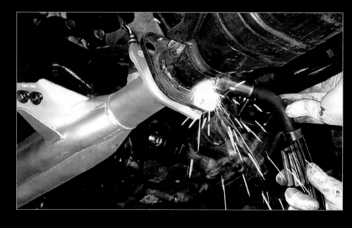

Engine durability

Why is there always money for the *go-fast* parts, but little for the *keep-alive* parts? That big ol' tow truck could be right around the corner waiting for you.

Most engine damage comes about from detonation during the tuner's "learning curve" – here are the results, a piece of block, half a mangled connecting rod, and a piston with a valve-head imbedded

Once you put on the slicks and open your header for action at the track, that's when any potential weakness is exposed, even on a combination that has worked fine on the street

It's a testament to the car designers and engineers that lots of power can be extracted from what are meant to be little more than efficient powerplants for economy cars. Our engines are lightweight, have good valvetrain dynamics, like to rev, and have amazing longevity in stock or mildly-modified form. However, when extracting maximum power from any engine not designed for this, durability begins to suffer as components are stressed beyond their design limits.

High-horsepower engines are built by teams that have learned through experience what it takes to make the engine live. When pressed, most tuners can reach under their bench and pull out a boxful of melted pistons and bent connecting rods accumulated along the way in the search for power and knowledge.

The wiser tuners with that box of parts under the bench will tell you it's better to spend some money now on beefing up the engine, than later on new parts *plus* the beefing up.

The average sport compact engine can handle a power increase in the neighborhood of 50% before you start needing to invest in "engine insurance." That covers most street engines with standard modifications. Where the real trouble starts is with either dragstrip action or the use of a power-adder.

Perhaps the modifications that result in the most stress on an engine are the ones that really increase cylinder pressure: high-compressions pistons; nitrous oxide; supercharging; and turbocharging.

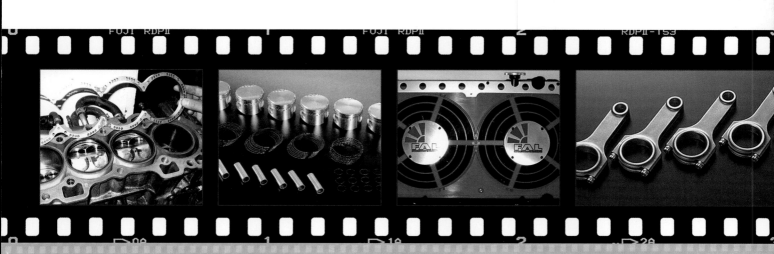

Pistons

The top of the piston usually takes the brunt of damage caused by increased cylinder pressure and detonation. The head gasket and the top of the cylinder walls are also affected by high pressures.

The stock cast-aluminum pistons in your engine now are perfect for what they do, they last a long time, run quietly and withstand all the normal pressures, even with some modifications. Different pistons, however, are required for more serious work.

In some cases the stock compression ratio may be too high for a big shot of nitrous or forced-induction boost, and you just need a replacement piston with lower compression to take advantage of the power-adder's potential. As long as you're replacing the pistons for a lower compression, it only makes sense to get stronger ones while you're at it.

Forged pistons are definitely stronger than your stock pistons, and most have many other subtle tricks to make them live under harsh conditions. Among these other factors are: lighter and stronger pins; full-floating pins that reduce friction losses; smooth edges on the crowns to prevent hot spots; uniform dome thickness for consistent strength; precise machining; heat-treating; and relocated and/or different size ring grooves.

If there's a downside to forged pistons, it is their expansion rate. They tend to expand more than cast pistons as the engine warms up, sometimes resulting in clatter when the engine is cold. Most of today's forged pistons make a little noise only at idle.

Today, the top piston manufacturers have several levels of forged pistons, with a variance in the exact alloy of aluminum used. For instance, for street/strip use with normal power-adder levels, piston manufacturers use a 4032 heat-treated aluminum alloy that has 12% silicon content to limit thermal expansion, and these pistons can be installed with close-to-stock clearances. For racing applications with higher power levels, they make their pistons from a 2618 alloy that is very low in silicon, but has other elements that contribute to a high-strength piston suited for elevated levels of heat and pressure in the cylinders. The low-silicon forgings do require more clearance.

Like a chain, the engine is only as strong as its weakest link, and once you have a stout piston that can take some punishment, the stress is going to be on the rod and its fasteners.

Aftermarket rods are very popular with racers, and a wide variety are available. The basic process of making a "forged" connecting rod goes like this: A red-hot chunk of metal is put into a machine that has dies that slam together to force it into something that resembles the desired finished part. These "blanks" are then machined and treated to produce the final product. The benefit of the forging process is that grains of the metal are packed together

Connecting rods and aftermarket crankshafts

and aligned into the desired shape, making a very strong, dense part that has less inherent tendency to fracture.

Aftermarket rods are available in a number of types of steel, and in various cross-sectional shapes. Many have names that describe the shape, like the H-beam, A-beam, I-beam, etc. While all of the manufacturers have their own features, they will all offer superior strength to any stock or race-prepped stock rod. They come with high-strength fasteners, are precision balanced, and in addition to being strong, are often lighter than the original stock rods!

There are a few companies making forged cranks for other sport compact engines. They are much stronger than a stock cast (stock crankshafts on Hondas are forged) crankshaft, and for racing use can even be made lighter than a stock crank, so the engine revs up quicker and has less reciprocating loads.

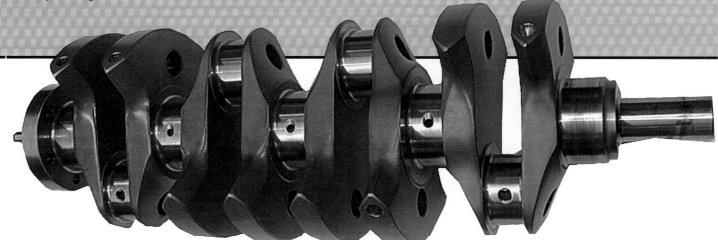

On Honda blocks the cylinders sit in the middle of the water jacket area, without connection to the deck – when your cylinder pressures are distorting them, you may want to try a block-guard like this one made by Midnight Performance, it taps in between the top of the cylinders and the block and has holes for water passage connection

The block

Most import engines have a lightweight block designed for efficiency, and with little extra material where it isn't needed. Basic high-performance machining techniques will assure you of a bottom-end that will stay together in all but extreme conditions. Among the blueprinting procedures that are useful is precisely 'decking" the top surface of the block so that it is flat and perfectly square to the crankshaft centerline. Align-boring the crankshaft saddles assure you that the crankshaft will run true with minimal friction and you can achieve an exact fit of the bearings.

If you're putting in new pistons, then you're putting in new rings and the cylinder walls need to be honed for a surface the new rings can seat against and "wear in." If your cylinder walls have any scores or deep scratches from a broken piston ring, then you'll have to bore the engine first to get rid of that and order oversize pistons.

For those eight and seven-second Honda-powered racecars, the ultimate solution to block problems could be this new block from Dart with a "conventional" deck, available in two bore sizes and complete with main caps and replaceable ductile-iron sleeves

Ecotec racers also have a race block available, Part#88958630, which is this steel-liner'ed aluminum block machined for stainless O-rings to contain serious boost

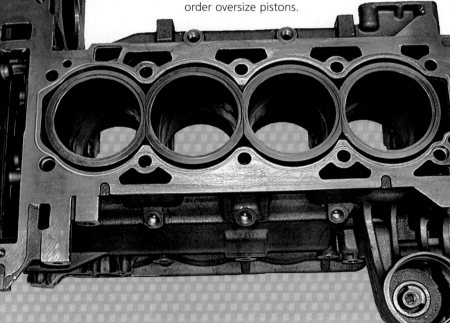

Regular maintenance could be your most important job

Let's assume that you're not running 20 psi of boost or a 200hp shot of nitrous, but you still want to do something within your budget to make your modified engine last longer. Good maintenance habits are always the first line of defense, modified engine or not. Your cooling system, fuel system and oiling system must be kept up at all times. Don't miss any oil changes (every 3,000 miles) and change the filter with every oil change. The Haynes repair manual for your car will have maintenance information specific to your make and model, plus a recommended maintenance schedule to follow.

Multi-valve engines

Most older car engines have one intake valve and one exhaust valve per cylinder - ie, two valves per cylinder. Many modern engines have three, four, or in a few cases even five valves per cylinder, although the most common configuration is four valves per cylinder. Such an engine has two inlet valves and two exhaust valves for each cylinder (so a four-cylinder engine would be a "16-valve" engine).

Using multiple valves gives improved efficiency, because they allow the fuel/air mixture to enter the cylinder, and the exhaust gases to leave, more easily.

Double-overhead-camshaft engines

Double-overhead-camshaft engines (or "twin-cam") engines have two camshafts, one operating the exhaust valves, and one operating the inlet valves. Multi-valve engines are almost always double-overhead-camshaft engines.

Cooling and Lubrication

The power in fuel is the heat generated when you light it, and a performance engine is going to make more heat. Worse yet, a turbocharger jammed between the engine and the radiator can really raise the underhood temperature.

Many import cars have factory oil coolers, usually in a sandwich between the oil filter and the block, and connected to coolant pipes. In stock form this is fine, but when you already have a big load on your cooling system with a modified engine, you don't want to add more heat to the cooling system by passing coolant through a container of hot oil.

The answer, for vehicles with or without a factory oil cooler may be to mount a radiator-type liquid-air cooler out in the car's airstream, although hopefully where it doesn't compete with the coolant radiator for airflow. The extra plumbing and the addition of the cooler to the system also increases the oil capacity of the engine.

The Honda engine has a great oiling system, but under hard, racing conditions the gears have been know to fail (above) – ProDrive makes these billet gears good for extreme use

This oil cooler kit, when mounted in the right place to get cool outside air, can keep engine temps down, even on a turbo application where engine oil must pass through "lubricant hell" to get back to the oil pan

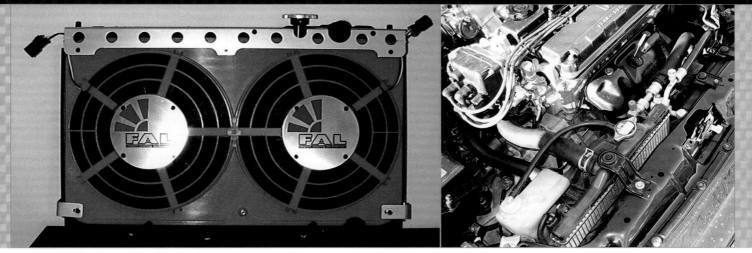

Aftermarket cooling fans keep the air moving faster than a stock fan, and the aftermarket fan/shroud packages are generally slimmer - this is an FAL (Flexalite) setup for a Civic

The small radiator in a compact (here a Honda) is light and handles normal loads, but doesn't have a lot of coolant capacity and is usually a one-row style

The radiator in most compacts is, well, *compact*. Luckily, the aftermarket companies have a wide variety of radiators with extra cooling capacity. Even in the conventional-construction category, your local radiator shop can supply you with a radiator just like your stock one, but with extra rows of tubes in it. Yours may be a one-row now, and you can replace it with a two-row for peace of mind.

Compare this Honda with the previous photo - this tuner has added a Fluidyne aluminum radiator – it's roughly the same size as the original but cools better – Fluidyne even has racing radiators that incorporate an electric water pump, which saves engine horsepower

Aftermarket aluminum radiators are rugged and available in sizes to fit almost any sport compact application for racing or street use

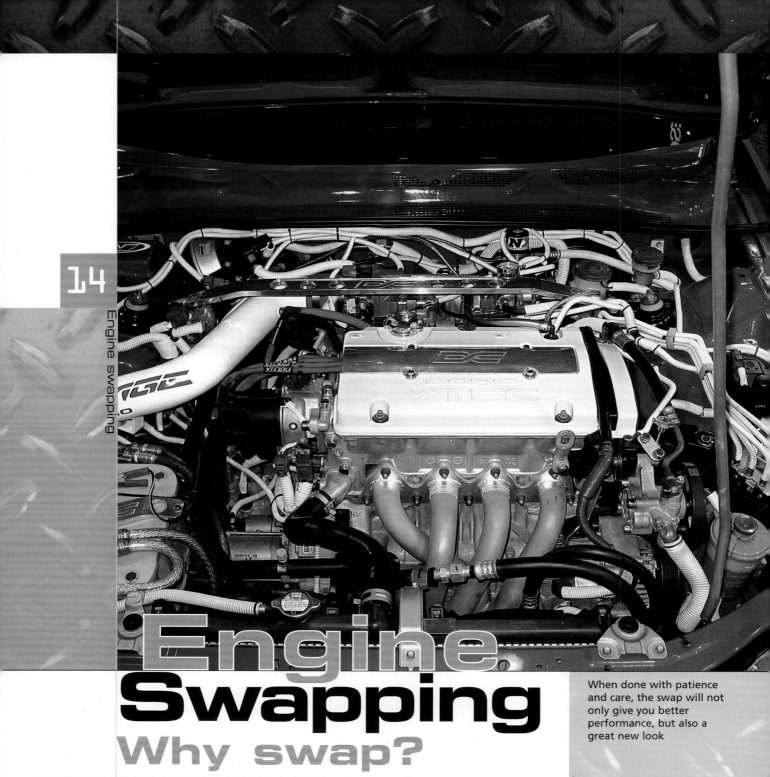

Engine
Swapping
Why swap?

When done with patience and care, the swap will not only give you better performance, but also a great new look

Sometimes it just makes sense to make a change

There are a few basic truths to creating horsepower. When all other factors are equal, the larger the engine displacement, the more power it will make. And the same modification made to a larger-displacement engine will generally gain more power over a smaller-displacement engine. For example, if you replace the 1.5L engine in your Honda Civic with a 2.2L Prelude engine, you will automatically get a substantial power increase, largely

How tough will the job be?
Do your research!

In a typical swap, you'll need to change the engine compartment wiring harness, engine mounts, radiator hoses, exhaust pipe and component mounting brackets. In some cases you may also need to change the transaxle (or shift rods), driveaxles, clutch, radiator and front suspension springs (to accommodate the heavier engine). Every swap is a little different, so it's important to study up before you pull out the wrenches.

In all probability, you're not the first person to try the swap you're planning. And why make the same mistakes the others made! Go to car shows and events. Find a car club. Go on the Internet. Basically, locate people who have already done the swap you're thinking about and pick their brain . . . see their car . . . find out what worked and what didn't.

because the engine has nearly 50-percent more displacement. Now let's say you want to add a header, cat-back exhaust system and cold-air intake. On the 1.5L engine, these modifications might have netted you 20 additional horsepower. These same modifications on the 2.2L engine would likely get you closer to 30 additional horsepower, or about 50-percent more. This is the simple, yet powerful math of displacement.

Another reason for engine swapping is to obtain the latest technology and tuning potential. For example, swapping your tired Single OverHead Cam (SOHC) Mitsubishi engine for a later-model Double OverHead Cam (DOHC) engine will get you some extra power, even though the displacement may be the same. The additional benefit is that the DOHC engine will respond better to tuning, since the cylinder head design is less restrictive and will allow better airflow when other modifications are made. And don't forget about the turbo that came stock on some of those DOHC engines!

Engine ID number

All engines have an ID number that uniquely identifies that particular engine. In some states, that number is printed on the title, so you'll have to notify your motor vehicles department when swapping

In some cases, the new engine number will have to be inspected by a state representative, who will assure the replacement engine has not been stolen. Have your receipts handy.

Engine ID numbers can be difficult to find on the engine block. Buy a Haynes manual to help.

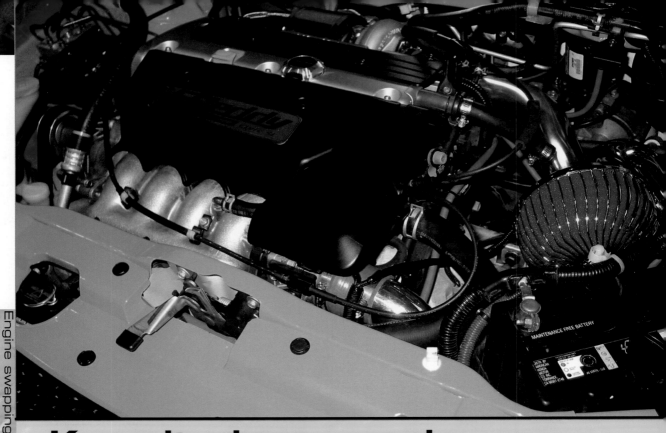

Keep it clean - engine swaps and emissions laws

More and more states and metropolitan areas are enacting some form of emissions control inspection. If you live in an emissions-inspection area, be sure to check the rules governing engine swaps. In many cases, you'll run into problems if you try to swap an early-model engine into your later-model car. Emissions-control requirements for manufacturers advance each year, and the equipment originally installed on an earlier-model engine will likely be inadequate for a later-model car. So, swapping in an engine that is at least the same year as your vehicle (and hopefully newer) is safest from the standpoint of emissions laws. Your state or metro area may also require that the vehicle meet the more stringent emissions standards of the newer engine that's installed. This may require the retrofitting of later-model equipment to your earlier-model vehicle.

And don't plan on being exempt from emissions concerns just because you live in an area that doesn't currently have inspections. As mentioned earlier, more and more areas are enacting laws; yours could be next. And what if you wind up moving to an area that does have inspections? When you go to sell your car, most potential buyers will want to be sure the vehicle is in stock, legal condition, no matter where you live. And if the car is sold in an area that has emissions inspections, you can be held liable for the cost of all repairs necessary to put the original emissions equipment back on the car. It's just not worth trying to skate around the laws. Keep your car legal and keep your peace of mind.

Who will do it?

Probably the most important question is who will actually do the work. Usually, the safest option is to have a tuning shop that specializes in your type of vehicle do the work for you. Often, this is the most costly option. But the advantage is that the work will be warrantied and done by people who are familiar with all the special considerations for your vehicle. If you also purchase the engine from the shop, you may get a warranty on the engine, as well. So if anything goes wrong, there won't be any finger-pointing.

If you want to save some money, you can purchase the engine separately and take it to a repair shop or tuning shop to have it installed. Many people choose this option and save the mark-up that the tuning shop is likely to add onto the engine price. But remember: You can't blame the shop if you purchase a bad engine. So if you're not sure of the quality of the engine, it's usually best to let the shop select the engine for you.

If you're a hands-on person who's pretty handy with tools, you may be able to handle the job yourself, with the guidance of someone who's done it before. The advantages to doing the job yourself are:

1) You'll save money.
2) You'll know exactly what was done, so, if you have repair issues later, you'll be able to knowledgeably explain to the technician what was done.
3) You can do the job the way you want to do it. There's a bit of art to this, as well, and since a shop will be doing the job quickly, they may not pay attention to the details the way you would. You may want to take some extra time to add artistic flair to your wiring or paint your engine differently. When you do it yourself, you can take the extra time.

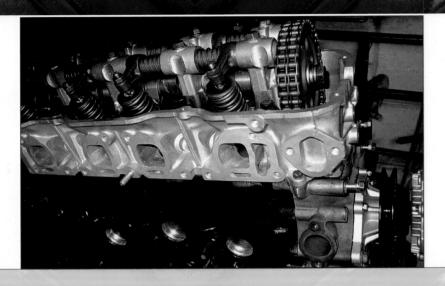

A remanufactured engine provides your best assurance of quality

Finding your engine

Remanufactured engines

Your best chance of getting a quality engine is to purchase it remanufactured from an automotive rebuilder. As you may have guessed, this is the most expensive option. But getting a warranty and being assured that the internals of the engine are "like-new" is usually worth the extra cost. Another advantage of a remanufactured engine is that you can often specify upgrades for internal parts. For example, if you'll be putting nitrous oxide to the engine, you'll probably want to pay the extra for forged pistons and high-strength connecting rod bolts.

Used engines

Used engines provide a more cost-effective option if you're on a budget. Since you probably won't be looking inside the engine, it will be difficult to know its condition. The best indicator of quality is the reputation of the seller. Find other people who are happy with their replacement engines and find out where they got theirs. Again, try to find a reputable seller who will provide a warranty on the engine. We've seen quite a few people who were told they were getting a good engine, but, when the engine was actually installed, they found it was in poor mechanical condition. Don't be caught like this without a warranty!

Engine retailers

As mentioned earlier, if you're not sure how to check the quality of a used engine, it's best to let the shop who's doing the work select the engine for you. The next best approach is to locate a source that warranties the engines they sell. There are many sources for used Japanese engines, especially in large metropolitan areas. If you're not lucky enough to have inexpensive used engines close by, check the Internet. Often, you can find prices so low that they're still a bargain, even after adding the shipping cost. But be sure you're dealing with a reputable company that will warranty the engine.

Used engines are a more economical solution. Japanese Domestic Market (JDM) engines are available from many sources and often have very low mileage

Best tips for roaming the wrecking yard
Check it out!

Checking out an engine at a wrecking yard can be difficult, since you're working in relatively primitive conditions. But if you know what to look for, you can do a pretty good job:

- If the engine is still installed in a vehicle, check the odometer for mileage.
- Aside from obvious body damage, look at the overall condition of the car. Chances are the owner who waxed the paint and vacuumed the carpets also changed the engine oil and replaced worn engine parts.
- Remove the oil cap and check for a "milkshake" look under the cap and in the oil itself. This is evidence that the cylinder head is cracked or the head gasket has blown – look for another engine if you see this. Also check the dipstick for the same evidence.
- Carefully look inside the valve cover (a small flashlight helps). Look for signs of carbon or sludge build-up, which indicate an abused engine (overheating and/or irregular oil changes).
- Compare the spark plugs to the condition chart in the Ignition Chapter to get a clue about the inside of the engine.

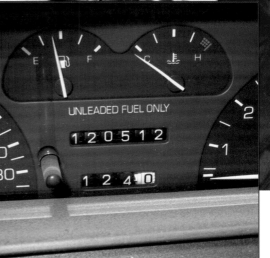

Gauges and monitoring
engine performance

Having the right gauges provides you with an early warning system to help you spot problems before they can cause major engine damage. On a stock street machine, the engine is so reliable that these situations are pretty rare. But when you start modifying your engine, stuff happens, which is why you better keep tabs on things.

Where do I put the gauges?

When cars were bigger, so were the dashboards. There was always room for extra gauges. On modern cars, however, there's not a lot of unused space for extra gauges. The one really flat space for gauges is of course the existing instrument "cluster" (the one-piece unit that houses the speedometer, tachometer and a few other gauges such as the fuel level and coolant temperature gauges). So, if you're swapping the old instrument cluster for a new unit, it should be a very straightforward procedure. But if you're planning to install additional gauges, then you'll have to be creative.

Gauge "cups" are the traditional strategy for housing gauges that can't be installed in the instrument cluster area. A cup is usually a black metal, chrome or plastic enclosure designed to house one gauge or a series of gauges. These are often simply mounted at the bottom edge of the dashboard. One drawback is that the wires between the gauge and the sender, voltage source, ground, etc. are exposed between the back of the cup and where they disappear into the dash.

All of the gauge manufacturers offer finished mounting plates, pre-cut to fit into storage recesses or ashtray receptacles in the dashboards of most modern cars. These empty spaces, which are usually located in the center of the dash, were intended for storing small sundries such as sunglasses, cell phones and other small items. If your car's dash is equipped with one of these storage areas, consider yourself lucky, because this is an easy way to add some gauges and make it look "factory."

There are gauge plates designed to fit into the ashtray receptacle of many makes and models. One neat thing about the ashtray is that the electrical lead to the cigarette lighter means that a convenient battery voltage source is already available.

Most of the gauge manufacturers also offer a wide range of "gauge pods," which are plastic housings designed to accept various sizes of gauges. There are pods for just about every vacant area on the dash: above the instrument cluster, to the left or right of the cluster, in the center of the dash, etc. Gauge pods usually have a black pebble-grain finish that blends nicely with most dashes.

One popular variation of the gauge pod is known as a "pillar pod." Pillar pods, which are designed to fit the driver's side A-pillar (the windshield pillar), are manufactured to accept one, two or three small gauges. A pillar pod is easy to install and looks as if it were installed at the factory, but be ready to do some drilling in the body and/or the dash to hide all the wires.

Gauge speak

Typical gauges

Air/fuel ratio gauge - The air/fuel ratio gauge indicates whether your air/fuel mixture ratio is rich or lean. It's a particularly helpful tuning tool if your engine is carbureted instead of fuel injected. Most air/fuel ratio gauges work with the existing oxygen sensor, according to the manufacturers, but how old is the existing oxygen sensor? Oxygen sensors become "lazy" before they actually fail. A lazy O2 sensor might still work, but if its signal is intermittent, irregular or slow (which it probably is if it's the original unit on a 10-year-old car), replace it. Or install another O2 sensor that's dedicated to the air/fuel ratio gauge.

Ammeter - An ammeter tells you how much current your alternator is putting out. Ammeters are not as popular as they once were (most people install a voltmeter instead).

Boost gauge - A boost gauge indicates the boost pressure on a supercharged or turbocharged engine. This is not an option on these vehicles. An overboost condition caused by a stuck wastegate can cause serious damage.

Coolant temperature gauge - The coolant temperature gauge indicates the temperature of the engine coolant. You might already have a coolant temperature gauge; if you're going to replace it, you'll need to consult the manufacturer to determine whether your new gauge will work with the existing sender for the old gauge. If you want to add a coolant temperature gauge - and you don't already have one - you'll need to install a coolant temperature sending unit. Also keep in mind that on many modern vehicles, a single Engine Coolant Temperature (ECT) sensor, which is the information sensor for the Powertrain Control Module (PCM), also functions as the coolant temperature sending unit for the coolant temperature gauge. On these models, you might want to install another sender dedicated to your new coolant temperature gauge.

Cylinder head temperature gauge - A cylinder head temperature gauge tells you the temperature of the cylinder head (obviously!), but its real value is that it can provide you with a general idea of the engine's operating temperature. For example, it can indicate whether an engine overheats under full power, or whether it has a tendency to run too cold, just right or too hot over a longer period. You will need to install a new sender for a cylinder head temperature gauge because this type of gauge is rarely found on cars as original equipment.

Exhaust gas temperature (EGT) gauge - An exhaust gas temperature gauge tells you the temperature of the exhaust gases as they're exiting the combustion chamber. An exhaust gas temperature of 1100 to 1200 degrees F. should result in nice tan-colored spark plug electrodes. A lower reading should produce darker colored plugs, and higher readings should give you gray or white plugs. Once you've identified the "normal" temperature range that produces tan plugs, all you have to do is monitor the EGT gauge(s) and watch for any deviation from normal. An EGT gauge is a valuable tuning tool when you're trying to set up the correct mixture ratio. A lean mixture will run hotter than normal, while a rich mixture will run cooler than normal (and will actually make increasingly less horsepower as it gets richer). An EGT can also help you identify "hot spots," which can occur when chopping the throttle from a full-throttle situation.

Fuel pressure gauge - A normally aspirated high performance engine, an engine equipped with nitrous oxide or a supercharged or turbocharged engine makes big demands on the fuel delivery system under acceleration, so you need a heavy-duty fuel pump capable of supplying sufficient fuel. And you need a fuel pressure gauge to make sure that the fuel pressure is adequate under all conditions. A fuel system that fails to deliver sufficient fuel under acceleration or high speed running leans out the air/fuel mixture ratio, which leads to detonation and/or preignition conditions, and it can ruin a motor in seconds! The fuel pressure gauge is primarily used for tuning. One reason for this is that you can't install it inside the car; you wouldn't want high-pressure fuel spraying the inside of the car if a compression fitting came loose!

Nitrous gauge - If you're running nitrous oxide, you need to know how much nitrous is in the tank. Running out of nitrous in the middle of a drag race will cause your air/fuel mixture to turn really rich in a hurry, which could cause big trouble. If you're going to install a nitrous kit, make sure you have a gauge to monitor the level in the tank.

Oil pressure gauge - The oil pressure gauge tells you the pressure of the engine oil. If you don't have an oil pressure gauge, this is one of the first gauges you should consider installing. An oil pressure gauge can save your engine from some expensive damage. If the engine loses oil pressure because of oil pump failure or a blocked oil passage, oil pressure will drop suddenly; without an oil pressure gauge, you might very well run the engine until it destroys itself. Many aftermarket oil pressure gauges can work with the existing oil pressure sending unit.

Oil temperature gauge - The oil temperature gauge tells you the temperature of the engine oil, which is generally considered a more accurate way of monitoring engine temperature.

Shift light - A shift light is a large, bright LED that can be programmed to come on at a specific, predetermined rpm level. You don't have to take your eyes off the road to watch a shift light; because of its intensity, a shift light can be seen out of the corner of your eye. A shift light can be located on the face of a special aftermarket drag racing tachometer or housed in a separate enclosure mounted on top of the dash.

Tachometer - The tachometer tells you the engine speed in revolutions-per-minute, or rpm. Some aftermarket tachs are also equipped with shift lights, which can be programmed to come on at the desired rpm. And some of the top-of-the-line units even make a recording of each run (or even multiple runs) so that you can analyze the data afterwards.

Voltmeter - The voltmeter tells you the voltage output of your alternator.

How much horsepower?
How fast?

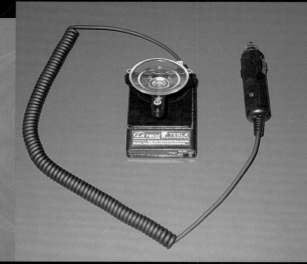

G-TECH/Pro tuning tools

One interesting and very helpful product in aftermarket instrumentation is the G-TECH/Pro, which is manufactured by Tesla Electronics of Duarte, California. The G-TECH/Pro uses a silicon accelerometer, which is a sensor that can measure acceleration, or G-force. The G-TECH/Pro measures the speed and distance traveled by integrating acceleration over time. It's all very complicated exactly how it works, but, bottom line, it does work. If you want to know how much power you really gained with those new headers, hook up the G-TECH before and after. Want to know 1/4-mile times without going to the drag strip? Plug in the G-TECH.

The G-TECH/Pro is ridiculously easy to install. Simply position the G-TECH/Pro in the middle of the dash (below the rear view mirror), push the rubber suction cup against the inside surface of the windshield, and plug it into your cigarette lighter. That's all there is to it. You're ready to go!

The G-TECH/Pro COMPETITION model can measure:

1/4-mile E.T. and top speed
1/8-mile E.T. and top speed
1000 foot time
Accelerating and braking Gs
Braking distance
Engine rpm
Engine rpm vs. time graph
Gs vs. time graph
Handling Gs
Horsepower
Horsepower and torque vs. rpm graph
Reaction time
Speed vs. distance graph
Speed vs. time graph
Torque
Zero-to-100 mph
Zero-to-330 feet
Zero-to-60 feet
Zero-to-60 mph

Another advantage is its portability. You can remove it from its mounting bracket to study your tuning data more closely. You can review the results, store logged runs that you want to save and even change the settings before putting the unit back in the car. Or in another car: Specific vehicle data such as weight and shift light settings can be stored and recalled for up to four vehicles.

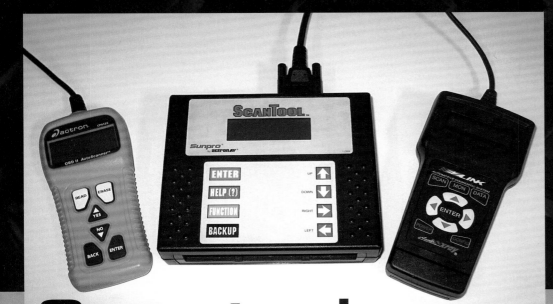

Scan tools:
Spend some quality time with your car's computer

All modern cars are equipped with sophisticated engine management systems run by a powerful computer. You don't have to be a dealer mechanic or shop with expensive equipment in order to tap into your car's computer.

Hand-held scan tools are the most powerful and versatile tools for troubleshooting the engine management systems on modern cars. Think of the scan tool as a way to peek inside your engine's brain. First, some terminology. OBD stands for On-Board Diagnostics; essentially a bunch of sensors feeding information to a computer. OBD cars started appearing in the early 90's. OBD-II is a much more sophisticatd system that was introduced in the mid-90's.

On some pre-OBD-II cars, if the dashboard Check Engine Light or Service Engine Soon light comes on, you might be able to extract stored diagnostic codes with a simple and inexpensive "code reader" which displays the code(s) when you plug it into the car's diagnostic connector. Or you might be able to put the computer into a diagnostic output mode in which it displays the code(s) by flashing the Check Engine light on and off. Refer to a Haynes repair manual for your vehicle for more information. But on all 1996 and later cars, you'll need a scan tool to extract and identify the code(s). And even

on earlier vehicles, a scan tool will tell you a lot more information than the diagnostic code number.

Little engine modifications like upgraded spark plug wires or a free-flowing air filter will likely have little if any effect on the serial data being exchanged between the information sensors, the computer and the actuators. But as the number and complexity of your engine mods increases, you will sooner or later do something that causes a sensor or its circuit to go out of range. A scan tool can help you understand how a recent modification affects the overall operation of your engine because you can "look" at the data.

A high-end scan tool can also help you diagnose the most maddening intermittent driveability problems by allowing you to retrieve freeze frame data from the memory of the computer. Freeze frame data is a digital recording for the interval during which a problem was detected.

Aftermarket scan tools are now widely available at automotive retailers. These tools, which are designed for the do-it-yourselfer, are not as powerful or versatile as professional units, but they can display all codes, and some of the better units can tell you a little about each code and can indicate whether a circuit is operating inside or outside its intended operating range. These are best used in conjuction with a Haynes repair manual.

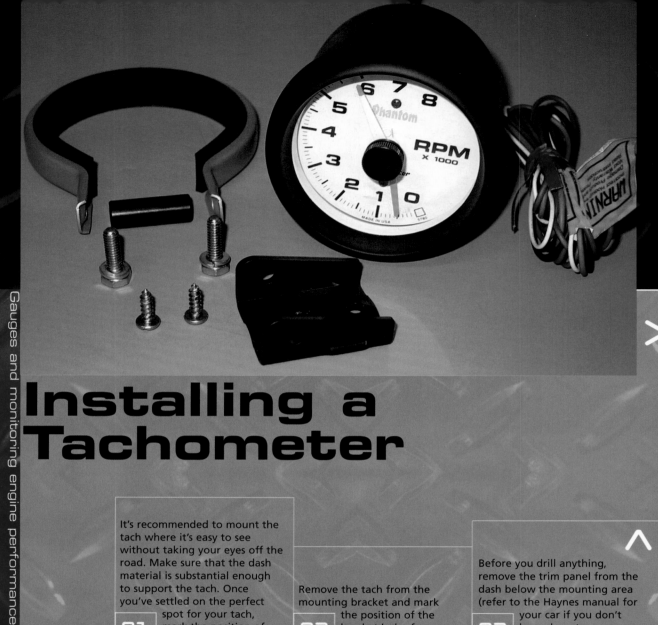

Installing a Tachometer

01 It's recommended to mount the tach where it's easy to see without taking your eyes off the road. Make sure that the dash material is substantial enough to support the tach. Once you've settled on the perfect spot for your tach, mark the position of the mounting bracket

02 Remove the tach from the mounting bracket and mark the position of the bracket holes for drilling

03 Before you drill anything, remove the trim panel from the dash below the mounting area (refer to the Haynes manual for your car if you don't know how to remove the trim panel) . . .

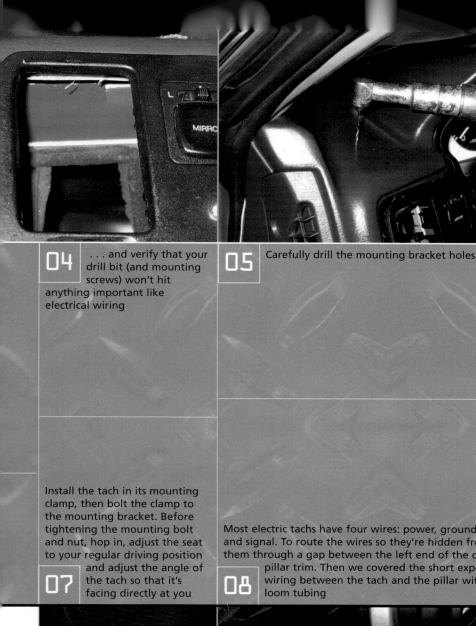

04 . . . and verify that your drill bit (and mounting screws) won't hit anything important like electrical wiring

05 Carefully drill the mounting bracket holes

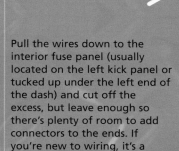

06 Place the tach mounting bracket in position, align it with your marks, install the bracket screws and tighten them securely, but don't overtorque them or you will strip out the dash material

>

07 Install the tach in its mounting clamp, then bolt the clamp to the mounting bracket. Before tightening the mounting bolt and nut, hop in, adjust the seat to your regular driving position and adjust the angle of the tach so that it's facing directly at you

08 Most electric tachs have four wires: power, ground, illumination and signal. To route the wires so they're hidden from view, we ran them through a gap between the left end of the dash and the A-pillar trim. Then we covered the short exposed section of wiring between the tach and the pillar with some split loom tubing

09 Pull the wires down to the interior fuse panel (usually located on the left kick panel or tucked up under the left end of the dash) and cut off the excess, but leave enough so there's plenty of room to add connectors to the ends. If you're new to wiring, it's a good idea to label the wires so that you don't mix them up

10 Now you're ready to start hooking up the wires. First, using a test light or continuity tester, find a pair of vacant 12-volt terminals on the fuse panel for your power (red) and illumination (white) wires. You want a switched 12-volt terminal for the power wire, which means that it's open circuit when the car is turned off, but hot when the ignition key is switched to ON. You'll also need a switched 12-volt terminal for the illumination wire that's open circuit when the lights are turned off, but hot when the parking lights are switched on

11 Strip off about 1/4 to 3/8-inch of insulation from each wire, crimp a connector the same size as the spade terminals you're going to hook up to and connect the power and illumination wires to the fuse panel. Those of you with sharp eyes will notice that these wires are oversize. That's because we plan to use these same wires for the illumination and power leads to the pillar pod gauges and the air/fuel ratio meter we'll be installing later

12 Look for a close and convenient fastener to connect the ground wire. Make sure that it grounds the wire to metal! We attached the ground wire to the body at this crossmember brace bolt. If you can't find a fastener nearby, drill a hole into the body and attach the ground wire with a self-tapping sheet metal screw

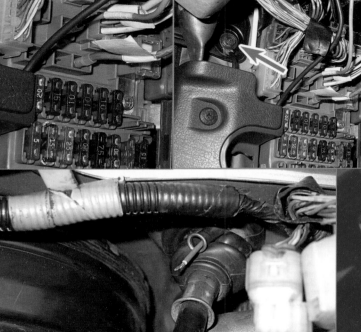

13 Unlike the other three wires, the signal wire must be routed through the firewall to the engine compartment. Look for a convenient cable grommet (throttle, clutch, hood release, etc.) in the firewall and make a hole in it with an awl. We used the clutch cable grommet because it's big and because it's easy to get to

14 Insert the signal wire through the plastic tube from under the dash and pull it through from the engine compartment side. Crimp on a suitable connector and connect the signal wire to the negative primary terminal on the ignition coil (standard-type coil) or to the auxiliary terminal meant for a tach wire (aftermarket, high-performance coil). That's it! You're done. Now set the telltale needle to the desired redline and be sure to not let the red needle go past it!

Installing pillar pod gauges

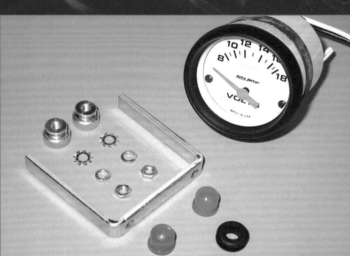

01 Unpack the oil pressure gauge kit and make sure you have everything you'll need to install it. If you're installing a mechanical type oil pressure gauge like this one, you will need to tap into the hole in the engine block or cylinder head for the oil pressure sender. So make sure that the kit includes all the adapter fittings you'll need to tee into the existing hole for the oil pressure sender

02 Unpack the voltmeter kit and make sure everything is there too. Unlike oil pressure gauges, voltmeters are pretty simple to install. Once you've inventoried everything for both kits, push them aside (but keep them separate!) and read the instructions that came with each kit. Pay close attention to all notes, cautions and warnings by the gauge manufacturer. For example, if a manufacturer specifies a certain gauge wire for a 12-volt connection, don't try to skimp by using a smaller wire than specified, or you might see smoke coming from your new gauges!

03 Okay, let's get started. Get your pillar pod and dummy it up exactly where you want to put it. Make sure it's a good fit before proceeding. Then, using a 3/16-inch bit, drill a hole at each corner of the pod as shown

04 Place the pod in position on the pillar and mark the locations of the four holes you're going to drill. Make sure the holes aren't going to be too close to the edges of the pillar

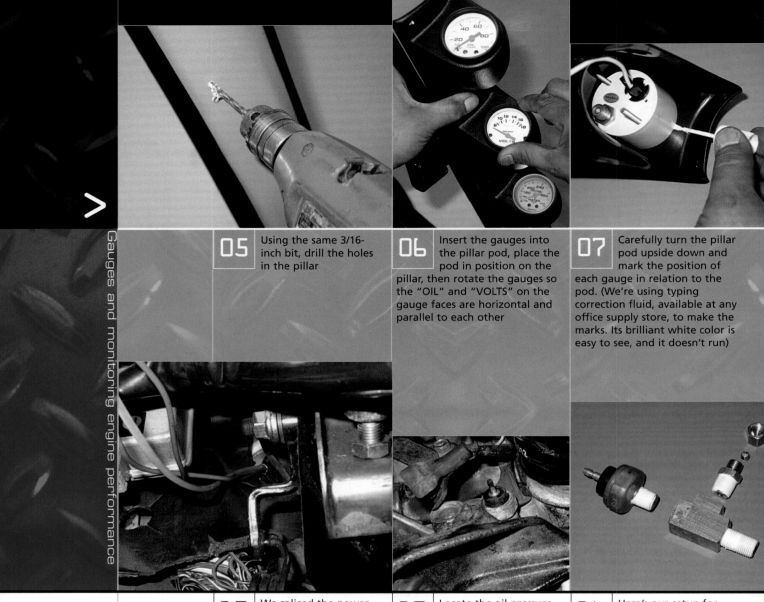

05 Using the same 3/16-inch bit, drill the holes in the pillar

06 Insert the gauges into the pillar pod, place the pod in position on the pillar, then rotate the gauges so the "OIL" and "VOLTS" on the gauge faces are horizontal and parallel to each other

07 Carefully turn the pillar pod upside down and mark the position of each gauge in relation to the pod. (We're using typing correction fluid, available at any office supply store, to make the marks. Its brilliant white color is easy to see, and it doesn't run)

12 We spliced the power, illumination and ground leads from all three pillar pod gauges into the same leads we used for the illumination and ground wires for the tachometer. Then we routed the oil line for the oil pressure gauge through the firewall to the engine compartment using the same tube that we installed in the clutch cable grommet for the signal wire to the tachometer

13 Locate the oil pressure sending unit and disconnect the electrical connector from the sender. The sender is usually - but not always - located somewhere near the oil filter. Refer to your Haynes manual if you have difficulty finding it. Be prepared to catch any oil that runs out when you remove the sender - the lower the sensor location on the head or block, the more oil you'll lose when you remove it

14 Here's our setup for tee-ing into the stock sending unit on our Acura project vehicle. Before assembling, be sure to wrap the threads of the sender, the adapter fitting and the compression fitting with Teflon tape to prevent leaks

08 Okay, remove the gauges from the pillar pod and connect the wires for power, ground and illumination . . .

09 . . . and on the oil pressure gauge, the tube that will carry oil from the oil pressure sender to the gauge

10 Reinstall the gauges in the pillar pod and clamp them into place with the clamps provided by the manufacturer. Note how we spliced the two illumination bulb wires and the two ground wires together

11 Route the wires and the oil line for the oil pressure gauge through the gap between the end of the dash and the A-pillar, then install the pillar pod/gauge assembly on the pillar and attach it with the four mounting screws. Don't overtighten the screws or you'll strip out the holes. When you're done with this phase, hide the wires with some split loom tubing

15 Screw the tee-fitting adapter into the block and tighten it securely. Make sure that the compression fitting is pointing in a direction that will allow easy connection of the oil pressure gauge line

16 Insert the line into the compression fitting, slide the olive down the line until it seats inside the open end of the fitting, thread the nut on and tighten it securely

17 Screw on the oil pressure sending unit, tighten it securely, reconnect the electrical connector to the sender and you're done!

Installing an air/fuel ratio gauge

01 Most gauge manufacturers offer a wide variety of mounting solutions for any gauge installation. We purchased this 2-1/16 inch diameter gauge bracket, which was designed for under-dash installations, but works just fine for this job

06 Using a hole saw bit, drill a hole in the exhaust, then clean up the edge around the hole with a small grinding tool until it's smooth and clean

07 Once you've drilled the hole and cleaned it up, place the weld-in boss over the hole, center it with a socket or an extension to keep it exactly in place

08 Tack weld the boss into place

09 With the boss tacked into position, remove the socket/extension, then weld the boss to the exhaust pipe

02 You'll also need to purchase an oxygen sensor and a weld-in boss from the manufacturer of the gauge. Don't buy a sensor from the manufacturer of your car. It will cost more money, and it won't include a weld-in boss, which you're going to need in order to screw the new sensor into the exhaust pipe

03 After removing the entire ashtray assembly, we discovered a couple of mounting holes that we could use for our under-dash mounting bracket. (If you need help removing the ashtray, refer to your Haynes manual.) We also discovered a big hole behind the ashtray receptacle through which we could route the wires (another reason why the ashtray receptacle is a good location for this or any other gauge which you might wish to install in this location)

04 For our installation, we removed the gauge and installed the bracket first, then installed the gauge in the bracket. Then we routed the power (red), ground (black) and illumination (white) wires over to the fuse panel and spliced them into the same connections that we created for the tachometer installation

05 Now for the fun part! There's no place to install your new oxygen sensor, so you're going to have to make one. First, mark the spot with a punch where you want to install the new sensor. For the best accuracy, it should be very near the oxygen sensor for the engine management computer (but be sure to offset it enough so the sensor tips don't touch each other)

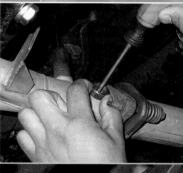

10 the exhaust pipe Inspect your work and make sure the weld completely surrounds the boss, with no holes. Any holes will allow air into the exhaust system and will cause false readings

11 Apply a film of anti-seize compound to the threads of the new sensor . . .

12 . . . then screw the sensor securely into the boss (a special oxygen sensor socket is being used here)

13 Finally, attach the sensor wire to the gauge wire; we used a butt connector here. Now lower the vehicle and test the gauge. Keep in mind that the gauge won't give you an accurate reading until the sensor has warmed up fully

Smokin' your tires can look cool, but to get your power to the pavement you better take a hard look at that driveline.

Driveline Upgrades

Once you have started modifying your machine, you can't go back to a stock clutch, or the combination of an aggressive driving style and an aggressive engine will fry a new stock clutch in short order. If you have done your clutch once already, you know much trouble it can be to get the car safely jacked up enough to be able to drop the transaxle out on the driveway. You don't want to have to do that too often. If you're having a shop do the installation, you have even more reason to do it once and do it right, since it can get expensive to re-clutch professionally. With an investment either way, in knuckle-busting labor or hard-earned cash, you need to choose your new clutch wisely.

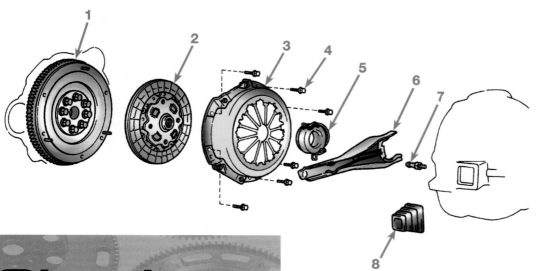

Typical clutch components

1 Flywheel
2 Clutch disc
3 Pressure plate
4 Pressure plate bolts
5 Release bearing
   (throwout bearing)
6 Release lever
7 Release lever ball
   stud (pivot point)
8 Release lever boot

Clutch and flywheel

When we say "clutch" we really mean the assembly that connects the engine to the transaxle and transfers power. It consists of four basic components: flywheel; clutch disc; pressure plate or cover; and the clutch release mechanism. The flywheel is a large metal disc bolted to the back of the crankshaft. The clutch cover or pressure plate is bolted to the flywheel, and sandwiched between the flywheel and pressure plate is the clutch disc. The disc is held tightly between the pressure plate and flywheel and power is transferred to the transaxle because the disc is splined in the center and rides on the splines of the transaxle's input shaft. When you need to "release the clutch," like to

A typical clutch system for performance use would include an aluminum flywheel, organic-faced clutch disc and higher-pressure clutch cover – this set is from Advanced Clutch Technology

Clutch disc friction materials run from like-stock to the exotic, but most street clutches use organic or Kevlar material for holding power with long life and good clutch "feel"– note the springs around the center of each disc hub; you've got to have these for a smooth street clutch engagement

shift, pushing the clutch pedal with your foot puts leverage against the pressure plate to let the disc spin independently of the flywheel. Let the pedal out and the power is again connected to the transaxle. This is a simplified explanation and there are a few smaller components to the system, but that's how it works.

For performance purposes, what we need to look at is the holding power and durability of a clutch system. From here on, by the way, we're going to use the term "clutch" to refer to the combination of clutch disc and pressure plate, because they normally are sold as a set, and it isn't recommended to intermix components of different brands. When you make more power, and tend to drive with race-style quick-shifting, the frictional load on the clutch is greatly increased, to the point where a stock clutch won't last.

While we may scoff at "stock" and want a manly clutch, you can go too far in that direction. A really stiff racing clutch is OK to use making a pass on the strip, since you only need to go through the gears once, but on the street your left leg is going to get cramped and muscle-bound in everyday driving.

Fortunately, the aftermarket clutch companies have divided their products into "stages" to make your choice easier. As you go up in stages, the clutches get stronger and stiffer; you basically match the clutch stage to your driving needs and horsepower level (or expected future level).

When you get into the clutches that have holding power for racing, things get expensive. There are disc designs with small metal or ceramic pucks instead of a full circle of friction material, discs without center springs (too harsh for street vehicles), an even multiple-disc designs. In the latter case, there would be studs on the flywheel, one disc goes against the flywheel then a "floater" plate slides over the studs, another disc is added and then the clutch cover. Essentially there's the frictional "grab" area of two complete clutches, and usually the discs are smaller than normal, so rotating weight is reduced.

When choosing your clutch components, ask clutch manufacturers, tuning shops and your friends about the clutches

Most import clutches are of the diaphragm style, in which a multi-fingered plate leverages against the pressure plate to clamp down on the clutch disc - most aftermarket clutch covers are similar to stock, but with altered leverage to increase clamping power without a big increase in pedal pressure

Not all aftermarket flywheels are aluminum, this Comptech flywheel for the Acura RSX is made of CNC-machined chrome-moly steel, yet still weighs only 8.75 pounds

they have used. What you're concerned about is the amount of pedal pressure, how the clutch engages (or its "feel"), and how long a particular clutch can be expected to handle performance use.

Flywheels are an important part of the clutch system as well, but the choices are fewer. A lighter flywheel allows an engine to rev quicker. For street use and only occassional racing with a mildly upgraded engine, the stock flywheel should be fine. As your driveline needs get more demanding, consider a performance flywheel at the same time your upgraded clutch is installed. And aftermarket companies have been making lightweight aluminum flywheels for performance use for fifty years.

Safety . . .
Shrapnel and scattershields

If you plan on racing at the dragstrip, you'd also be wise to check that the clutch has a certification sticker from SFI, the racing safety organization. At many events, you must have an SFI-approved clutch and flywheel if you go quicker than 12 seconds.

Under extreme racing use, an OEM-type clutch and flywheel combination can literally explode in the car. The continued heat from hard shifts can crack a flywheel or clutch pressure plate to the point where the component eventually comes apart. Flying pieces of clutch/flywheel shrapnel can injure the driver or cut a fuel line and cause a disastrous fire. This we don't want, so invest in a lightweight flywheel that has the SFI certification. Even with the SFI clutch and flywheel, there are some events and classes in which you will also have to have a "scattershield" which is a 1/4 - inch-thick steel shield that goes around your bellhousing to contain shrapnel if anything happens. We should also mention that when installing a performance clutch and or flywheel, you should use only top-quality, new, high-strength bolts to secure them. Go fast, but be safe.

Racing clutches have solid hubs (no springs) and usually have exotic materials for the friction surfaces, like ceramic or metallic pads, either in a full circle or in pucks like these

There aren't a lot of gear ratio choices for sport compacts, and a new ring and pinion set like this is expensive, but if you're racing and determine that you need the extra gearing because you're running much bigger tires (slicks) these could be just what you need

Driveline
improvements

Once you have a decent clutch that can handle your engine's new output, you will probably never have a driveline problem on the street. It's possible, of course, but the major limit to your car's hookup is "where the rubber meets the road." Street tires will just go up in smoke when you apply too much throttle on a high-horsepower car; this could cause an engine problem if you over-rev during the tire spin, but the driveline shouldn't break. Once you put on a pair of slicks or a wider, softer tire that really grabs, that's when things can snap!

If you have a stock differential in your car, most of your engine load is going to wind up going to one axle when you're taking off the line. This increases the chances of breaking that axle. One solution that can take the extra burden off that axle is a limited-slip differential (LSD). This differential has a type of clutch in it that "locks up" under acceleration, providing more equal distribution of power to the two axles, giving you more traction and each axle has less load on it than one axle getting all the torque. This sounds perfect but there are catches, of course. An LSD is expensive, and most home tuners have someone experienced do the installation, which adds to the cost.

How the LSD hooks up is the other consideration. Such differentials differ in style of clutches but also in how much percentage of lockup, or "hook" they offer. The units with a higher percentage of lockup are less fun to drive around corners on the street, making ratcheting or clunking sounds because one axle (on the outside of the corner) is trying to turn faster than the other. The LSD's that are better for the street have less hook, but they are still a major improvement in traction for street or strip.

For serious *strip-only* use, the complete answer is a spool. This is a solid unit that takes the place of the differential and absolutely provides half the power to each axle.

The disadvantage is that it doesn't like to go around corners

A limited-slip differential works great on the street for providing increased traction, but for track-only use, a nearly-unbreakable spool like this Pro Drive gives equal torque to each axle

Since all your new power is getting transferred very suddenly to your new slicks, you may need to upgrade your hub assembly to one with a billet flange and stronger wheel studs – this one is from Pro Drive

at all, not real practical for the street.

With plenty of power and plenty of traction, the only thing missing in the equation is plenty of axle strength. Your axles typically have a CV joint on the outside, an axleshaft, and a tripod-type joint at the inner end of the axle. One or all of these components will fail with enough force against them on the starting line. Once you have upgraded your driveline, you'll be fine until the tire companies come out with a stickier or bigger slick, then you'll have to upgrade to the next level of axles.

If you have been reading our book up to this point, and you're making enough new power and torque to start worrying about driveline breakage, that makes us feel good. Not that you're breaking parts, but that our advice in the power-making department has served you well!

As engine builders keep finding more power and use bigger slicks, for extreme drag use you need a completely-new drivetrain – this package from Moore Performance includes big axles, billet joint components, billet spool, and chrome-moly knuckles with hubs, bearings and lightweight disc brakes

Stronger axleshafts and bigger CV joints will handle the extra loads imposed by running slicks – once you upgrade, you won't have to carry spare stock axleshafts to the track with you

Glossary

A

Acceleration - The time rate of change in velocity; velocity (speed) can be measured in feet-per-second, acceleration in feet-per-second-per-second, or feet-per-second-squared.

Adhesion - The property of oil which causes it to cling to metal surfaces such as bearings. Also, the ability of a tire to remain in contact with a road surface. Also, the ability of a paint to stick to the surface being painted.

Advance - Moving the timing of the camshaft, distributor spark or valve operation ahead so that an event - such as firing of the spark plug or the opening of a valve - occurs earlier in the cycle. This term is also used to describe the mechanism used for accomplishing this.

Air-fuel mixture - The air and fuel traveling to the combustion chamber after being mixed by the carburetor, or after fuel is injected into the airstream by an injector. The mass of air supplied to the engine, divided by the mass of fuel supplied in the same period of time. The *stoichiometric*, or chemically correct, air-fuel ratio (*AFR*, or *A/F ratio*) is the exact ratio necessary to burn all the carbon and hydrogen in the fuel, leaving no other combustion by-products except carbon dioxide and water. See *stoichiometric*.

Air-fuel ratio - The ratio of air to the *weight* of the fuel supplied to the mixture for combustion. See *stoichiometric*.

Air gap - Space between spark plug electrodes, starting motor and generator armatures, field shoes, etc.

Air pressure - Atmospheric pressure (14.7 psi).

Air-to-air intercooler - A heat exchanger, used on a turbocharged engine, which uses ambient air to cool the air coming from the turbo into the intake manifold.

Air-to-water intercooler - A heat exchanger, used on a turbocharged engine, which uses liquid coolant from the radiator to cool the air coming from the turbo into the intake manifold.

Alloy - A metal containing two or more elements. Adding one or more elements to a pure metal alters its properties such as elongation, strength, etc. For example: solder is an alloy of lead and tin.

Alloy wheel - A generic term used to describe any non-steel road wheel. The alloys are usually aluminum of magnesium (hence the term *mag wheel*, which refers to any non-steel wheel).

All-wheel-drive (AWD) - A vehicle drivetrain with every wheel under power. On a four-wheeled vehicle, all-wheel-drive generally refers to a full-time four-wheel-drive system with a center differential.

Anti-seize compound - A coating that reduces the risk of seizing on fasteners that are subjected to high temperatures, such as exhaust manifold bolts and nuts.

Aspect ratio - The ratio of section height to section width on a tire.

ATDC - "After Top Dead Center," the point at which a piston starts to move downward in the cylinder on either the intake stroke or the combustion stroke.

B

Backpressure - Any resistance to free flow in the exhaust system. For example, catalytic converters and mufflers cause backpressure.

Ball bearing - An anti-friction bearing consisting of a hardened inner and outer race with hardened steel balls interposed between two races.

Balance shaft(s) - The rotating shaft or shafts, incorporating eccentric counterweights, designed to counter-act the natural vibration of other reciprocating parts, such as the pistons, connecting rods and crankshaft.

Balancing - The process of checking every engine part for conformity to its specified dimensions. The specified working clearances for all moving parts are also checked. Balancing improves engine performance, smoothness and reliability. Also referred to as *blueprinting*.

Banjo fitting - A type of hydraulic fitting, shaped like a banjo, through which a hollow bolt passes, allowing fluid transfer from a hydraulic line to a hydraulic component.

Barometric pressure (or Bar) - Atmospheric pressure, expressed in inches of Mercury (in-Hg). Barometric pressure is determined by how high atmospheric pressure (relative to zero absolute pressure) forces Mercury up a glass tube. 14.5 psi = 29.92 inches.

BDC - "Bottom Dead Center." The lowest point of piston and connecting rod travel in the cylinder; the ends of the intake and power strokes, respectively, in a four-stroke engine.

Black smoke - Incompletely burned fuel in the exhaust.

Block deck - The cylinder head gasket surface.

Blow-by - The leakage of the compressed air-fuel mixture or the burned gases from the combustion chamber past the piston rings and into the crankcase. this leakage results in power loss and oil contamination.

Blower - A pump-like device which forces air into the cylinders at higher-than-atmospheric pressure. Because of this higher pressure, the cylinder gets more air per intake stroke, which means it can burn more fuel, which means more horsepower. There are two types of blowers - A turbocharger uses some of the waste heat energy in the exhaust gases to drive a compressor and pump the air; a belt-driven supercharger uses engine power to pump air. See *turbocharger* and *supercharger*. The term also refers to the *blower motor fan* assembly in the heating/air conditioning system.

Blow-off valve - A control valve on a turbocharged engine, installed on the intake side of the system, which relieves pressure if it exceeds a predetermined value.

Blueprinting - Dismantling an engine and reassembling it to EXACT specifications.

Blue smoke - Caused by blow-by allowing crankcase oil in the combustion chamber due to bad rings, valve seals or other faulty components.

Bore diameter - Diameter of the cylinders.

Bottom end - A term which refers collectively to the engine block, crankshaft, main bearings and the big ends of the connecting rods.

Brake horsepower (bhp) - The power produced by the engine (as measured at the output shaft) that is available for driving the vehicle. It's called brake horsepower because the shaft power is usually measured by an absorption dynamometer or *brake*.

Break-in - The period of operation between installation of new or rebuilt parts and the point in time at which the parts are worn to the correct fit. The time or mileage period during which the rough edges and friction between newly assembled moving parts and surfaces are gradually reduced. Generally calls for moderate loads and driving at reduced and varying speed for a specified mileage to permit parts to wear to the correct fit.

BTDC - "Before Top Dead Center;" any position of the piston between bottom dead center and top dead center, on the upward stroke.

C

Cam - A rotating lobe or eccentric which, when used with a cam follower, can change rotary motion to the reciprocating motion. For example, the multi-lobed *breaker cam* rotating in the inanition distributor interrupts the primary circuit to induce a high tension spark for ignition. Some brake adjuster designs use a cam (or cams) to set the clearance between the brake shoes and brake drum.

Cam follower - A device that follows the cam contour as it rotates. Also called a lifter, valve lifter or tappet.

Camshaft - A rotating shaft on which a series of *cam lobes* operate the valve mechanisms. The camshaft is driven by gears or sprockets and a timing chain. Usually referred to simply as the *cam*.

Camshaft gear - The sprocket used to drive the camshaft.

Case harden - To harden the surface of steel.

Cast iron - An alloy of iron and more than two percent carbon, used for engine blocks and heads because it's relatively inexpensive and easy to mold into complex shapes.

Catalytic converter - A muffler-like device in the exhaust system that catalyzes a chemical reaction which converts certain air pollutants in the exhaust gases into less harmful substances.

Cavitation - A condition in which a partial vacuum forms around the blades or impeller wheels of a pump, reducing the pump's output because part of the pump blades lose contact with the liquid. It can be a problem in fuel and water pumps, fluid couplings and torque converters and, when severe, can result in erosion of pump blades and other internal surfaces.

Central Fuel Injection (CFI) - A computer-controlled fuel metering system which sprays atomized fuel into a throttle body mounted on the intake manifold.

Chamfer - To bevel across - or, a bevel on - the sharp edge of an object or a hole.

Closed loop - An operating condition or mode which enables modification of programmed instructions based on a feedback system.

Closed loop fuel control - The normal operating mode for a fuel injection system. Once the engine is warmed up the computer can interpret an analog voltage signal from an exhaust gas oxygen sensor and alter the air/fuel ratio accordingly through the fuel injectors.

Closed loop mode - Once the engine has reached "warm-up" temperature, the engine management computer collects the precise data from all the sensors (coolant temperature sensor, throttle position sensor, oxygen sensor etc.) to determine the most efficient air/fuel mixture for combustion.

Clutch - Any device which connects and disconnects a driven component from the driving component. For example a clutch is used to disengage the engine from the transmission in vehicles with a manual transmission.

Coil binding - Compressing a valve spring to the point at which each coil touches the adjacent coil.

Cold lash - The valve lash clearance, measured between the rocker arm and valve tip, when the engine is cold.

Collapsed piston - A piston whose skirt diameter has been reduced by heat and the forces imposed upon it during service in engine.

Combustion chamber - The cavity in the cylinder head (or the cylinder head and the piston) into which the air/fuel mixture is compressed by the piston when the piston is at the top of its compression stroke. In other words, the volume of the cylinder above the piston with the piston at top dead center.

Compression - Reduction in volume, and increase in pressure and temperature, of a gas, caused by squeezing it into a smaller space.

Compression ratio - The relationship between cylinder volume (clearance volume) when the piston is at top dead center and cylinder volume when the piston is at bottom dead center. The clearance volume of an engine cylinder divided by its total volume.

Compression ring - The upper ring, or rings, on a piston, designed to hold the compression in the combustion chamber and prevent blow-by.

Compression stroke - The piston's movement from bottom dead center to top dead center immediately following the intake stroke, during which both the intake and exhaust valves are closed while the air-fuel mixture in the cylinder is compressed.

Compressor - The part of a turbocharger that compresses the intake air.

Compressor pressure ratio - In a turbocharger system, the ratio between the absolute pressure at the compressor outlet and the absolute pressure at the compressor inlet.

Compressor ratio - In a turbocharged engine, the ratio between the volume in the cylinder when the piston is at the bottom of its stroke and the volume in the cylinder when the piston is at the top of its stroke.

Computer - A device that takes information, processes it, makes decisions and outputs those decisions.

Connecting rod - The rod that connects the crank on the crankshaft with the piston. Sometimes called a con rod.

Connecting rod cap - The part of the connecting rod assembly that attaches the rod to the crankpin.

Constant velocity (CV) joint - A universal joint whose output shaft travels at the same velocity as the input shaft, through 360-degrees, with no fluctuations in speed.

Coolant temperature sensor - A device that senses the engine coolant temperature, and passes that information to the electronic control module as an analog (variable) voltage signal.

Core plug - Soft metal plug used to plug the casting holes for the coolant passages in the block. See *freeze plug*.

Counterbalancing - Additional weight placed at the crankshaft vibration damper an/or flywheel to balance the crankshaft.

Counterbore - Concentric machine surface around a hole opening. To enlarge a hole to a given depth.

Crankcase - The lower part of the engine in which the crankshaft rotates; includes the lower section of the cylinder block and the oil pan.

Crankcase breather - A port or tube that vents fumes from the crankcase. An inlet breather allows fresh air into the crankcase.

Crankcase dilution - Under certain conditions of operation, unburned portions of fuel get past piston rings into the crankcase where they "thin" the engine lubricating oil.

Crank kit - A reground or reconditioned crankshaft and new main and connecting rod bearings.

Crankpin - The part of a crankshaft to which a connecting rod is attached.

Crankshaft - The main rotating member, or shaft, running the length of the crankcase, with offset throws to which the connecting rods are attached; changes the reciprocating motion of the pistons into rotating motion.

Crankshaft counterbalance - Series of weights attached to, or forged integrally, with the crankshaft and placed to offset reciprocating weight of each piston and rod assembly.

Crankshaft gear - The gear on the front of the crankshaft which drives the camshaft gear.

Cylinder block - Largest single part of an engine. Basic or main mass of metal in which cylinders are bored or placed.

Cylinder head - A detachable portion of an engine fastened securely to cylinder block which contains all or a portion of combustion chamber.

Cylinder head gasket - Seal between engine block and cylinder head.

Cylinder sleeve - A replaceable sleeve, or liner, pressed into the cylinder block to form the cylinder bore and provide a replaceable friction surface for the piston and rings.

D

Deck - The flat upper surface of the engine block where the cylinder head mounts.

Deck height - The center of the crankshaft main-bearing bores to the block deck surface.

Degree wheel - A disc divided into 360 equal parts that can be attached to a shaft to measure angle of rotation.

Density - The weight or mass per unit volume of a gas, liquid or solid. Density is an indicator of relative compactness of a mass of matter in a given volume.

Detonation - The uncontrolled spontaneous explosion of air/fuel mixture in the combustion chamber - after the spark occurs at the spark plug - which spontaneously combusts the remaining air/fuel mixture, resulting in a "pinging" noise, and causing a loss of power and possible engine damage. Commonly referred to as spark knock or ping.

Detonation-activated ignition retard - A system which retards the ignition timing when the detonation knock sensor picks up vibration at frequencies typical of detonation.

Detonation sensor - A device, usually piezoelectric, which senses frequencies typical of detonation and converts this information into an analog voltage signal. Also called a *knock sensor*.

Dial indicator - A precision measuring instrument that indicates movement to a thousandth of an inch with a needle sweeping around dial face.

Dish - A depression in the top of a piston.

Displacement - The total volume of an engine's cylinders, usually measured in cubic inches, cubic centimeters or liters. The total volume of air-fuel mixture an engine is theoretically capable of drawing into all cylinders during one operating cycle. Also refers to the volume swept out by the piston as it moves from bottom dead center to top dead center.

Distributor - In the ignition system on a spark-ignition engine, a mechanical device designed to switch a high voltage secondary circuit from an ignition coil to the spark plugs in the proper firing sequence.

Double-overhead cam (DOHC) - An engine that uses two overhead camshafts, one for the intake valves and one for the exhaust valves. The cams are driven by a timing chain or by a timing belt.

Draw-through - A turbocharger system in which the turbocharger sucks the air/fuel mixture through the carburetor or fuel injector, i.e. the air and fuel mixing occurs upstream from the turbocharger.

Drivebelt(s) - The belt(s) used to drive accessories such as the alternator, water pump, power steering pump, air conditioning compressor, etc. off the crankshaft pulley.

Drivetrain - The power-transmitting components in a vehicle. Usually consists of the clutch (on vehicles with a manual transmission), the (manual or automatic) transmission, the driveshaft, the universal joints, the differential and the driveaxle assemblies.

Dry sump - A lubrication system in which the engine's supply of oil isn't contained in the crankcase (sump), but is pumped to the engine from an external container. Allows the crankcase to be reduced in size and the engine to be reduced in size and the engine to be installed lower in the chassis, and eliminates the oil starvation most conventional oiling systems suffer when subjected to the acceleration, braking and cornering forces generated by a racing vehicle.

Duration - The period of time during which anything lasts. For a camshaft, the time each valve is open, measured in crankshaft degrees of rotation.

Duty cycle - Many solenoid-operated metering devices cycle on and off. The duty cycle is a measurement of the amount of time a device is energized, or turned on, expressed as a percentage of the complete on-off cycle of that device. In other words, the duty cycle is the ratio of the pulse width to the complete cycle width.

Dynamometer - A device for measuring the power output, or brake horsepower, of an engine. An engine dynamometer measures the power output at the flywheel. A chassis dynamometer measures power at the drive wheels.

E

Eccentric - One circle within another circle not having the same center. A disk, or offset section (of a shaft, for example) used to convert rotary motion to reciprocating motion. Sometimes called a cam.

EGR valve - A valve used to introduce exhaust gases into the intake air stream to lower exhaust emissions, principally oxides of nitrogen (NOx).

Electronically-controlled wastegate - A turbocharger wastegate that's activated by an electric signal from a computer.

Electronic Control Module (ECM) - A generic term referring to the computer. The ECM is the brain of the engine control systems receiving information from various sensors in the engine compartment. The ECM calculates what is required for proper engine operation and controls the different actuators to achieve it.

Electronic Fuel Injection (EFI) - A computer-controlled fuel system that distributes fuel through an injector located in each intake port of the engine.

Electronic ignition - An ignition system that uses electronic switching devices to relieve the mechanical breaker points of part of their duties or replace them. Electronic ignitions can be divided into three basic classifications - contact controlled, mechanically controlled and capacitor controlled. In the first type, the breaker points are retained but merely serve to trigger a transistor which switches the heavy primary current. In a magnetically controlled (also known as a *contactless* or *all-electronic*) system, transistors are used as the switching device for the primary current and the points are eliminated. A capacitive discharge system can be either all-electronic or breaker-point controlled (although points haven't been used since the Seventies).

Engine block - The iron or aluminum casting which encloses the crankshaft, connecting rods, connecting rods and pistons.

Engine displacement - The sum of piston displacement of all engine cylinders.

Exhaust manifold – Attached to the cylinder head, the exhaust manifold collects the exhaust from all engine exhaust ports and routes the exhaust gasses into a single exhaust pipe. Exhaust manifolds are usually made from cast iron, which contains heat and noise well and has excellent durability at high temperatures. A common performance modification is to replace the exhaust manifold with a tubular-steel header, which often offers better performance, but usually is not as durable and increases underhood heat and noise.

Exhaust oxygen sensor - Also known as an *oxygen sensor* or an *02 sensor*. Device that detects the amount of oxygen in the exhaust stream, and sends that information to the ECM.

Exhaust ports - The passages in the cylinder head, connecting the exhaust valves and the exhaust manifold, through which the exhaust gases pass on their way to the exhaust manifold.

Exhaust stroke - The portion of the piston's movement devoted to expelling burned gases from the cylinder. The exhaust stroke lasts from bottom dead center to top dead center, immediately following the power stroke, during which the exhaust valve opens so the exhaust gases can escape from the cylinder to the exhaust manifold.

Exhaust system - The pipes, resonators and mufflers that carry the exhaust gases from the exhaust manifold out into the atmosphere.

Exhaust valve - The valve through which the burned air-fuel charge passes on its way from the cylinder to the exhaust manifold during the exhaust stroke.

F

Feeler gauge - A thin strip or blade of hardened steel, ground to an exact thickness, used to check and/or measure clearances between parts. Feeler gauges are graduated in thickness by increments of .001 inch.

Firing order - The order in which the engine cylinders fire, or deliver their power strokes, beginning with the number one cylinder.

Flare-nut wrench - A wrench designed for loosening hydraulic fitting tube nuts (flare-nuts) without damaging them. Flare-nut wrenches are kind of like a six-point box-end wrench with one of the flats missing, which allows the wrench to pass over the tubing but still maintain a maximum amount of contact with the nut.

Float - Float occurs when the valve train loses contact with the cam lobe and the parts "float" on air until control is regained.

Flywheel - A heavy, usually metal, spinning wheel in which energy is absorbed and stored by means of momentum. On cars, the heavy metal wheel that's attached to the crankshaft to smooth out firing impulses. It provides inertia to keep the crankshaft turning smoothly during periods when no power is being applied. It also serves as part of the clutch and engine cranking systems.

Foot-pound - A unit of measurement for work, equal to lifting one pound one foot.

Four-stroke cycle - The four piston strokes - intake, compression, power and exhaust - that make up the complete cycle of events in the four-stroke cycle engine. Also referred to as four-cycle and four-stroke.

Freeze plug - A disc or cup-shaped metal device inserted in a hole in a casting through which core was removed when casting was formed. Also known as a *core hole plug* or *expansion plug*. See *core plug*.

Friction horsepower - The amount of power consumed by an engine in driving itself. It includes the power absorbed in mechanical friction and in driving auxiliaries plus, in the case of four-stroke engines, some pumping power.

Fuel injection - A type of fuel system using a pump and injectors instead of a carburetor to meter fuel. There are two main types of injection - continuous, or mechanical (such as Bosch Continuous Injection Systems), and electronic. Mechanical injection systems are no longer manufactured but a wide variety of electronic injection systems can be found on new vehicles. Earlier versions of electronic injection were throttle body designs; these systems utilize one or two injectors in a throttle body above the intake manifold. The latest electronic systems are port injection designs; these systems use one injector at each intake port.

Fuel injector - In electronic fuel-injection systems, a spring-loaded, solenoid (electromagnetic) valve which delivers fuel into the intake manifold, in response to electrical signals from the control module.

Fuel pressure regulator - A pressure-activated diaphragm valve that maintains the pressure in a fuel system to a pre-set value above manifold pressure, particularly in a fuel injection system.

Fuel rail - A special manifold designed to provide a large reservoir of pressurized fuel for the fuel injectors, which are attached between the rail and the intake runners or the cylinder head. The fuel rail also serves as a mounting place for the fuel damper (if equipped) and the fuel pressure regulator.

G

Gallery - A large passage in the engine block that forms a reservoir for engine oil pressure.

Gap - Generally refers to the distance the spark must travel in jumping from the center electrode to the side electrode in a spark plug. Also refers to the spacing between the points in a contact breaker assembly in a conventional points-type ignition, or to the distance between the reluctor or rotor and the pickup coil in an electronic ignition.

Gasket - Any thin, soft material - usually cork, cardboard, asbestos or soft metal - installed between two metal surfaces to ensure a good seal between two components such as the block and the cylinder head.

Gear ratio - Number of revolutions made by a driving gear as compared to number of revolutions made by a driven gear of different size. For example, if one gear makes three revolutions while the other gear makes one revolution, the gear ratio is 3 to 1 or (3:1).

H

Header - A high-performance exhaust manifold that replaces the stock exhaust manifold. Designed with smooth flowing lines to prevent back pressure caused by sharp bends, rough castings, etc. See *Exhaust Manifold*.

Heat range - The ability of a spark plug to transfer heat from the combustion chamber to the cylinder head. The speed of this transfer is commonly described by the terms cold plug and hot plug. A hot plug transfers heat slowly, causing the plug to operate at a higher temperature. A cold plug transfers heat at a faster rate, thus operating at a lower temperature. Plugs are available in different heat ranges to accommodate the operating conditions of different engines and driving conditions. A plug must operate hot enough to prevent fouling, but cold enough to prevent pre-ignition.

High tension - Secondary or induced high voltage electrical current. Circuit includes wiring from ignition distributor cap to coil and to each spark plug.

Horsepower - A measure of mechanical power, or the rate at which work is done. One horsepower is the amount of power required to lift 550 pounds one foot per second. One horsepower equals 33,000 ft-lbs of work per minute. It's the amount of power necessary to raise 33,000 pounds a distance of one foot in one minute.

Hot lash - The valve adjustment on an engine equipped with solid lifters.

I

Ideal air/fuel mixture, or ideal mixture - The air/fuel ratio which provides the best performance while maintaining maximum conversion of exhaust emissions, typically 14.7:1. See *stoichiometric ratio*.

Idle - Rotational speed of an engine with vehicle at rest and accelerator pedal not depressed.

Idle Air Control (IAC) valve - On fuel-injected vehicles, a valve that allows air to bypass the throttle plate(s), increasing idle speed. The valve is operated by an electric solenoid or motor. The vehicle's computer controls the amount of opening to regulate idle speed for varying conditions such as cold starting and air conditioning compressor load.

Ignition system - The system responsible for igniting fuel in the cylinders. Includes the ignition module, the coil, the coil wire, the distributor, the spark plug wires, the plugs, and a voltage source.

Ignition timing - The moment at which the spark plug fires, usually expressed in the number of crankshaft degrees before the piston reaches the top of its stroke.

Intake manifold - A tube or housing with passages through which flows the air-fuel mixture (carbureted vehicles and vehicles with throttle body injection) or air only (port fuel-injected vehicles) to the port openings in the cylinder head.

Intake ports - The passages in the cylinder head connecting the intake valves and the intake manifold through which the air-fuel mixture flows on its way to the cylinders.

Intake stroke - The portion of the piston's movement, between top dead center and bottom dead center, devoted to drawing fuel mixture into engine cylinder. The intake stroke is the stroke immediately following the exhaust stroke, during which the intake valve opens and the cylinder fills with air-fuel mixture from the intake manifold.

Intake valve - The valve through which the air-fuel mixture is admitted to the cylinder.

Intercooler - A radiator used to reduce the temperature of the compressed air or air/fuel mixture before it enters the combustion chamber. Either air-to-water or, more commonly, air-to-air.

Internal combustion engine - An engine that burns its fuel within cylinders and converts the power of this burning directly into mechanical work.

K

Keeper - The split lock that holds the valve spring retainer in position on the valve stem.

Keyway - A slot cut in a shaft, pulley hub, etc. A square key is placed in the slot and engages a similar keyway in the mating piece.

Knock - The sharp, metallic sound produced when two pressure fronts collide in the combustion chamber of an engine, usually because of *detonation*. Also, a general term used to describe various noises occurring in an engine; can be used to describe noises made by loose or worn mechanical parts, such as a bad bearing. Connecting rod or main bearing knocks are created by too much oil clearance or insufficient lubrication. Also referred to as *detonation*, *pinging* and *spark knock*.

Knurl - A roughened surface caused by a sharp wheel that displaces metal outward as its sharp edges push into the metal surface. To indent or roughen a finished surface.

L

Lean - A term used to describe an air/fuel mixture that's got either too much air or too little fuel.

Lift - Maximum distance and intake or exhaust valve head is raised off its seat.

Lifter - The part that rides against the cam to transfer motion to the rest of the valve train.

Limited slip differential (LSD) - A differential that uses cone or disc clutches to lock the two independent axleshafts together, forcing both wheels to transmit their respective drive torque regardless of the available traction. It allows a limited amount of slip between the two axleshafts to accommodate the differential action. This design doubles the number of drive wheels in low-traction situation.

Lubricant - Any substance, usually oil or grease, applied to moving parts to reduce friction between them.

M

Manifold - Any device designed to collect, route and/or distribute air, air/fuel mixture, exhaust gases, fluids, etc. In air conditioning, a device which controls refrigerant flow for system test purposes by means of hand valves which can open or close various passageways connected together inside the manifold. Used in conjunction with manifold gauges and service hoses. See *exhaust manifold* and *intake manifold*.

Manifold Absolute Pressure (MAP) sensor - A pressure-sensitive disk capacitor used to measure air pressure inside the intake manifold. The MAP sensor sends a signal to the computer which uses this information to determine load conditions so it can adjust spark timing and fuel mixture.

N

Net horsepower - Brake horsepower remaining at flywheel of engine after power required by engine accessories (fan, water pump, alternator, etc.).

Normally-aspirated - An engine which draws its air/fuel mixture into its cylinders solely by piston-created vacuum, i.e. not supercharged or turbocharged.

O

Oil control ring - The third piston ring from the top (and the fourth, if four are used) that scrapes off excess oil from the cylinder walls and returns it to the oil pan via vents in the ring and the piston itself. This action prevents oil from getting into the combustion chamber where it could burn and form carbon that could clog valves and piston rings, short out spark plugs and increase exhaust emissions.

Oil gallery - A pipe or drilled passageway in the engine used to carry engine oil from one area to another.

Oil pan - The detachable lower part of the engine, usually made of stamped steel, which encloses the crankcase and acts as an oil reservoir.

Oil pump - An engine-driven pump that delivers oil to all the moving engine parts. Oil pumps are usually driven from the camshaft either by gears or cams and the two common types are the gear and the rotor pump.

Open-loop fuel control - A non-feedback mode of operation which an engine management system resorts to when the engine is started while it's still cold. During this period, the oxygen sensor isn't yet able to supply reliable data to the computer for controlling the air/fuel mixture ratio because the engine isn't yet warmed up. So mixture control is handled by a program stored in computer memory. Open loop is also used when the engine management system is malfunctioning.

Overhead cam (ohc) engine - An engine with the camshaft(s) located on top of the cylinder head(s) instead of in the engine block. This design eliminates pushrods; some designs also dispense with the rocker arms too. The advantage of an ohc engine are quicker and more accurate valve response because of the shorter path between the cam(s) and the valves.

Overlap - The overlap period occurs at the end of the exhaust stroke and the beginning of the next intake stroke. The exhaust valve closes late to give the burned gases as much time as possible to leave the combustion chamber after they have expended most of their useful work; the intake valve opens early to give the fresh mixture enough time to fill the combustion chamber. The overlap is the number of degrees of crankshaft rotation during which the intake and exhaust valves in one cylinder are open at the same time.

Oxygen sensor - A device installed in the engine exhaust manifold, which senses the oxygen content in the exhaust and converts this information into an electric current.

P

Piston pin (or wrist pin) - The cylindrical and usually hollow steel pin that passes through the piston. The piston pin fastens the piston to the upper end of the connecting rod and serves as the journal for the bearing in the small end of the connecting rod.

Piston ring - The split ring fitted to the groove in a piston. The ring contacts the sides of the ring groove and also rubs against the cylinder wall, thus sealing space between piston and wall. There are two types of rings: Compression rings seal the compression pressure in the combustion chamber; oil rings scrape excessive oil off the cylinder wall.

Piston slap - A sound made by a piston with excess skirt clearance as the crankshaft goes across top center.

Port injection - A fuel injection system in which the fuel is sprayed by individual injectors into each intake port, upstream of the intake valve.

Ports - Openings in the cylinder block for the valves, the intake and exhaust manifolds and coolant plumbing. In two-cycle engines, openings for inlet and exhaust purposes.

Positive Crankcase Ventilation (PCV) system - An emission control system that routes engine crankcase fumes into the intake manifold or air cleaner, where they are drawn into the cylinders and burned along with the air-fuel mixture.

Powertrain - The components through which motive power is generated and transmitted to the driven axles. See *drivetrain*.

Preignition - Short for *premature ignition*. The premature burning of the air/fuel mixture in the combustion chamber, caused by combustion chamber heat and/or fuel instability. Preignition begins before the spark plug fires.

R

Relay - An electromechanical device which enables one circuit to open or close another circuit. A relay is usually operated by a low current circuit, but it controls the opening and closing of another circuit of higher current capacity.

Ring gap - The distance between the ends of the piston ring when installed in the cylinder.

rpm - Engine speed, measured in crankshaft *revolutions per minute*.

S

Scan Tool - A device that interfaces with and communicates information on a data link. Commonly used to get data from automotive computers.

Sending unit - Used to operate a gauge or indicator light. In indicator light circuits, contains contact points, like a switch. In gauge circuits, contains a variable resistance that modifies current flow in accordance with the condition or system being monitored.

Sensor - The generic name for a device that senses either the absolute value or a change in a physical quantity such as temperature, pressure, or flow rate, and converts that change into an electrical signal which is monitored by a computer.

Serpentine drivebelt - A single, long, wide accessory drivebelt that's used on some newer vehicles to drive all the accessories, instead of a series of smaller, shorter belts. Serpentine drivebelts are usually tensioned by an automatic tensioner.

Short block - An engine block complete with crankshaft and piston and, usually, camshaft assemblies.

Single-overhead cam (SOHC) - See *overhead cam*.

Spark gap - The space between the electrodes of a spark plug through which the spark jumps. Also, a safety device in a magneto to provide an alternate path for current when it exceeds a safe value.

Spark knock - See *detonation* or *preignition*.

Spark plug - An electrical device which protrudes into the combustion chamber of an engine. The spark plug contains an insulated center electrode for conducting high tension current from the distributor. This insulated electrode is spaced a predetermined distance from the side electrode to control the dimensions of the gap for the spark to jump across.

Stoichiometric - The ideal ratio of air to fuel, in terms of mass; results in the most complete and efficient combustion, converting the carbon and hydrogen content of the fuel into (mainly) water and carbon dioxide. The stoichiometric ratio varies with the heating value of the fuel: For example, it's around 15.1:1 by weight for 100-octane gasoline, 14.6:1 for regular, 9.0:1 to ethanol, 6.45:1 for methanol and so on.

Stroke - The distance the piston moves when traveling from top dead center to bottom dead center, or from bottom dead center to top dead center.

Sump - The lowest part of the oil pan. The part of oil pan that contains oil. See *oil pan*.

Supercharger - A mechanically-driven device that pressurizes the intake air, thereby increasing the density of charge air and the consequent power output from a given engine displacement. Superchargers are usually belt-driven by the engine crankshaft pulley. See *blower*.

T

Throttle body - On carburetors, the casting which houses the throttle plate(s) and shaft(s) and the throttle linkage for the primary and, if equipped, the secondary bores. The throttle body is a separate component that's bolted to the underside of the carburetor main body. On fuel-injection systems, the carburetor-like aluminum casting that houses the throttle valve, the idle air bypass (if equipped), the throttle position sensor (TPS), the idle air control (IAC) motor and, on TBI systems, one or two injectors.

Throttle Body Injection (TBI) - Any of several injection systems which have the fuel injector(s) mounted in a centrally located throttle body, as opposed to positioning the injectors close to the intake ports.

Throttle Position Sensor (TPS) - A potentiometric sensor that tells the computer the position (angle) of the throttle plate. The sensor wiper position is proportional to throttle position. The computer uses this information to control fuel flow.

Throw-out bearing - The bearing in the clutch assembly that is moved in to the release levers by clutch-pedal action to disengage the clutch. Also referred to as a *release bearing*.

Timing marks (ignition) - Marks, usually located on the crankshaft pulley, used to synchronize the ignition system so the spark plugs will fire at the correct time.

Timing marks (valves) - Marks placed on the crankshaft and camshaft sprockets or gears which must be aligned with their corresponding marks so that the camshaft(s) and crankshaft are synchronized.

Torque - A turning or twisting force, such as the force imparted on a fastener by a torque wrench. Usually expressed in foot-pounds (ft-lbs).

Turbocharger - A centrifugal device, driven by exhaust gases, that pressurizes the intake air, thereby increasing the density of the charge air, and therefore the resulting power output, from a given engine displacement.

V

Valve clearance - The clearance between the valve tip (the end of the valve stem) and the rocker arm. The valve clearance is measured when the valve is closed.

Valve float - The condition which occurs when the valves are forced back open before they've had a chance to seat. Valve float is usually caused by extremely high rpm.

Valve grinding - The process of refacing a valve in a valve refacing machine.

Valve guide - The cast-iron bore that's part of the head, or the bronze or silicon-bronze tube that's pressed into the head, to provide support and lubrication for the valve stem.

Valve head - The portion of a valve upon which the valve face is machined.

Valve keeper - Also referred to as valve key. Small half-cylinder of steel that snaps into a groove in the upper end of valve stem. Two keepers per valve are used. Designed to secure valve spring, valve retainer and valve stem together. Also referred to as a *valve key* or *valve lock*.

Valve lifter - A cylindrical device that contacts the end of the cam lobe and the lower end of the pushrod. The lifter rides on the camshaft. When the cam lobe moves it upward, it pushes on the pushrod, which pushes on the lifer and opens the valve. Also referred to as a *lifter*, *tappet*, *valve tappet* or *cam follower*.

Valve overlap - The number of degrees of crankshaft rotation during which both the intake and the exhaust valve are partially open (the intake is starting to open while the exhaust is not yet closed).

Valve stem - The long, thin, cylindrical bearing surface of the valve that slides up and down in the valve guide.

W

Wastegate - A device which bleeds off exhaust gases before they reach the turbocharger when boost pressure reaches a set limit.

Water pump - A pump, usually mounted on the front of the engine and driven by an accessory drivebelt, which forces coolant through the cooling system.

White smoke - Unburned fuel emitted by the exhaust that indicates low combustion chamber temperatures.

Wrist pin - A journal for bearing in small end of an engine connecting rod which also passes through piston walls. See *piston pin*.

Safety First

Regardless of how enthusiastic you may be about getting on with the job at hand, take the time to ensure that your safety is not jeopardized. A moment's lack of attention can result in an accident, as can failure to observe certain simple safety precautions. The possibility of an accident will always exist, and the following points should not be considered a comprehensive list of all dangers. Rather, they are intended to make you aware of the risks and to encourage a safety conscious approach to all work you carry out on your vehicle.

Essential DOs and DON'Ts

DON'T rely on a jack when working under the vehicle. Always use approved jackstands to support the weight of the vehicle and place them under the recommended lift or support points.

DON'T attempt to loosen extremely tight fasteners (i.e. wheel lug nuts) while the vehicle is on a jack - it may fall.

DON'T start the engine without first making sure that the transmission is in Neutral (or Park where applicable) and the parking brake is set.

DON'T remove the cooling system pressure cap from a hot cooling system - let it cool or cover it with a cloth and release the pressure gradually.

DON'T attempt to drain the engine oil until you are sure it has cooled to the point that it will not burn you.

DON'T touch any part of the engine or exhaust system until it has cooled sufficiently to avoid burns.

DON'T siphon toxic liquids such as gasoline, antifreeze and brake fluid by mouth, or allow them to remain on your skin.

DON'T inhale brake lining dust - it is potentially hazardous (see **Asbestos**).

DON'T allow spilled oil or grease to remain on the floor - wipe it up before someone slips on it.

DON'T use loose fitting wrenches or other tools which may slip and cause injury.

DON'T push on wrenches when loosening or tightening nuts or bolts. Always try to pull the wrench toward you. If the situation calls for pushing the wrench away, push with an open hand to avoid scraped knuckles if the wrench should slip.

DON'T attempt to lift a heavy component alone - get someone to help you.

DON'T rush or take unsafe shortcuts to finish a job.

DON'T allow children or animals in or around the vehicle while you are working on it.

DO wear eye protection when using power tools such as a drill, sander, bench grinder, etc. and when working under a vehicle.

DO keep loose clothing and long hair well out of the way of moving parts.

DO make sure that any hoist used has a safe working load rating adequate for the job.

DO get someone to check on you periodically when working alone on a vehicle.

DO carry out work in a logical sequence and make sure that everything is correctly assembled and tightened.

DO keep chemicals and fluids tightly capped and out of the reach of children and pets.

DO remember that your vehicle's safety affects that of yourself and others. If in doubt on any point, get professional advice.

Steering, suspension and brakes

These systems are essential to driving safety, so make sure you have a qualified shop or individual check your work. Also, compressed suspension springs can cause injury if released suddenly - be sure to use a spring compressor.

Airbag

Airbags are explosive devices that can cause injury if they deploy while you're working on the car. Follow the manufacturer's instructions to disable the airbag whenever you're working in the vicinity of airbag components.

Asbestos

Certain friction, insulating, sealing, and other products - such as brake linings, brake bands, clutch linings, torque converters, gaskets, etc. - may contain asbestos or other hazardous friction material. Extreme care must be taken to avoid inhalation of dust from such products, since it is hazardous to health. If in doubt, assume that they are harmful.

Fire

Remember at all times that gasoline is highly flammable. Never smoke or have any kind of open flame around when working on a vehicle. But the risk does not end there. A spark caused by an electrical short circuit, by two metal surfaces contacting each other, by a tool falling on concrete, or even by static electricity built up in your body under certain conditions, can ignite gasoline vapors, which in a confined space are highly explosive. Do not, under any circumstances, use gasoline for cleaning parts. Use an approved safety solvent.

Always disconnect the battery ground (-) cable at the battery before working on any part of the fuel system or electrical system. Never risk spilling fuel on a hot engine or exhaust component. It is strongly recommended that a fire extinguisher suitable for use on fuel and electrical fires be kept handy in the garage or workshop at all times. Never try to extinguish a fuel or electrical fire with water.

Fumes

Certain fumes are highly toxic and can quickly cause unconsciousness and even death if inhaled to any extent. Gasoline vapor falls into this category, as do the vapors from some cleaning solvents. Any draining or pouring of such volatile fluids should be done in a well ventilated area.

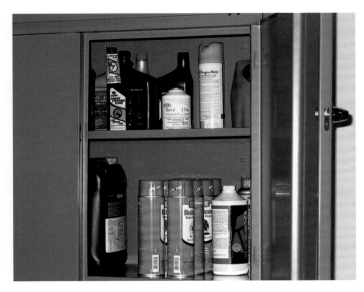

When using cleaning fluids and solvents, read the instructions on the container carefully. Never use materials from unmarked containers.

Never run the engine in an enclosed space, such as a garage. Exhaust fumes contain carbon monoxide, which is extremely poisonous. If you need to run the engine, always do so in the open air, or at least have the rear of the vehicle outside the work area.

The battery

Never create a spark or allow a bare light bulb near a battery. They normally give off a certain amount of hydrogen gas, which is highly explosive.

Always disconnect the battery ground (-) cable at the battery before working on the fuel or electrical systems.

If possible, loosen the filler caps or cover when charging the battery from an external source (this does not apply to sealed or maintenance-free batteries). Do not charge at an excessive rate or the battery may burst.

Take care when adding water to a non maintenance-free battery and when carrying a battery. The electrolyte, even when diluted, is very corrosive and should not be allowed to contact clothing or skin.

Always wear eye protection when cleaning the battery to prevent the caustic deposits from entering your eyes.

Household current

When using an electric power tool, inspection light, etc., which operates on household current, always make sure that the tool is correctly connected to its plug and that, where necessary, it is properly grounded. Do not use such items in damp conditions and, again, do not create a spark or apply excessive heat in the vicinity of fuel or fuel vapor.

Secondary ignition system voltage

A severe electric shock can result from touching certain parts of the ignition system (such as the spark plug wires) when the engine is running or being cranked, particularly if components are damp or the insulation is defective. In the case of an electronic ignition system, the secondary system voltage is much higher and could prove fatal.

Source List

AEM (Advanced Engine Management)
2205 126th St., Unit A
Hawthorne, CA 90250
(310) 484-2322
www.aempower.com

A'PEX Integration
(intercoolers, intakes, blow-off valves, more)
330 West Taft
Orange, CA 92865
(714) 685-5700
www.apexi.com

B&M Racing and Performance Parts
(fuel system and many other parts)
9142 Independence Ave.
Chatsworth, CA 91311
(818) 882-6422
www.bmracing.com

Blitz
(intakes, turbo components, other parts)
4879 East La Palma Ave., Suite 202
Anaheim, CA 92807
(714) 777-9766
www.blitz-na.com

Competition Cams
(cams, valvetrain parts, ZEX nitrous kits)
3406 Democrat Road
Memphis, TN 38118
(888) 817-1008
www.zex.com

Comptech USA
(blower kits, Honda/Acura performance parts)
4717 Golden Foothill Parkway
El Dorado Hills, CA 95762
(916) 933-1080
www.comptechusa.com

Clutch Masters
267 E. Valley Blvd.
Rialto, CA 92376
(909) 877-6800
www.clutchmasters.com

Crane Cams
530 Fentress Blvd.
Daytona Beach, FL 32114
(386) 258-6174
www.cranecams.com

Dart Industries
(race cylinder heads and blocks)
353 Oliver Street
Troy, MI 48084
(248) 362-1188
www.dartheads.com

DC Sports
(cold air intakes, exhausts, other parts)
1451 East 6th Street
Corona, CA 92879
(909) 734-2020
www.dcsports.com

Edelbrock Corp.
(intake components, nitrous)
2700 California Street
Torrance, CA 90503
(310) 781-2222
www.edelbrock.com

Flexalite
(FAL fans)
P.O. Box 580
Milton, WA 98354
(253) 922-2700
www.flex-a-lite.com

Fluidyne
(aluminum radiators)
2605 East Cedar St.
Ontario, CA 91761
(800) 358-4396
www.fluidyne.com

Ford Racing Performance Parts
(Ford sport compact catalog)
P.O. Box 51394
Livonia, MI 48151
(586) 468-1356
www.fordracing.com/performance parts

GM Performance Parts
(GM sport compact catalog)
(800) 468-7387
www.goodwrench.com

GReddy Performance Products
(large catalog of performance parts)
9 Vanderbilt
Irvine, CA 92618
(949) 588-8300
www.greddy.com

Gude
(camshafts, valvetrain, ported heads)
29885 2nd St., Suite Q
Lake Elsinore, CA 92530
www.gude.com

Holley Performance Products
(Airmass Exhaust, Holley Ignition, NOS, Earl's)
1801 Russellville Road, P.O. Box 10360
Bowling Green, KY 42102-7360
(800) Holley-1
www.holley.com

Hondata
(engine management electronics)
2341 W. 205th St, #106
Torrance, CA 90501
(301) 782-8278
www.hondata.com

Innovative Turbo Systems
845 Easy Street
Simi Valley, CA 93065
(805) 526-5400
www.innovativeturbo.com

Jackson Racing
(supercharger kits and more)
440 Rutherford Street
Goleta, CA 93117
(888) 888-4079
www.jacksonracing.com

Jacobs Electronics
2519 Dana Drive
Laurinburg, NC 28352
(800) 782-3379
www.jacobselectronics.com

JE Pistons
15312 Connector Lane
Huntington Beach, CA 92649
(714) 898-9763
www.jepistons.com

Jim Wolf Technology
(electronics, Toyota performance parts)
212 Millar Avenue
El Cajon, CA 92020
(619) 442-0680
www.jimwolftechnology.com

K&N Engineering
(air filters, intake kits)
P.O. Box 1329
Riverside, CA 92502
(888) 949-1832
www.knfilters.com

Midnight Performance
(import tuning shop, products)
3324 Monier Circle, #1and 2
Rancho Cordova, CA 95742
(916) 852-6887
www.midnightperformance.com

Moore Performance
(racing driveline components)
3740 Greenwood Street
San Diego, CA 92110
(619) 296-9180

MSD
(ignition products)
1490 Henry Brennan Drive
El Paso, TX 79936
(915) 857-5200
www.msdignition.com

Neuspeed
(full range of performance parts, accessories)
3300 Corte Malpaso
Camarillo, CA 93012
(805) 388-7171
www.neuspeed.com

Nitrous Express (NX)
1808 Southwest Parkway
Wichita Falls, TX 76302
(888) 463-2781
www.nitrousexpress.com

NOS
(see Holley)

ProDrive
(driveline components)
6530 Alondra Blvd.
Paramount, CA 90723
(888) 340-4753
www.prodriveusa.com

Racers Against Street Racing (RASR)
A coalition of auto manufacturers, aftermarket parts companies, professional drag racers, sanctioning bodies, race tracks and automotive magazines devoted to promoting safe and legal alternatives to illegal street racing on a national level. The message is simple: *If you want to race, go to a racetrack!*
www.racersagainststreetracing.org

RC Engineering
(injectors, injection specialists)
1728 Border Avenue
Torrance, CA 90501
(310) 320-2277
www.rceng.com

Split-Second
(engine management electronics)
1949 East Deere Avenue
Santa Ana, CA 92705
(949) 863-1359
www.splitsec.com

STR
(racing intakes)
1161 California Ave.
Corona, CA 92881
(909) 272-2150
www.strspeedlab.com

Tanabe
(Japanese exhaust systems)
see your sport compact tuner or dealer

Toyota Racing Development (TRD)
see your Toyota dealer
or www.toyota-trd.com

Turbo Specialties
(turbo kits)
17906 Crusader Avenue
Cerritos, CA 90703
(562) 403-7039

Turbonetics
(turbochargers)
2255 Agate Court
Simi Valley, CA 93065
(805) 581-0333
www.turboneticsinc.com

Veilside USA
(performance and appearance parts)
1250 E. 223rd St., #105
Carson, CA 90745
(310) 835-5684
www.veilside.com

Vortech Engineering
(supercharger kits)
1650 Pacific Avenue
Channel Islands, CA 93033
(805) 247-0226
www.vortechsuperchargers.com

Whipple Superchargers
3292 N. Weber
Fresno, CA 93722
(559) 442-1261
www.whipplesuperchargers.com

ZEX
(nitrous oxide kits)
3406 Democrat Road
Memphis, TN 38118
(888) 817-1008
www.zex.com